The Riddle Of The Universe At The Close Of The Nineteenth Century

Ernst Haeckel

Copyright © BiblioLife, LLC

This book represents a historical reproduction of a work originally published before 1923 that is part of a unique project which provides opportunities for readers, educators and researchers by bringing hard-to-find original publications back into print at reasonable prices. Because this and other works are culturally important, we have made them available as part of our commitment to protecting, preserving and promoting the world's literature. These books are in the "public domain" and were digitized and made available in cooperation with libraries, archives, and open source initiatives around the world dedicated to this important mission.

We believe that when we undertake the difficult task of re-creating these works as attractive, readable and affordable books, we further the goal of sharing these works with a global audience, and preserving a vanishing wealth of human knowledge.

Many historical books were originally published in small fonts, which can make them very difficult to read. Accordingly, in order to improve the reading experience of these books, we have created "enlarged print" versions of our books. Because of font size variation in the original books, some of these may not technically qualify as "large print" books, as that term is generally defined; however, we believe these versions provide an overall improved reading experience for many.

THE RIDDLE OF THE UNIVERSE

AT THE CLOSE OF THE NINETEENTH CENTURY

BY

ERNST HAECKEL

(Ph.D., M.D., LL.D., Sc.D., and Professor at the
University of Jena)

AUTHOR OF "THE HISTORY OF CREATION"
"THE EVOLUTION OF MAN" ETC.

TRANSLATED BY

JOSEPH McCABE

HARPER & BROTHERS PUBLISHERS
NEW YORK AND LONDON
1901

Copyright, 1900, by HARPER & BROTHERS.

All rights reserved.

CONTENTS

	PAGE
AUTHOR'S PREFACE	v
TRANSLATOR'S PREFACE	xi

CHAPTER I
THE NATURE OF THE PROBLEM 1

CHAPTER II
OUR BODILY FRAME 22

CHAPTER III
OUR LIFE 39

CHAPTER IV
OUR EMBRYONIC DEVELOPMENT 53

CHAPTER V
THE HISTORY OF OUR SPECIES 71

CHAPTER VI
THE NATURE OF THE SOUL 88

CHAPTER VII
PSYCHIC GRADATIONS 108

CHAPTER VIII
THE EMBRYOLOGY OF THE SOUL 132

CHAPTER IX
THE PHYLOGENY OF THE SOUL 148

CONTENTS

CHAPTER X
CONSCIOUSNESS 170

CHAPTER XI
THE IMMORTALITY OF THE SOUL 188

CHAPTER XII
THE LAW OF SUBSTANCE 211

CHAPTER XIII
THE EVOLUTION OF THE WORLD 233

CHAPTER XIV
THE UNITY OF NATURE. 254

CHAPTER XV
GOD AND THE WORLD 275

CHAPTER XVI
KNOWLEDGE AND BELIEF 292

CHAPTER XVII
SCIENCE AND CHRISTIANITY 308

CHAPTER XVIII
OUR MONISTIC RELIGION. 331

CHAPTER XIX
OUR MONISTIC ETHICS. 347

CHAPTER XX
SOLUTION OF THE WORLD-PROBLEMS 365

CONCLUSION 380

INDEX 385

AUTHOR'S PREFACE

THE present study of the monistic philosophy is intended for thoughtful readers of every condition who are united in an honest search for the truth. An intensification of this effort of man to attain a knowledge of the truth is one of the most salient features of the nineteenth century. That is easily explained, in the first place, by the immense progress of science, especially in its most important branch, the history of humanity, it is due, in the second place, to the open contradiction that has developed during the century between science and the traditional "Revelation"; and, finally, it arises from the inevitable extension and deepening of the rational demand for an elucidation of the innumerable facts that have been recently brought to light, and for a fuller knowledge of their causes.

Unfortunately, this vast progress of empirical knowledge in our "Century of Science" has not been accompanied by a corresponding advancement of its theoretical interpretation—that higher knowledge of the causal nexus of individual phenomena which we call philosophy. We find, on the contrary, that the abstract and almost wholly metaphysical science which has been taught in our universities for the

AUTHOR'S PREFACE

last hundred years under the name of "philosophy" is far from assimilating our hard-earned treasures of experimental research. On the other hand, we have to admit, with equal regret, that most of the representatives of what is called "exact science" are content with the special care of their own narrow branches of observation and experiment, and deem superfluous the deeper study of the universal connection of the phenomena they observe—that is, philosophy. While these pure empiricists "do not see the wood for the trees," the metaphysicians, on the other hand, are satisfied with the mere picture of the wood, and trouble not about its individual trees. The idea of a "philosophy of nature," to which both those methods of research, the empirical and the speculative, naturally converge, is even yet contemptuously rejected by large numbers of representatives of both tendencies.

This unnatural and fatal opposition between science and philosophy, between the results of experience and of thought, is undoubtedly becoming more and more onerous and painful to thoughtful people. That is easily proved by the increasing spread of the immense popular literature of "natural philosophy" which has sprung up in the course of the last half-century. It is seen, too, in the welcome fact that, in spite of the mutual aversion of the scientific observer and the speculative philosopher, nevertheless eminent thinkers from both camps league themselves in a united effort to attain the solution of that highest object of inquiry which we briefly denominate the "world-riddles." The studies of these "world-riddles" which I offer in the present work cannot reasonably claim to give a perfect solution of them; they merely offer to a wide circle of readers a critical inquiry into the prob-

AUTHOR'S PREFACE

lem, and seek to answer the question as to how nearly we have approached that solution at the present day. What stage in the attainment of truth have we actually arrived at in this closing year of the nineteenth century? What progress have we really made during its course towards that immeasurably distant goal?

The answer which I give to these great questions must, naturally, be merely subjective and only partly correct; for my knowledge of nature and my ability to interpret its objective reality are limited, as are those of every man. The one point that I can claim for it, and which, indeed, I must ask of my strongest opponents, is that my Monistic Philosophy is sincere from beginning to end—it is the complete expression of the conviction that has come to me, after many years of ardent research into Nature and unceasing reflection, as to the true basis of its phenomena. For fully half a century has my mind's work proceeded, and I now, in my sixty-sixth year, may venture to claim that it is mature; I am fully convinced that this "ripe fruit" of the tree of knowledge will receive no important addition and suffer no substantial modification during the brief spell of life that remains to me.

I presented all the essential and distinctive elements of my monistic and genetic philosophy thirty-three years ago, in my *General Morphology of Organisms*, a large and laborious work, which has had but a limited circulation. It was the first attempt to apply in detail the newly established theory of evolution to the whole science of organic forms. In order to secure the acceptance of at least one part of the new thought which it contained, and to kindle a wider interest in the greatest advancement of knowledge that our century has witnessed, I published my *Natural History of Creation*

AUTHOR'S PREFACE

two years afterwards. As this less complicated work, in spite of its great defects, ran into nine large editions and twelve different translations, it has contributed not a little to the spread of monistic views. The same may be said of the less known *Anthropogeny** (1874), in which I set myself the difficult task of rendering the most important facts of the theory of man's descent accessible and intelligible to the general reader; the fourth, enlarged, edition of that work appeared in 1891. In the paper which I read at the fourth International Congress of Zoology at Cambridge, in 1898, on "Our Present Knowledge of the Descent of Man"† (a seventh edition of which appeared in 1899), I treated certain significant and particularly valuable advances which this important branch of anthropology has recently made. Other isolated questions of our modern natural philosophy, which are peculiarly interesting, have been dealt with in my *Collected Popular Lectures on the Subject of Evolution* (1878). Finally, I have briefly presented the broad principles of my monistic philosophy and its relation to the dominant faith in my *Confession of Faith of a Man of Science : Monism as a Connecting Link between Religion and Science* ‡ (1892, eighth edition, 1899).

The present work on *The Riddle of the Universe* is the continuation, confirmation, and integration of the views which I have urged for a generation in the aforesaid volumes. It marks the close of my studies on the monistic conception of the universe. The earlier

---

* There are two English translations, *The Evolution of Man* (1879) and *The Pedigree of Man* (1880).

† The English translation, by Dr. Hans Gadow, bears the title of *The Last Link*.

‡ English translation, by J. Gilchrist, with the title of *Monism*.

AUTHOR'S PREFACE

plan, which I projected many years ago, of constructing a complete "System of Monistic Philosophy" on the basis of evolution will never be carried into effect now. My strength is no longer equal to the task, and many warnings of approaching age urge me to desist. Indeed, I am wholly a child of the nineteenth century, and with its close I draw the line under my life's work.

The vast extension of human knowledge which has taken place during the present century, owing to a happy division of labor, makes it impossible to-day to range over all its branches with equal thoroughness, and to show their essential unity and connection. Even a genius of the highest type, having an equal command of every branch of science, and largely endowed with the artistic faculty of comprehensive presentation, would be incapable of setting forth a complete view of the cosmos in the space of a moderate volume. My own command of the various branches of science is uneven and defective, so that I can attempt no more than to sketch the general plan of such a world-picture, and point out the pervading unity of its parts, however imperfect be the execution. Thus it is that this work on the world-enigma has something of the character of a sketch-book, in which studies of unequal value are associated. As the material of the book was partly written many years ago, and partly produced for the first time during the last few years, the composition is, unfortunately, uneven at times; repetitions, too, have proved unavoidable. I trust those defects will be overlooked.

In taking leave of my readers, I venture the hope that, through my sincere and conscientious work—in spite of its faults, of which I am not unconscious—

AUTHOR'S PREFACE

I have contributed a little towards the solution of the great enigma. Amid the clash of theories, I trust that I have indicated to many a reader who is absorbed in the zealous pursuit of purely rational knowledge that path which, it is my firm conviction, alone leads to the truth—the path of empirical investigation and of the Monistic Philosophy which is based upon it.

ERNST HAECKEL.

JENA, GERMANY.

PREFACE

THE hour is close upon us when we shall commence our retrospect of one of the most wonderful sections of time that was ever measured by the sweep of the earth. Already the expert is at work, dissecting out and studying his particular phase of that vast world of thought and action we call the nineteenth century. Art, literature, commerce, industry, politics, ethics—all have their high interpreters among us; but in the chance of life it has fallen out that there is none to read aright for us, in historic retrospect, what after ages will probably regard as the most salient feature of the nineteenth century—the conflict of theology with philosophy and science. The pens of our Huxleys, and Tyndalls, and Darwins lie where they fell; there is none left in strength among us to sum up the issues of that struggle with knowledge and sympathy.

In these circumstances it has been thought fitting that we should introduce to English readers the latest work of Professor Haeckel. Germany, as the reader will quickly perceive, is witnessing the same strange reaction of thought that we see about us here in England, yet *Die Weltrathsel* found an immediate and very extensive circle of readers. One of the most prominent

PREFACE

zoologists of the century, Professor Haeckel, has a unique claim to pronounce with authority, from the scientific side, on what is known as "the conflict of science and religion." In the contradictory estimates that are urged on us—for the modern ecclesiastic is as emphatic in his assurance that the conflict has ended favorably to theology as the rationalist is with his counter-assertion—the last words of one of the leading combatants of the second half of the century, still, happily, in full vigor of mind, will be heard with respect and close attention.

A glance at the index of the work suffices to indicate its comprehensive character. The judgment of the distinguished scientist cannot fail to have weight on all the topics included; yet the reader will soon discover a vein of exceptionally interesting thought in the chapters on evolution. The evolution of the human body is no longer a matter of serious dispute. It has passed the first two tribunals—those of theology and of an *à priori* philosophy—and is only challenged at the third and last—that of empirical proof—by the decorative heads of scientific bodies and a few isolated thinkers.

"*Apparent rari nantes in gurgite vasto.*"

But the question of the evolution of the human mind, or soul, has been successfully divorced from that of the body. Roman Catholic advanced theologians, whose precise terminology demanded a clear position, admit the latter and deny the former categorically. Other theologians, and many philosophers, have still a vague notion that the evidence for the one does not impair their sentimental objection to the other. Dr. Haeckel's work summarizes the evidence for the evo-

PREFACE

lution of mind in a masterly and profoundly interesting fashion. It seems impossible to follow his broad survey of the psychic world, from protist to man, without bearing away a conviction of the natural origin of every power and content of the human soul.

TRANSLATOR.

October, 1900.

THE RIDDLE OF THE UNIVERSE

CHAPTER I

THE NATURE OF THE PROBLEM

The Condition of Civilization and of Thought at the Close of the Nineteenth Century—Progress of Our Knowledge of Nature, of the Organic and Inorganic Sciences—The Law of Substance and the Law of Evolution—Progress of Technical Science and of Applied Chemistry—Stagnancy in other Departments of Life: Legal and Political Administration, Education, and the Church—Conflict of Reason and Dogma—Anthropism—Cosmological Perspective—Cosmological Theorems—Refutation of the Delusion of Man's Importance—Number of "World-Riddles"—Criticism of the "Seven" Enigmas—The Way to Solve Them—Function of the Senses and of the Brain—Induction and Deduction—Reason, Sentiment, and Revelation—Philosophy and Science—Experience and Speculation—Dualism and Monism

THE close of the nineteenth century offers one of the most remarkable spectacles to the thoughtful observer. All educated people are agreed that it has in many respects immeasurably outstripped its predecessors, and has achieved tasks that were deemed impracticable at its commencement. An entirely new character has been given to the whole of our modern civilization, not only by our astounding theoretical progress in sound knowledge of nature, but also by the remarkably fertile practical application of that knowledge in technical science, industry, commerce, and so forth. On the other hand, however, we have made little or no progress in moral and social life, in comparison with earlier centuries; at times there has been serious reaction. And from this obvious conflict there have arisen, not only an uneasy sense of dismemberment and falseness, but even the danger of grave catastrophes in the political and social world. It is, then, not merely the right, but the sacred duty, of every honorable and humanitarian thinker to devote himself conscientiously to the settlement of that conflict, and to warding off the dangers that it brings in its train. In our conviction this can only be done by a courageous effort to attain the truth, and by the formation of a clear view of the world —a view that shall be based on truth and conformity to reality.

If we recall to mind the imperfect condition of science at the beginning of the century, and compare this with the magnificent structure of its closing years, we are compelled to admit that marvellous progress has been made during its course. Every single branch of science can boast that it has, especially during the latter half of the century, made numerous acquisitions of the utmost value. Both in our microscopic knowledge of the little and in our telescopic investigation of the great we have attained an invaluable insight that seemed inconceivable a hundred years ago. Improved methods of microscopic and biological research have not only revealed to us an invisible world of living things in the kingdom of the protists, full of an infinite wealth of forms, but they have taught us to recognize in the tiny cell the all-pervading "elementary organism" of whose social communities—the tissues—the body of every

THE NATURE OF THE PROBLEM

multicellular plant and animal, even that of man, is composed. This anatomical knowledge is of extreme importance; and it is supplemented by the embryological discovery that each of the higher multicellular organisms is developed out of one simple cell, the impregnated ovum. The "cellular theory," which has been founded on that discovery, has given us the first true interpretation of the physical, chemical, and even the psychological processes of life—those mysterious phenomena for whose explanation it had been customary to postulate a supernatural "vital force" or "immortal soul." Moreover, the true character of disease has been made clear and intelligible to the physician for the first time by the cognate science of Cellular Pathology.

The discoveries of the nineteenth century in the inorganic world are no less important. Physics has made astounding progress in every section of its province—in optics and acoustics, in magnetism and electricity, in mechanics and thermo-dynamics; and, what is still more important, it has proved the unity of the forces of the entire universe. The mechanical theory of heat has shown how intimately they are connected, and how each can, in certain conditions, transform itself directly into another. Spectral analysis has taught us that the same matter which enters into the composition of all bodies on earth, including its living inhabitants, builds up the rest of the planets, the sun, and the most distant stars. Astro-physics has considerably enlarged our cosmic perspective in revealing to us, in the immeasurable depths of space, millions of circling spheres larger than our earth, and, like it, in endless transformation, in an eternal rhythm of life and death. Chemistry has introduced us to a multitude of new substances, all of

THE RIDDLE OF THE UNIVERSE

which arise from the combination of a few (about seventy) elements that are incapable of further analysis; some of them play a most important part in every branch of life. It has been shown that one of these elements —carbon—is the remarkable substance that effects the endless variety of organic syntheses, and thus may be considered "the chemical basis of life." All the particular advances, however, of physics and chemistry yield in theoretical importance to the discovery of the great law which brings them all to one common focus, the "Law of Substance." As this fundamental cosmic law establishes the eternal persistence of matter and force, their unvarying constancy throughout the entire universe, it has become the pole-star that guides our Monistic Philosophy through the mighty labyrinth to a solution of the world-problem.

Since we intend to make a general survey of the actual condition of our knowledge of nature and its progress during the present century in the following chapters, we shall delay no longer with the review of its particular branches. We would only mention one important advance, which was contemporary with the discovery of the law of substance, and which supplements it—the establishment of the theory of evolution. It is true that there were philosophers who spoke of the evolution of things a thousand years ago; but the recognition that such a law dominates the entire universe, and that the world is nothing else than an eternal "evolution of substance," is a fruit of the nineteenth century. It was not until the second half of this century that it attained to perfect clearness and a universal application. The immortal merit of establishing the doctrine on an empirical basis, and pointing out its world-wide application, belongs to the great scientist Charles Darwin;

THE NATURE OF THE PROBLEM

he it was who, in 1859, supplied a solid foundation for the theory of descent, which the able French naturalist Jean Lamarck had already sketched in its broad outlines in 1809, and the fundamental idea of which had been almost prophetically enunciated in 1799 by Germany's greatest poet and thinker, Wolfgang Goethe. In that theory we have the key to "the question of all questions," to the great enigma of "the place of man in nature," and of his natural development. If we are in a position to-day to recognize the sovereignty of the law of evolution—and, indeed, of a monistic evolution—in every province of nature, and to use it, in conjunction with the law of substance, for a simple interpretation of all natural phenomena, we owe it chiefly to those three distinguished naturalists; they shine as three stars of the first magnitude amid all the great men of the century.

This marvellous progress in a theoretical knowledge of nature has been followed by a manifold practical application in every branch of civilized life. If we are to-day in the "age of commerce," if international trade and communication have attained dimensions beyond the conception of any previous age, if we have transcended the limits of space and time by our telegraph and telephone, we owe it, in the first place, to the technical advancement of physics, especially in the application of steam and electricity. If, in photography, we can, with the utmost ease, compel the sunbeam to create for us in a moment's time a correct picture of any object we like; if we have made enormous progress in agriculture, and in a variety of other pursuits; if, in surgery, we have brought an infinite relief to human pain by our chloroform and morphia, our antiseptics and serous therapeutics, we owe it all to applied chemistry. But it is so well known how much we have surpassed all earlier centuries through these and other scientific discoveries that we need linger over the question no longer.

While we look back with a just pride on the immense progress of the nineteenth century in a knowledge of nature and in its practical application, we find, unfortunately, a very different and far from agreeable picture when we turn to another and not less important province of modern life. To our great regret we must endorse the words of Alfred Wallace: "Compared with our astounding progress in physical science and its practical application, our system of government, of administrative justice, and of national education, and our entire social and moral organization, remain in a state of barbarism." To convince ourselves of the truth of this grave indictment we need only cast an unprejudiced glance at our public life, or look into the mirror that is daily offered to us by the press, the organ of public sentiment.

We begin our review with justice, the *fundamentum regnorum*. No one can maintain that its condition today is in harmony with our advanced knowledge of man and the world. Not a week passes in which we do not read of judicial decisions over which every thoughtful man shakes his head in despair; many of the decisions of our higher and lower courts are simply unintelligible. We are not referring in the treatment of this particular "world-problem" to the fact that many modern states, in spite of their paper constitutions, are really governed with absolute despotism, and that many who occupy the bench give judgment less in accordance with their sincere conviction than with wishes expressed in higher quarters. We readily ad-

THE NATURE OF THE PROBLEM

mit that the majority of judges and counsel decide conscientiously, and err simply from human frailty. Most of their errors, indeed, are due to defective preparation. It is popularly supposed that these are just the men of highest education, and that on that very account they have the preference in nominations to different offices. However, this famed " legal education " is for the most part rather of a formal and technical character. They have but a superficial acquaintance with that chief and peculiar object of their activity, the human organism, and its most important function, the mind. That is evident from the curious views as to the liberty of the will, responsibility, etc., which we encounter daily. I once told an eminent jurist that the tiny spherical ovum from which every man is developed is as truly endowed with life as the embryo of two, or seven, or even nine months; he laughed incredulously. Most of the students of jurisprudence have no acquaintance with anthropology, psychology, and the doctrine of evolution—the very first requisites for a correct estimate of human nature. They have " no time " for it; their time is already too largely bespoken for an exhaustive study of beer and wine and for the noble art of fencing. The rest of their valuable study-time is required for the purpose of learning some hundreds of paragraphs of law books, a knowledge of which is supposed to qualify the jurist for any position whatever in our modern civilized community.

We shall touch but lightly on the unfortunate province of politics, for the unsatisfactory condition of the modern political world is only too familiar. In a great measure its evils are due to the fact that most of our officials are jurists—that is, men of high technical education, but utterly devoid of that thorough knowledge of human nature which is only obtained by the study of comparative anthropology and the monistic psychology—men without an acquaintance with those social relations of which we find the earlier types in comparative zoology and the theory of evolution, in the cellular theory, and the study of the protists. We can only arrive at a correct knowledge of the structure and life of the social body, the state, through a scientific knowledge of the structure and life of the individuals who compose it, and the cells of which they are in turn composed. If our political rulers and our " representatives of the people " possessed this invaluable biological and anthropological knowledge, we should not find our journals so full of the sociological blunders and political nonsense which at present are far from adorning our parliamentary reports, and even many of our official documents. Worst of all is it when the modern state flings itself into the arms of the reactionary Church, and when the narrow-minded self-interest of parties and the infatuation of short-sighted party-leaders lend their support to the hierarchy. Then are witnessed such sad scenes as the German Reichstag puts before our eyes even at the close of the nineteenth century. We have the spectacle of the educated German people in the power of the ultramontane Centre, under the rule of the Roman papacy, which is its bitterest and most dangerous enemy. Then superstition and stupidity reign instead of right and reason. Never will our government improve until it casts off the fetters of the Church and raises the views of the citizens on man and the world to a higher level by a general scientific education. That does not raise the question of any special form of constitution. Whether a monarchy or a republic be preferable, whether the constitution should be

THE NATURE OF THE PROBLEM

aristocratic or democratic, are subordinate questions in comparison with the supreme question: Shall the modern civilized state be spiritual or secular? Shall it be *theocratic*—ruled by the irrational formulæ of faith and by clerical despotism—or *nomocratic*—under the sovereignty of rational laws and civic right? The first task is to kindle a rational interest in our youth, and to uplift our citizens and free them from superstition. That can only be achieved by a timely reform of our schools.

Our education of the young is no more in harmony with modern scientific progress than our legal and political world. Physical science, which is so much more important than all other sciences, and which, properly understood, really embraces all the so-called moral sciences, is still regarded as a mere accessory in our schools, if not treated as the Cinderella of the curriculum. Most of our teachers still give the most prominent place to that dead learning which has come down from the cloistral schools of the Middle Ages. In the front rank we have grammatical gymnastics and an immense waste of time over a " thorough knowledge " of classics and of the history of foreign nations. Ethics, the most important object of practical philosophy, is entirely neglected, and its place is usurped by the ecclesiastical creed. Faith must take precedence over knowledge—not that scientific faith which leads to a monistic religion, but the irrational superstition that lays the foundation of a perverted Christianity. The valuable teaching of modern cosmology and anthropology, of biology and evolution, is most inadequately imparted, if not entirely unknown, in our higher schools; while the memory is burdened with a mass of philological and historical facts which are utterly useless, either from the point of view of theoretical education or for the practical purposes of life. Moreover, the antiquated arrangements and the distribution of faculties in the universities are just as little in harmony with the point we have reached in monistic science as the curriculum of the primary and secondary schools.

The climax of the opposition to modern education and its foundation, advanced natural philosophy, is reached, of course, in the Church. We are not speaking here of ultramontane papistry, nor of the orthodox evangelical tendencies, which do not fall far short of it in ignorance and in the crass superstition of their dogmas. We are imagining ourselves for the moment to be in the church of a liberal Protestant minister, who has a good average education, and who finds room for "the rights of reason" by the side of his faith. There, besides excellent moral teaching, which is in perfect harmony with our own monistic ethics, and humanitarian discussion of which we cordially approve, we hear ideas on the nature of God, of the world, of man, and of life which are directly opposed to all scientific experience. It is no wonder that physicists and chemists, doctors and philosophers, who have made a thorough study of nature, refuse a hearing to such preachers. Our theologians and our politicians are just as ignorant as our philosophers and our jurists of that elementary knowledge of nature which is based on the monistic theory of evolution, and which is already far exceeded in the triumph of our modern learning.

From this opposition, which we can only briefly point out at present, there arise grave conflicts in our modern life which urgently demand a settlement. Our modern education, the outcome of our great advance in knowledge, has a claim upon every department of public and private life; it would see humanity raised, by the in-

THE NATURE OF THE PROBLEM

strumentality of reason, to that higher grade of culture, and, consequently, to that better path towards happiness which has been opened out to us by the progress of modern science. That aim, however, is vigorously opposed by the influential parties who would detain the mind in the exploded views of the Middle Ages with regard to the most important problems of life; they linger in the fold of traditional dogma, and would have reason prostrate itself before their "higher revelation." That is the condition of things, to a very large extent, in theology and philosophy, in sociology and jurisprudence. It is not that the motives of the latter are to be attributed, as a rule, to pure self-interest; they spring partly from ignorance of the facts, and partly from an indolent acquiescence in tradition. The most dangerous of the three great enemies of reason and knowledge is not malice, but ignorance, or, perhaps, indolence. The gods themselves still strive in vain against these two latter influences when they have happily vanquished the first.

One of the main supports of that reactionary system is still what we may call "anthropism." I designate by this term "that powerful and world-wide group of erroneous opinions which opposes the human organism to the whole of the rest of nature, and represents it to be the preordained end of the organic creation, an entity essentially distinct from it, a godlike being." Closer examination of this group of ideas shows it to be made up of three different dogmas, which we may distinguish as the *anthropocentric*, the *anthropomorphic*, and the *anthropolatrous*.*

I. The *anthropocentric* dogma culminates in the idea

* E. Haeckel, *Systematische Phylogenie*, 1895, vol. iii., pp. 646–50. (Anthropolatry means " A divine worship of human nature.")

that man is the preordained centre and aim of all terrestrial life—or, in a wider sense, of the whole universe. As this error is extremely conducive to man's interest, and as it is intimately connected with the creation-myth of the three great Mediterranean religions, and with the dogmas of the Mosaic, Christian, and Mohammedan theologies, it still dominates the greater part of the civilized world.

II. The *anthropomorphic* dogma is likewise connected with the creation-myth of the three aforesaid religions, and of many others. It likens the creation and control of the world by God to the artificial creation of a talented engineer or mechanic, and to the administration of a wise ruler. God, as creator, sustainer, and ruler of the world, is thus represented after a purely human fashion in his thought and work. Hence it follows, in turn, that man is godlike. "God made man to His own image and likeness." The older, naïve mythology is pure "homotheism," attributing human shape, flesh, and blood to the gods. It is more intelligible than the modern mystic theosophy that adores a personal God as an invisible—properly speaking, gaseous—being, yet makes him think, speak, and act in human fashion; it gives us the paradoxical picture of a "gaseous vertebrate."

III. The *anthropolatric* dogma naturally results from this comparison of the activity of God and man; it ends in the apotheosis of the human organism. A further result is the belief in the personal immortality of the soul, and the dualistic dogma of the twofold nature of man, whose "immortal soul" is conceived as but the temporary inhabitant of the mortal frame. Thus these three anthropistic dogmas, variously adapted to the respective professions of the different religions, came at

THE NATURE OF THE PROBLEM

length to be vested with an extraordinary importance, and proved the source of the most dangerous errors. The anthropistic view of the world which springs from them is in irreconcilable opposition to our monistic system; indeed, it is at once disproved by our new cosmological perspective.

Not only the three anthropistic dogmas, but many other notions of the dualistic philosophy and orthodox religion, are found to be untenable as soon as we regard them critically from the cosmological perspective of our monistic system. We understand by that the comprehensive view of the universe which we have from the highest point of our monistic interpretation of nature. From that stand-point we see the truth of the following "cosmological theorems," most of which, in our opinion, have already been amply demonstrated:

(1) The universe, or the cosmos, is eternal, infinite, and illimitable. (2) Its substance, with its two attributes (matter and energy), fills infinite space, and is in eternal motion. (3) This motion runs on through infinite time as an unbroken development, with a periodic change from life to death, from evolution to devolution. (4) The innumerable bodies which are scattered about the space-filling ether all obey the same "law of substance;" while the rotating masses slowly move towards their destruction and dissolution in one part of space others are springing into new life and development in other quarters of the universe. (5) Our sun is one of these unnumbered perishable bodies, and our earth is one of the countless transitory planets that encircle them. (6) Our earth has gone through a long process of cooling before water, in liquid form (the first condition of organic life), could settle thereon. (7) The ensuing biogenetic process, the slow development and

THE RIDDLE OF THE UNIVERSE

transformation of countless organic forms, must have taken many millions of years—considerably over a hundred.* (8) Among the different kinds of animals which arose in the later stages of the biogenetic process on earth the vertebrates have far outstripped all other competitors in the evolutionary race. (9) The most important branch of the vertebrates, the mammals, were developed later (during the triassic period) from the lower amphibia and the reptilia. (10) The most perfect and most highly developed branch of the class mammalia is the order of primates, which first put in an appearance, by development from the lowest prochoriata, at the beginning of the Tertiary period—at least three million years ago. (11) The youngest and most perfect twig of the branch primates is man, who sprang from a series of manlike apes towards the end of the Tertiary period. (12) Consequently, the so-called history of the world "—that is, the brief period of a few thousand years which measures the duration of civilization—is an evanescently short episode in the long course of organic evolution, just as this, in turn, is merely a small portion of the history of our planetary system; and as our mother-earth is a mere speck in the sunbeam in the illimitable universe, so man himself is but a tiny grain of protoplasm in the perishable framework of organic nature.

Nothing seems to me better adapted than this magnificent cosmological perspective to give us the proper standard and the broad outlook which we need in the solution of the vast enigmas that surround us. It not only clearly indicates the true place of man in nature, but it dissipates the prevalent illusion of man's supreme

* Cf. my Cambridge lecture, *The Last Link*, " Geological Time and Evolution."

THE NATURE OF THE PROBLEM

importance, and the arrogance with which he sets himself apart from the illimitable universe, and exalts himself to the position of its most valuable element. This boundless presumption of conceited man has misled him into making himself "the image of God," claiming an "eternal life" for his ephemeral personality, and imagining that he possesses unlimited "freedom of will." The ridiculous imperial folly of Caligula is but a special form of man's arrogant assumption of divinity. Only when we have abandoned this untenable illusion, and taken up the correct cosmological perspective, can we hope to reach the solution of the "riddles of the universe."

The uneducated member of a civilized community is surrounded with countless enigmas at every step, just as truly as the savage. Their number, however, decreases with every stride of civilization and of science; and the monistic philosophy is ultimately confronted with but one simple and comprehensive enigma—the "problem of substance." Still, we may find it useful to include a certain number of problems under that title. In the famous speech which Emil du Bois-Reymond delivered in 1880, in the Leibnitz session of the Berlin Academy of Sciences, he distinguished seven world-enigmas, which he enumerated as follows: (1) The nature of matter and force. (2) The origin of motion. (3) The origin of life. (4) The (apparently preordained) orderly arrangement of nature. (5) The origin of simple sensation and consciousness. (6) Rational thought, and the origin of the cognate faculty, speech. (7) The question of the freedom of the will. Three of these seven enigmas are considered by the orator of the Berlin Academy to be entirely transcendental and insoluble —they are the first, second, and fifth; three others (the third, fourth, and sixth) he considers to be capable of solution, though extremely difficult; as to the seventh and last "world-enigma," the freedom of the will, which is the one of the greatest practical importance, he remains undecided

As my monism differs materially from that of the Berlin orator, and as his idea of the "seven great enigmas" has been very widely accepted, it may be useful to indicate their true position at once. In my opinion, the three transcendental problems (1, 2, and 5) are settled by our conception of substance (*vide* chap. xii.); the three which he considers difficult, though soluble, (3, 4, and 6), are decisively answered by our modern theory of evolution; the seventh and last, the freedom of the will, is not an object for critical, scientific inquiry at all, for it is a pure dogma, based on an illusion, and has no real existence.

The means and methods we have chosen for attaining the solution of the great enigma do not differ, on the whole, from those of all purely scientific investigation—firstly, experience; secondly, inference. Scientific experience comes to us by observation and experiment, which involve the activity of our sense-organs in the first place, and, secondly, of the inner sense-centres in the cortex of the brain. The microscopic elementary organs of the former are the sense-cells; of the latter, groups of ganglionic cells The experiences which we derive from the outer world by these invaluable instruments of our mental life are then moulded into ideas by other parts of the brain, and these, in their turn, are united in a chain of reasoning by association. The construction of this chain may take place in two different ways, which are, in my opinion, equally valuable and indispensable: *induction* and *deduction*. The higher

THE NATURE OF THE PROBLEM

cerebral operations, the construction of complicated chains of reasoning, abstraction, the formation of concepts, the completion of the perceptive faculty by the plastic faculty of the imagination—in a word, consciousness, thought, and speculation—are functions of the ganglionic cells of the cortex of the brain, just like the preceding simpler mental functions. We unite them all in the supreme concept of *reason*.*

By reason only can we attain to a correct knowledge of the world and a solution of its great problems. Reason is man's highest gift, the only prerogative that essentially distinguishes him from the lower animals. Nevertheless, it has only reached this high position by the progress of culture and education, by the development of knowledge. The uneducated man and the savage are just as little (or just as much) "rational" as our nearest relatives among the mammals (apes, dogs, elephants, etc.). Yet the opinion still obtains in many quarters that, besides our godlike reason, we have two further (and even surer!) methods of receiving knowledge—emotion and revelation. We must at once dispose of this dangerous error. Emotion has nothing whatever to do with the attainment of truth. That which we prize under the name of "emotion" is an elaborate activity of the brain, which consists of feelings of like and dislike, motions of assent and dissent, impulses of desire and aversion. It may be influenced by the most diverse activities of the organism, by the cravings of the senses and the muscles, the stomach, the sexual organs, etc. The interests of truth are far from promoted by these conditions and vacillations of emotion; on the contrary, such circumstances often dis-

* As to induction and deduction, *vide The Natural History of Creation.*

turb that reason which alone is adapted to the pursuit of truth, and frequently mar its perceptive power. No cosmic problem is solved, or even advanced, by the cerebral function we call emotion. And the same must be said of the so-called "revelation," and of the "truths of faith" which it is supposed to communicate; they are based entirely on a deception, consciously or unconsciously, as we shall see in the sixteenth chapter.

We must welcome as one of the most fortunate steps in the direction of a solution of the great cosmic problems the fact that of recent years there is a growing tendency to recognize the two paths which alone lead thereto—*experience* and *thought*, or *speculation*—to be of equal value, and mutually complementary. Philosophers have come to see that pure speculation—such, for instance, as Plato and Hegel employed for the construction of their *idealist* systems—does not lead to knowledge of reality. On the other hand, scientists have been convinced that mere experience—such as Bacon and Mill, for example, made the basis of their *realist* systems—is insufficient of itself for a complete philosophy For these two great paths of knowledge, sense-experience and rational thought, are two distinct cerebral functions; the one is elaborated by the sense-organs and the inner sense-centres, the other by the thought-centres, the great "centres of association in the cortex of the brain," which lie between the sense-centres. (Cf cc. vii. and x.) True knowledge is only acquired by combining the activity of the two. Nevertheless, there are still many philosophers who would construct the world out of their own inner consciousness, and who reject our empirical science precisely because they have no knowledge of the real world. On the other hand, there are many

THE NATURE OF THE PROBLEM

scientists who still contend that the sole object of science is "the knowledge of facts, the objective investigation of isolated phenomena"; that "the age of philosophy" is past, and science has taken its place.* This one-sided over-estimation of experience is as dangerous an error as the converse exaggeration of the value of speculation Both channels of knowledge are mutually indispensable The greatest triumphs of modern science—the cellular theory, the dynamic theory of heat, the theory of evolution, and the law of substance —are *philosophic achievements*; not, however, the fruit of pure speculation, but of an antecedent experience of the widest and most searching character.

At the commencement of the nineteenth century the great idealistic poet, Schiller, gave his counsel to both groups of combatants, the philosophers and the scientists:

"Does strife divide your efforts—no union bless your toil?
Will truth e'er be delivered if ye your forces rend?"

Since then the situation has, happily, been profoundly modified; while both schools, in their different paths, have pressed onward towards the same high goal, they have recognized their common aspiration, and they draw nearer to a knowledge of the truth in mutual covenant. At the end of the nineteenth century we have returned to that monistic attitude which our greatest realistic poet, Goethe, had recognized from its very commencement to be alone correct and fruitful †

* Rudolph Virchow, *Die Gründung der Berliner Universität und der Uebergang aus dem philosophischen in das naturwissenschaftliche Zeitalter*. (Berlin; 1893.)

† Cf. chap. iv. of my *General Morphology*, 1866; *Kritik der naturwissenschaftlichen Methoden.*

THE RIDDLE OF THE UNIVERSE

All the different philosophical tendencies may, from the point of view of modern science, be ranged in two antagonistic groups; they represent either a *dualistic* or a *monistic* interpretation of the cosmos. The former is usually bound up with teleological and idealistic dogmas, the latter with mechanical and realistic theories. Dualism, in the widest sense, breaks up the universe into two entirely distinct substances — the material world and an immaterial God, who is represented to be its creator, sustainer, and ruler. Monism, on the contrary (likewise taken in its widest sense), recognizes one sole substance in the universe, which is at once "God and nature"; body and spirit (or matter and energy) it holds to be inseparable. The extramundane God of dualism leads necessarily to theism; and the intra-mundane God of the monist leads to pantheism

The different ideas of *monism* and *materialism*, and likewise the essentially distinct tendencies of theoretical and practical materialism, are still very frequently confused. As this and other similar cases of confusion of ideas are very prejudicial, and give rise to innumerable errors, we shall make the following brief observations, in order to prevent misunderstanding:

I. Pure monism is identical neither with the theoretical materialism that denies the existence of spirit, and dissolves the world into a heap of dead atoms, nor with the theoretical spiritualism (lately entitled "energetic" spiritualism by Ostwald) which rejects the notion of matter, and considers the world to be a specially arranged group of "energies" or immaterial natural forces.

II. On the contrary, we hold, with Goethe, that "matter cannot exist and be operative without spirit,

THE NATURE OF THE PROBLEM

nor spirit without matter." We adhere firmly to the pure, unequivocal monism of Spinoza: Matter, or infinitely extended substance, and spirit (or energy), or sensitive and thinking substance, are the two fundamental attributes or principal properties of the all-embracing divine essence of the world, the universal substance. (Cf. chap. xii.)

CHAPTER II

OUR BODILY FRAME

Fundamental Importance of Anatomy—Human Anatomy—Hippocrates, Aristotle, Galen, Vesalius—Comparative Anatomy—Georges Cuvier—Johannes Muller—Karl Gegenbaur—Histology—The Cellular Theory—Schleiden and Schwann—Kölliker—Virchow—Man a Vertebrate, a Tetrapod, a Mammal, a Placental, a Primate—Prosimiæ and Simiæ—The Catarrhinæ—Papiomorphic and Anthropomorphic Apes—Essential Likeness of Man and the Ape in Corporal Structure.

ALL biological research, all investigation into the forms and vital activities of organisms, must first deal with the visible body, in which the morphological and physiological phenomena are observed. This fundamental rule holds good for man just as much as for all other living things. Moreover, the inquiry must not confine itself to mere observation of the outer form; it must penetrate to the interior, and study both the general plan and the minute details of the structure. The science which pursues this fundamental investigation in the broadest sense is anatomy.

The first stimulus to an inquiry into the human frame arose, naturally, in medicine. As it was usually practised by the priests in the older civilizations, we may assume that these highest representatives of the education of the time had already acquired a certain

OUR BODILY FRAME

amount of anatomical knowledge two thousand years before Christ, or even earlier. We do not, however, find more exact observations, founded on the dissection of mammals, and applied, by analogy, to the human frame, until we come to the Greek scientists of the sixth and fifth centuries before Christ—Empedocles (of Agrigentum) and Democritus (of Abdera), and especially the most famous physician of classic antiquity, Hippocrates (of Cos). It was from these and other sources that the great Aristotle, the renowned "father of natural history," equally comprehensive as investigator and philosopher, derived his first knowledge. After him only one anatomist of any consequence is found in antiquity, the Greek physician Claudius Galenus (of Pergamus), who developed a wealthy practice in Rome in the second century after Christ, under the Emperor Marcus Aurelius. All these ancient anatomists acquired their knowledge, as a rule, not by the dissection of the human body itself—which was then sternly forbidden—but by a study of the bodies of the animals which most closely resembled man, especially the apes; they were all, indeed, comparative anatomists.

The triumph of Christianity and its mystic theories meant retrogression to anatomy, as it did to all the other sciences. The popes were resolved above all things to detain humanity in ignorance; they rightly deemed a knowledge of the human organism to be a dangerous source of enlightenment as to our true nature. During the long period of thirteen centuries the writings of Galen were almost the only source of human anatomy, just as the works of Aristotle were for the whole of natural history. It was not until the sixteenth century, when the spiritual tyranny of the papacy was broken by the Reformation, and the geocentric theory, so intimately connected with papal doctrine, was destroyed by the new cosmic system of Copernicus, that the knowledge of the human frame entered upon a new period of progress. The great anatomists, Vesalius (of Brussels), and Eustachius and Fallopius (of Modena), advanced the knowledge of our bodily structure so much by their own thorough investigations that little remained for their numerous followers to do, with regard to the more obvious phenomena, except the substantiation of details. Andreas Vesalius, as courageous as he was talented and indefatigable, was the pioneer of the movement; he completed in his twenty-eighth year (1543) that great and systematic work *De humani corporis fabrica;* he gave to the whole of human anatomy a new and independent scope and a more solid foundation. On that account he was, at a later date, at Madrid—where he was physician to Charles V. and Philip II.—condemned to death by the Inquisition as a magician. He only escaped by undertaking a pilgrimage to Jerusalem; in returning he suffered shipwreck on the Isle of Zante, and died there in misery and destitution.

The great merit of the nineteenth century, as far as our knowledge of the human frame is concerned, lies in the founding of two new lines of research of immense importance—comparative anatomy and histology, or microscopic anatomy. The former was intimately associated with human anatomy from the very beginning; indeed, it had to supply the place of the latter so long because the dissection of human corpses was a crime visited with capital punishment—that was the case even in the fifteenth century! But the many anatomists of the next three centuries devoted themselves mainly to a more accurate study of the human organism. The

OUR BODILY FRAME

elaborate science which we now call comparative anatomy was born in the year 1803, when the great French zoologist Georges Cuvier (a native of Mömpelgard, in Alsace) published his profound *Leçons sur l'anatomie comparée*, and endeavored to formulate, for the first time, definite laws as to the organism of man and the beasts. While his predecessors—among whom was Goethe in 1790—had mainly contented themselves with comparing the skeleton of man with those of other animals, Cuvier's broader vision took in the whole of the animal organization. He distinguished therein four great and mutually independent types: Vertebrata, Articulata, Mollusca, and Radiata. This advance was of extreme consequence for our "question of all questions," since it clearly brought out the fact that man belonged to the vertebral type, and differed fundamentally from all the other types. It is true that the keen-sighted Linné had already, in his *Systema Naturae*, made a great step in advance by assigning man a definite place in the class of mammals; he had even drawn up the three groups of half-apes, apes, and men (*Lemur, simia,* and *homo*) in the order of primates. But his keen, systematic mind was not furnished with that profound empirical foundation, supplied by comparative anatomy, which Cuvier was the first to attain. Further developments were added by the great comparative anatomists of our own century—Friedrich Meckel (Halle), Johannes Müller (Berlin), Richard Owen, T. Huxley, and Karl Gegenbaur (Jena, subsequently Heidelberg). The last-named, in applying the evolutionary theory, which Darwin had just established, to comparative anatomy, raised his science to the front rank of biological studies. The numerous comparative anatomical works of Gegenbaur are, like his well-known

THE RIDDLE OF THE UNIVERSE

Manual of Human Anatomy, equally distinguished by a thorough empirical acquaintance with their immense multitudes of facts, and by a comprehensive control of his material, and its philosophic appreciation in the evolutionary sense. His recent *Comparative Anatomy of the Vertebrata* establishes the solid foundation on which our conviction of the vertebral character of man in every aspect is chiefly based.

Microscopic anatomy has been developed, in the course of the present century, in a very different fashion from comparative anatomy. At the beginning of the century (1802) a French physician, Bichat, made an attempt to dissect the organs of the human body into their finer constituents by the aid of the microscope, and to show the connection of these various *tissues* (*histа*, or *tela*). This first attempt led to little result, because the scientist was ignorant of the one common element of all the different tissues. This was first discovered (1838) in the shape of the *cell*, in the plant world, by Matthias Schleiden, and immediately afterwards proved to be the same in the animal world by Theodor Schwann, the pupil and assistant of Johannes Müller at Berlin. Two other distinguished pupils of this great master, who are still living, Albert Kölliker and Rudolph Virchow, took up the cellular theory, and the theory of tissues which is founded on it, in the sixties, and applied them to the human organism in all its details, both in health and disease; they proved that, in man and all other animals, every tissue is made up of the same microscopic particles, the *cells*, and these "elementary organisms" are the real, self-active citizens which, in combinations of millions, constitute the "cellular state," our body. All these cells spring from one simple cell, the *cytula*, or im-

OUR BODILY FRAME

pregnated ovum, by continuous subdivision. The general structure and combination of the tissues are the same in man as in the other vertebrates. Among these the mammals, the youngest and most highly developed class take precedence, in virtue of certain special features which were acquired late. Such are, for instance, the microscopic texture of the hair, of the glands of the skin, and of the breasts, and the corpuscles of the blood, which are quite peculiar to mammals, and different from those of the other vertebrates; man, even in these finest histological relations, is a *true mammal*.

The microscopic researches of Albert Kölliker and Franz Leydig (at Würzburg) not only enlarged our knowledge of the finer structure of man and the beasts in every direction, but they were especially important in the light of their connection with the evolution of the cell and the tissue; they confirmed the great theory of Carl Theodor Siebold (1845) that the lowest animals, the Infusoria and the Rhizopods, are unicellular organisms.

Our whole frame, both in its general plan and its detailed structure, presents the characteristic type of the vertebrates. This most important and most highly developed group in the animal world was first recognized in its natural unity in 1801 by the great Lamarck; he embraced under that title the four higher animal groups of Linné—mammals, birds, amphibia, and fishes. To these he opposed the two lower classes, insects and worms, as invertebrates. Cuvier (1812) established the unity of the vertebrate type on a firmer basis by his comparative anatomy. It is quite true that all the vertebrates, from the fish up to man, agree in every essential feature; they all have a firm internal skeleton, a framework of cartilage and bone, consisting principally of a vertebral column and a skull; the advanced construction of the latter presents many variations, but, on the whole, all may be reduced to the same fundamental type. Further, in all vertebrates the "organ of the mind," the central nervous system, in the shape of a spinal cord and a brain, lies at the back of this axial skeleton. Moreover, what we said of its bony environment, the skull, is also true of the brain—the instrument of consciousness and all the higher functions of the mind; its construction and size present very many variations in detail, but its general characteristic structure remains always the same.

We meet the same phenomenon when we compare the rest of our organs with those of the other vertebrates; everywhere, in virtue of heredity, the original plan and the relative distribution of the organs remain the same, although, through adaptation to different environments, the size and the structure of particular sections offer considerable variation. Thus we find that in all cases the blood circulates in two main blood-vessels, of which one—the aorta—passes over the intestine, and the other—the principal vein—passes underneath, and that by the broadening out of the latter in a very definite spot a heart has arisen; this "ventral heart" is just as characteristic of all vertebrates as the "dorsal heart" is of the articulata and mollusca. Equally characteristic of all vertebrates is the early division of the intestinal tube into a "head-gut" (or gill-gut), which serves in respiration, and a "body-gut" (or liver-gut), which co-operates with the liver in digestion; so are, likewise, the ramification of the muscular system, the peculiar structure of the urinary and

OUR BODILY FRAME

sexual organs, and so forth. In all these anatomical relations *man is a true vertebrate.*

Aristotle gave the name of four-footed, or tetrapoda, to all the higher warm-blooded animals which are distinguished by the possession of two pairs of legs. The category was enlarged subsequently, and its title changed into the Latin "quadrupeda," when Cuvier proved that even "two-legged" birds and men are really "four-footed"; he showed that the internal skeleton of the four legs in all the higher land-vertebrates, from the amphibia up to man, was originally constructed after the same pattern out of a definite number of members. The "arm" of man and the "wing" of bats and birds have the same typical skeleton as the foreleg of the animals which are conspicuously "four-footed"

The anatomical unity of the fully developed skeleton in the four limbs of all tetrapods is very important. In order to appreciate it fully one has only to compare carefully the skeleton of a salamander or a frog with that of a monkey or a man. One perceives at once that the humeral zone in front and the pelvic zone behind are made up of the same principal parts as in the rest of the quadrupeds. We find in all cases that the first section of the leg proper consists of one strong marrow-bone (the *humerus,* in the forearm; the *femur,* behind); the second part, on the contrary, originally always consists of two bones (the *ulna* and *radius,* in front; the *fibula* and *tibia,* behind). When we further compare the developed structure of the foot proper we are surprised to find that the small bones of which it is made up are also similarly arranged and distributed in every case: in the front limb the three groups of bones of the forefoot (or "hand") correspond in all classes of the tetrapoda. (1) the *carpus*, (2) the *metacarpus*, (3) the five fingers (*digiti anteriores*); in the rear limb, similarly, we have always the same three osseous groups of the hind foot: (1) the *tarsus*, (2) the *metatarsus*, and (3) the five toes (*digiti posteriores*). It was a very difficult task to reduce all these little bones to one primitive type, and to establish the equivalence (or homology) of the separate parts in all cases; they present extreme variations of form and construction in detail, sometimes being partly fused together and losing their individuality. This great task was first successfully achieved by the most eminent comparative anatomist of our day, Karl Gegenbaur. He pointed out, in his *Researches into the Comparative Anatomy of the Vertebrata* (1864), how this characteristic "five-toed leg" of the land tetrapods originally (not before the Carboniferous period) arose out of the radiating fin (the breast-fin, or the belly-fin) of the ancient fishes. He had also, in his famous *Researches into the Skull of the Vertebrata* (1872), deduced the younger skull of the tetrapods from the oldest cranial form among the fishes, that of the shark.

It is especially remarkable that the original number of the toes (five) on each of the four feet, which first appeared in the old amphibia of the Carboniferous period, has, in virtue of a strict heredity, been preserved even to the present day in man. Also, naturally and harmoniously, the typical construction of the joints, ligaments, muscles, and nerves of the two pairs of legs has, in the main, remained the same as in the rest of the "four-footed." In all these important relations *man is a true tetrapod*.

The mammals are the youngest and most advanced class of the vertebrates. It is true they are derived

OUR BODILY FRAME

from the older class of amphibia, like birds and reptiles; yet they are distinguished from all the other tetrapods by a number of very striking anatomical features. Externally, there is the clothing of the skin with hair, and the possession of two kinds of skin glands—the sweat glands and the sebaceous glands. A local development of these glands on the abdominal skin gave rise (probably during the Triassic period) to the organ which is especially characteristic of the class, and from which it derives its name—the *mammarium*. This important instrument of lactation is made up of milk glands (*mammae*) and the "mammar-pouches" (folds of the abdominal skin); in its development the teats appear, through which the young mammal sucks its mother's milk. In internal structure the most remarkable feature is the possession of a complete diaphragm, a muscular wall which, in all mammals—and *only* in mammals— separates the thoracic from the abdominal cavity; in all other vertebrates there is no such separation. The skull of mammals is distinguished by a number of remarkable formations, especially in the maxillary apparatus (the upper and lower jaws, and the temporal bones). Moreover, the brain, the olfactory organ, the heart, the lungs, the internal and external sexual organs, the kidneys, and other parts of the body present special peculiarities, both in general and detailed structure, in the mammals; all these, taken collectively, point unequivocally to an early derivation of the mammals from the older groups of the reptiles and amphibia, which must have taken place, at the latest, in the Triassic period — at least twelve million years ago! In all these important characteristics *man is a true mammal*.

The numerous orders (12-33) which modern systematic zoology distinguishes in the class of mammals had been arranged in 1816 (by Blainville) in three natural groups, which still hold good as sub-classes: (1) the monotrema, (2) the marsupialia, and (3) the placentalia. These three sub-classes not only differ in the important respect of bodily structure and development, but they correspond, also, to three different historical stages in the formation of the class, as we shall see later on. The monotremes of the Triassic period were followed by the marsupials of the Jurassic, and these by the placentals of the Cretaceous. Man belongs to this, the youngest, sub-class; for he presents in his organization all the features which distinguish the placentals from the marsupials and the still older monotremes. First of all, there is the peculiar organ which gives a name to the placentals—the *placenta*. It serves the purpose of nourishing the young mammal embryo for a long time during its enclosure in the mother's womb; it consists of blood-bearing tufts which grow out of the chorion surrounding the embryo, and penetrate corresponding cavities in the mucous membrane of the maternal uterus; the delicate skin between the two structures is so attenuated in this spot that the nutriment in the mother's blood can pass directly into the blood of the child. This excellent contrivance for nourishing the embryo, which makes its first appearance at a somewhat late date, gives the fœtus the opportunity of a longer maintenance and a higher development in the protecting womb; it is wanting in the *implacentalia*, the two older sub-classes of the marsupials and the monotremes. There are, likewise, other anatomical features, particularly the higher development of the brain and the absence of the marsupial bone, which raise the placentals above all their implacental ances-

OUR BODILY FRAME

tors. In all these important particulars *man is a true placental.*

The very varied sub-class of the placentals has been recently subdivided into a great number of orders; they are usually put at from ten to sixteen, but when we include the important extinct forms which have been recently discovered the number runs up to from twenty to twenty-six. In order to facilitate the study of these numerous orders, and to obtain a deeper insight into their kindred construction, it is very useful to form them into great natural groups, which I have called " legions." In my latest attempt* to arrange the advanced system of placentals in phylogenetic order I have substituted eight of these legions for the twenty-six orders, and shown that these may be reduced to four main groups. These, in turn, are traceable to one common ancestral group of all the placentals, their fossil ancestors, the *prochoriata* of the Cretaceous period. These are directly connected with the marsupial ancestors of the Jurassic period. We will only specify here, as the most important living representatives of these four main groups, the rodentia, the ungulata, the carnivora, and the primates. To the legion of the primates belong the prosimiæ (half-apes), the simiæ (real apes), and man. All the members of these three orders agree in many important features, and are at the same time distinguished by these features from the other twenty-three orders of placentals. They are especially conspicuous for the length of their bones, which were originally adapted to their arboreal manner of life. Their hands and feet are five-fingered, and the long fingers are excellently suited for grasping and embracing the

* *Systematische Phylogenie,* 1896, part iii., pp. 490, 494, and 496.

branches of trees; they are provided, either partially or completely, with nails, but have no claws. The dentition is complete, containing all four classes—incisors, canine, premolars, and molars. Primates are also distinguished from all the other placentals by important features in the special construction of the skull and the brain; and these are the more striking in proportion to their development and the lateness of their appearance in the history of the earth. In all these important anatomical features our human organism agrees with that of all the other primates: *man is a true primate*.

An impartial and thorough comparison of the bodily structure of the primates forces us to distingiush two orders in this most advanced legion of the mammalia —half-apes (*prosimiae* or *hemipitheci*) and apes (*simiae* or *pitheci*). The former seem in every respect to be the lower and older, the latter to be the higher and younger order. The womb of the half-ape is still double, or two-horned, as it is in all the other mammals. In the true ape, on the contrary, the right and left wombs have completely amalgamated; they blend into a pear-shaped womb, which the human mother possesses besides the ape. In the skull of the apes, just as in that of man, the orbits of the eyes are completely separated from the temporal cavities by an osseous partition; in the *prosimiae* this is either entirely wanting or very imperfect. Finally, the cerebrum of the *prosimia* is either quite smooth or very slightly furrowed, and proportionately small; that of the true ape is much larger, and the gray bed especially, the organ of higher psychic activity, is much more developed; the characteristic convolutions and furrows appear on its surface exactly in proportion as the ape approaches to man. In these and other important respects, par-

OUR BODILY FRAME

ticularly in the construction of the face and the hands, *man presents all the anatomical marks of a true ape.*

The extensive order of apes was divided by Geoffroi, in 1812, into two sub-orders, which are still universally accepted in systematic zoology—New World and Old World monkeys, according to the hemisphere they respectively inhabit. The American " New World " monkeys are called *Platyrrhinae* (flat-nosed); their nose is flat, and the nostrils divergent, with a broad partition. The " Old World " monkeys, on the contrary, are called collectively *Catarrhinae* (narrow-nosed); their nostrils point downward, like man's, and the dividing cartilage is narrow. A further difference between the two groups is that the tympanum is superficial in the *platyrrhinae*, but lies deeper, inside the petrous bone, in the *catarrhinae*; in the latter a long and narrow bony passage has been formed, while in the former it is still short and wide, or even altogether wanting. Finally, we have a much more important and decisive difference between the two groups in the circumstance that all the Old World monkeys have the same teeth as man—*i.e.*, twenty deciduous and thirty-two permanent teeth (two incisors, one canine, two premolars, and three molars in each half of the jaw). The New World monkeys, on the other hand, have an additional premolar in each half-jaw, or thirty-six teeth altogether. The fact that these anatomical differences of the two simian groups are universal and conspicuous, and that they harmonize with their geographical distribution in the two hemispheres, fully authorizes a sharp systematic division of the two, as well as the phylogenetic conclusion that for a very long period (for more than a million years) the two sub-orders have been developing quite independently of each other in the western and eastern hemispheres. That is a most important point in view of the geneaology of our race, for man bears all the marks of *a true catarrhina;* he has descended from some extinct member of this sub-order in the Old World.

The numerous types of *catarrhinae* which still survive in Asia and Africa have been formed into two sections for some time—the tailed, doglike apes (the *cynopitheci*) and the tailless, manlike apes (the *anthropomorpha*). The latter are much nearer to man than the former, not only in the absence of a tail and in the general build of the body (especially of the head), but also on account of certain features which are unimportant in themselves but very significant in their constancy. The sacrum of the anthropoid ape, like that of man, is made up of the fusion of five vertebræ; that of the *cynopithecus* consists of three (more rarely four) sacral vertebræ. The premolar teeth of the *cynopitheci* are greater in length than breadth; those of the *anthropomorpha* are broader than they are long; and the first molar has four protuberances in the former, five in the latter. Furthermore, the outer incisor of the lower jaw is broader than the inner one in the manlike apes and man; in the doglike ape it is the smaller. Finally, there is a special significance in the fact, established by Selenka in 1890, that the anthropoid apes share with man the peculiar structure of the discoid *placenta,* the *decidua reflexa,* and the pedicle of the allantois. In fact, even a superficial comparison of the bodily structure of the *anthropomorpha* which still survive makes it clear that both the Asiatic (the orang-outang and the gibbous ape) and the African (the gorilla and chimpanzee) representatives of this group are nearer to man in build than any of the *cynopitheci.* Under the latter group we include the dog-faced papiomorpha, the baboon, and

OUR BODILY FRAME

the long-tailed monkey, at a very low stage. The anatomical difference between these low papiomorpha and the most highly developed anthropoid apes is greater in every respect, whatever organ we take for comparison, than the difference between the latter and man. This instructive fact was established with great penetration by the anatomist Robert Hartmann, in his work on *The Anthropoid Apes*;* he proposed to divide the order of *Simiae* in a new way—namely, into the two great groups of *primaria* (man and the anthropoid ape) and the *simiae* proper, or *pitheci* (the rest of the catarrhinæ and all the platyrrhinæ). In any case, we have a clear proof of *the close affinity of man and the anthropoid ape.*

Thus comparative anatomy proves to the satisfaction of every unprejudiced and critical student the significant fact that the body of man and that of the anthropoid ape are not only peculiarly similar, but they are practically one and the same in every important respect The same two hundred bones, in the same order and structure, make up our inner skeleton; the same three hundred muscles effect our movements; the same hair clothes our skin; the same groups of ganglionic cells build up the marvellous structure of our brain; the same four chambered heart is the central pulsometer in our circulation; the same thirty-two teeth are set in the same order in our jaws; the same salivary, hepatic, and gastric glands compass our digestive process; the same reproductive organs insure the maintenance of our race.

It is true that we find, on close examination, certain minor differences in point of size and shape in most of the organs of man and the ape, but we discover the

* Translated in the International Science Series, 1872.

same, or similar, differences between the higher and lower races of men, when we make a careful comparison—even, in fact, in a minute comparison of the various individuals of our own race. We find no two persons who have exactly the same size and form of nose, ears, eyes, and so forth. One has only to compare attentively these special features in many different persons in any large company to convince one's self of the astonishing diversity of their construction and the infinite variability of specific forms. Not infrequently even two sisters are so much unlike as to make their origin from the same parents almost incredible. Yet all these individual variations do not weaken the significance of the fundamental similarity of structure; they are traceable to certain minute differences in the growth of the individual features.

CHAPTER III

OUR LIFE

Development of Physiology in Antiquity and the Middle Ages: Galen—Experiment and Vivisection—Discovery of the Circulation of the Blood by Harvey—Vitalism: Haller—Teleological and Vitalistic Conception of Life—Mechanical and Monistic View of the Physiological Processes—Comparative Physiology in the Nineteenth Century · Johannes Müller—Cellular Physiology: Max Verworn—Cellular Pathology: Virchow—Mammal Physiology—Similarity of all Vital Activity in Man and the Ape

IT is only in the nineteenth century that our knowledge of human life has attained the dignity of a genuine, independent science; during the course of the century it has developed into one of the highest, most interesting, and most important branches of knowledge. This "science of the vital functions," physiology, had, it is true, been regarded at a much earlier date as a desirable, if not a necessary, condition of success in medical treatment, and had been constantly associated with anatomy, the science of the structure of the body. But it was only much later, and much more slowly, than the latter that it could be thoroughly studied, as it had to contend with much more serious difficulties.

The idea of life, as the opposite of death, naturally became the subject of speculation at a very early age. In the living man, just as in other living animals, there were certain peculiar changes, especially movements, which were wanting in lifeless nature: spontaneous locomotion, the beat of the heart, the drawing of the breath, speech, and so forth. But the discrimination of such "organic movements" from similar phenomena in inorganic bodies was by no means easy, and was frequently impossible, the flowing stream, the flickering flame, the rushing wind, the falling rock, seemed to man to exhibit the same movements. It was quite natural that primitive man should attribute an independent life to these "dead" bodies. He knew no more of the real sources of movement in the one case than in the other.

We find the earliest scientific observations on the nature of man's vital functions (as well as on his structure) in the Greek natural philosophers and physicians of the sixth and fifth centuries before Christ. The best collection of the physiological facts which were known at that time is to be found in the *Natural History* of Aristotle; a great number of his assertions were probably taken from Democritus and Hippocrates. The school of the latter had already made attempts to explain the mystery; it postulated as the ultimate source of life in man and the beasts a volatile "spirit of life" (Pneuma); and Erasistratus (280 B.C.) already drew a distinction between the lower and the higher "spirit of life," the *pneuma zoticon* in the heart and the *pneuma psychicon* in the brain.

The credit of gathering these scattered truths into unity, and of making the first attempt at a systematic physiology, belongs to the great Greek physician Galen; we have already recognized in him the first great anatomist of antiquity (cf. p 23). In his researches into the organs of the body he never lost sight

OUR LIFE

of the question of their vital activity, their functions; and even in this direction he proceeded by the same comparative method, taking for his principal study the animals which approach nearest to man. Whatever he learned from these he applied directly to man. He recognized the value of physiological experiment; in his vivisection of apes, dogs, and swine he made a number of interesting experiments. Vivisection has been made the object of a violent attack in recent years, not only by the ignorant and narrow-minded, but by theological enemies of knowledge and by perfervid sentimentalists, it is, however, one of the *indispensable* methods of research into the nature of life, and has given us invaluable information on the most important questions. This was recognized by Galen seventeen hundred years ago.

Galen reduces all the different functions of the body to three groups, which correspond to the three forms of the *pneuma*, or vital spirit. The *pneuma psychicon*—the soul—which resides in the brain and nerves, is the cause of thought, sensation, and will (voluntary movement); the *pneuma zoticon*—the heart—is responsible for the beat of the heart, the pulse, and the temperature; the *pneuma physicon*, seated in the liver, is the source of the so-called vegetative functions, digestion and assimilation, growth and reproduction. He especially emphasized the renewal of the blood in the lungs, and expressed a hope that we should some day succeed in isolating the permanent element in the atmosphere—the *pneuma*, as he calls it—which is taken into the blood in respiration. More than fifteen centuries elapsed before this *pneuma*—oxygen—was discovered by Lavoisier.

In human physiology, as well as in anatomy, the

great system of Galen was for thirteen centuries the *Codex aureus,* the inviolable source of all knowledge. The influence of Christianity, so fatal to scientific culture, raised the same insuperable obstacles in this as in every other branch of secular knowledge. Not a single scientist appeared from the third to the sixteenth century who dared to make independent research into man's vital activity, and transcend the limits of the Galenic system. It was not until the sixteenth century that experiments were made in that direction by a number of distinguished physicians and anatomists (Paracelsus, Servetus, Vesalius, and others). In 1628 Harvey published his great discovery of the circulation of the blood, and showed that the heart is a pump, which drives the red stream unceasingly through the connected system of arteries and veins by a rhythmic, unconscious contraction of its muscles. Not less important were Harvey's researches into the procreation of animals, as a result of which he formulated the well-known law: " Every living thing comes from an egg " (*omne vivum ex ovo*).

The powerful impetus which Harvey gave to physiological observation and experiment led to a great number of discoveries in the sixteenth and seventeenth centuries. These were co-ordinated for the first time by the learned Albrecht Haller about the middle of the last century; in his great work, *Elementa Physiologiae,* he established the inherent importance of the science, independently of its relation to practical medicine. In postulating, however, a special " sensitive force or sensibility " for neural action, and a special "irritability" for muscular movement, Haller gave strong support to the erroneous idea of a specific "vital force " (*vis vitalis*).

OUR LIFE

For more than a century afterwards, from the middle of the eighteenth until the middle of the nineteenth century, medicine and (especially) physiology were dominated by the old idea that a certain number of the vital processes may be traced to physical and chemical causes, but that others are the outcome of a special vital force which is independent of physical agencies. However much scientists differed in their conceptions of its nature and its relation to the "soul," they were all agreed as to its independence of, and essential distinction from, the chemico-physical forces of ordinary "matter"; it was a self-contained force (*archaeus*), unknown in inorganic nature, which compelled ordinary forces into its service. Not only the distinctly psychical activity, the sensibility of the nerves and the irritability of the muscles, but even the phenomena of sense activity, of reproduction, and of development seemed so wonderful and so mysterious in their sources that it was impossible to attribute them to simple physical and chemical processes. As the free activity of the vital force was purposive and conscious, it led, in philosophy, to a complete *teleology*; especially did this seem indisputable when even the "critical" philosopher Kant had acknowledged, in his famous critique of the teleological position, that, though the mind's authority to give a mechanical interpretation of all phenomena is theoretically unlimited, yet its actual capacity for such interpretation does not extend to the phenomena of organic life; here we are compelled to have recourse to a *purposive*—therefore *supernatural*—principle. This divergence of the *vital* phenomena from the *mechanical* processes of life became, naturally, more conspicuous as science advanced in the chemical and physical explanation of the latter. The circulation of the blood

THE RIDDLE OF THE UNIVERSE

and a number of other phenomena could be traced to mechanical agencies; respiration and digestion were attributable to chemical processes like those we find in inorganic nature. On the other hand, it seemed impossible to do this with the wonderful performances of the nerves and muscles, and with the characteristic life of the mind; the co-ordination of all the different forces in the life of the individual seemed also beyond such a mechanical interpretation. Hence there arose a complete physiological dualism—an essential distinction was drawn between inorganic and organic nature, between mechanical and vital processes, between material force and life force, between the body and the soul. At the beginning of the nineteenth century this vitalism was firmly established in France by Louis Dumas, and in Germany by Reil. Alexander Humboldt had already published a poetical presentation of it in 1795, in his narrative of the *Legend of Rhodes;* it is repeated, with critical notes, in his *Views of Nature.*

In the first half of the seventeenth century the famous philosopher Descartes, starting from Harvey's discovery of the circulation of the blood, put forward the idea that the body of man, like that of other animals, is merely an intricate machine, and that its movements take place under the same mechanical laws as the movements of an automaton of human construction. It is true that Descartes, at the same time, claimed for man the exclusive possession of a perfectly independent, immaterial soul, and held that its subjective experience, thought, was the only thing in the world of which we have direct and certain cognizanze ("*Cogito, ergo sum*"). Yet this dualism did not prevent him from doing much to advance our knowledge of the mechanical life processes in detail. Borelli followed (1660)

OUR LIFE

with a reduction of the movements of the animal body to purely physical laws, and Sylvius endeavored, about the same time, to give a purely chemical explanation of the phenomena of digestion and respiration; the former founded the *iatromechanical*, the latter the *iatrochemical*, school of medicine. However, these rational tendencies towards a natural, mechanical explanation of the phenomena of life did not attain to a universal acceptance and application; in the course of the eighteenth century they fell entirely away before the advance of teleological vitalism. The final disproof of the latter and a return to mechanism only became possible with the happy growth of the new science of comparative physiology in the forties of the present century.

Our knowledge of the vital functions, like our knowledge of the structure of the human body, was originally obtained, for the most part, not by direct observation of the human organism itself, but by a study of the more closely related animals among the vertebrates, especially the mammals. In this sense the very earliest beginning of human anatomy and physiology was "comparative." But the distinct science of "comparative physiology," which embraces the whole sphere of life phenomena, from the lowest animal up to man, is a triumph of the nineteenth century. Its famous creator was Johannes Müller, of Berlin (born, the son of a shoemaker, at Coblentz, in 1801). For fully twenty-five years—from 1833 to 1858—this most versatile and most comprehensive biologist of our age evinced an activity at the Berlin University, as professor and investigator, which is only comparable with the associated work of Haller and Cuvier. Nearly every one of the great biologists who have taught and worked in Germany for the last sixty years was, directly or indirectly, a pupil of Johannes Müller. Starting from the anatomy and physiology of man, he soon gathered all the chief groups of the higher and lower animals within his sphere of comparison. As, moreover, he compared the structure of extinct animals with the living, and the healthy organism with the diseased, endeavoring to bring together all the phenomena of life in a truly philosophic fashion, he attained a biological knowledge far in advance of his predecessors.

The most valuable fruit of these comprehensive studies of Johannes Müller was his *Manual of Human Physiology*. This classical work contains much more than the title indicates; it is the sketch of a comprehensive "comparative biology." It is still unsurpassed in respect of its contents and range of investigation. In particular, we find the methods of observation and experiment applied in it as masterfully as the philosophic processes of induction and deduction. Müller was originally a vitalist, like all the physiologists of his time. Nevertheless, the current idea of a vital force took a novel form in his speculations, and gradually transformed itself into the very opposite. For he attempted to explain the phenomena of life mechanically in every department of physiology. His "transfigured" vital force was not *above* the physical and chemical laws of the rest of nature but entirely bound up with them. It was, in a word, nothing more than life itself—that is, the sum of all the movements which we perceive in the living organism. He sought especially to give them the same mechanical interpretation in the life of the senses and of the mind as in the working of the muscles; the same in the phenomena of circulation, respiration, and digestion as in generation and development. Müller's success was chiefly due to the fact

OUR LIFE

that he always began with the simplest life phenomena of the lowest animals, and followed them step by step in their gradual development up to the very highest, to man. In this his method of *critical comparison* proved its value both from the physiological and from the anatomical point of view. Johannes Müller is, moreover, the only great scientist who has equally cultivated these two branches of research, and combined them with equal brilliancy. Immediately after his death his vast scientific kingdom fell into four distinct provinces, which are now nearly always represented by four or more chairs—human and comparative anatomy, pathological anatomy, physiology, and the history of evolution. This sudden division of Müller's immense realm of learning in 1858 has been compared to the dissolution of the empire which Alexander the Great had consolidated and ruled.

Among the many pupils of Johannes Müller who, either during his lifetime or after his death, labored hard for the advancement of the various branches of biology, one of the most fortunate—if not the most important—was Theodor Schwann. When the able botanist Schleiden, in 1838, indicated the cell as the common elementary organ of all plants, and proved that all the different tissues of the plant are merely combinations of cells, Johannes Müller recognized at once the extraordinary possibilities of this important discovery. He himself sought to point out the same composition in various tissues of the animal body—for instance, in the spinal cord of vertebrates—and thus led his pupil, Schwann, to extend the discovery to all the animal tissues. This difficult task was accomplished by Schwann in his *Microscopic Researches into the Accordance in the Structure and Growth of Plants and Animals* (1839).

THE RIDDLE OF THE UNIVERSE

Thus was the foundation laid of the "cellular theory," the profound importance of which, both in physiology and anatomy, has become clearer and more widely recognized in each subsequent year. Moreover, it was shown by two other pupils of Johannes Müller that the activity of all organisms is, in the ultimate analysis, the activity of the components of their tissues, the microscopic cells—these were the able physiologist Ernst Brücke, of Vienna, and the distinguished histologist Albert Kölliker, of Würzburg. Brücke correctly denominated the cells the "elementary organisms," and showed that, in the body of man and of all other animals, they are the only actual, independent factors of the life process. Kölliker earned special distinction, not only in the construction of the whole science of histology, but particularly by showing that the animal ovum and its products are simple cells.

Still, however widely the immense importance of the cellular theory for all biological research was acknowledged, the "cellular physiology" which is based on it only began an independent development very recently. In this Max Verworn (of Jena) earned a twofold distinction. In his *Psycho-physiological Studies of the Protistae* (1889) he showed, as a result of an ingenious series of experimental researches, that the "theory of a cell-soul" which I put forward in 1866[*] is completely established by an accurate study of the unicellular protozoa, and that "the psychic phenomena of the protistæ form the bridge which unites the chemical processes of inorganic nature with the mental life of the highest animals." Verworn has further developed these views, and based them on the modern theory of

[*] *Zell-Seelen und Seelen-Zellen.* Ernst Haeckel, *Gesammelte populare Vortrage.* I. *Heft.* 1878.

OUR LIFE

evolution, in his *General Physiology*. This distinguished work returns to the comprehensive point of view of Johannes Müller, in opposition to the one-sided and narrow methods of those modern physiologists who think to discover the nature of the vital phenomena by the exclusive aid of chemical and physical experiments. Verworn showed that it is only by Müller's comparative method and by a profound study of the physiology of the cell that we can reach the higher stand-point which will give us a comprehensive survey of the wonderful realm of the phenomena of life. Only thus do we become convinced that the vital processes in man are subject to the same physical and chemical laws as those of all other animals.

The fundamental importance of the cellular theory for all branches of biology was made clear in the second half of the nineteenth century, not only by the rapid progress of morphology and physiology, but also by the entire reform of that biological science which has always been deemed most important on account of its relation to practical medicine—pathology, or the science of disease. Many even of the older physicians were convinced that human diseases were natural phenomena, like all other manifestations of life, and should be studied scientifically, like other vital functions. Particular schools of medicine—the Iatrophysical and the Iatrochemical—had already, in the seventeenth century, attempted to trace the sources of disease to certain physical and chemical changes. However, the imperfect condition of science at that period precluded any lasting results of these efforts. Many of the older theories, which sought the nature of disease in supernatural and mystical causes, were almost universally accepted down to the middle of the nineteenth century.

THE RIDDLE OF THE UNIVERSE

It was then that Rudolf Virchow, another pupil of Müller, conceived the happy idea of transferring the cellular theory from the healthy to the diseased organism; he sought in the more minute metamorphoses of the diseased cells and the tissues they composed the true source of those larger changes which, in the form of disease, threaten the living organism with peril and death. Especially during the seven years of his professorship at Würzburg (1849-56) Virchow pursued his great task with such brilliant results that his *Cellular Pathology* (published in 1858) turned, at one stroke, the whole of pathology and the dependent science of practical medicine into new and eminently fruitful paths. This reform of medicine is significant for our present purpose in that it led us to a monistic and purely scientific conception of disease. In sickness, no less than in health, man is subject to the same eternal "iron laws" of physics and chemistry as all the rest of the organic world.

Among the numerous classes of animals which modern zoology distinguishes the mammals occupy a pre-eminent position, not only on morphological grounds, but also for physiological reasons. As man belongs to the class of mammals (see p. 27) by every portion of his frame, we must expect him to share his characteristic functions with the rest of the mammals. Such we find to be the case. The circulation of the blood and respiration are accomplished in man under precisely the same laws and in the same manner as in all the other mammals—*and in these alone;* they are determined by the peculiar structure of their heart and lungs. In mammals only is all the arterial blood conducted from the left ventricle of the heart to the body by one, the *left*, branch of the aorta, while in birds it

OUR LIFE

passes along the *right* branch, and in reptiles along both branches. The blood of mammals is distinguished from that of any other vertebrate by the circumstance that its red cells have lost their nucleus (by reversion). The respiratory movements are effected largely by the diaphragm in this class of animals alone, because only in them does it form a complete partition between the pectoral and abdominal cavities. Special importance, however, in this highest class of animals, attaches to the production of milk in the breasts (*mammae*), and to the peculiar method of the rearing of the young, which entails the supplying of the offspring with the mother's milk. As this nutritive process reacts most powerfully on the other vital functions, and the maternal affection of mammals must have arisen from this intimate form of rearing, the name of the class justly reminds us of its great importance In millions of pictures, most of them produced by painters of the highest rank, the "madonna with the child" is revered as the purest and noblest type of maternal love—the instinct which is found in its extreme form in the exaggerated tenderness of the mother-ape.

As the apes approach nearest to man of all the mammals in point of structure, we shall expect to hear the same of their vital functions; and that we find to be the case. Everybody knows how closely the habits, the movements, the sense activity, the mental life, and the parental customs of apes resemble those of man. Scientific physiology proves the same significant resemblance in other less familiar processes, particularly in the working of the heart, the division of the breasts, and the sexual life. In the latter connection it is especially noteworthy that the mature females of many kinds of apes suffer a periodical discharge of blood from the womb, which corresponds to the menstruation of the human female. The secretion of the milk in the glands and the suctorial process also take place in the female ape in precisely the same fashion as in women.

Finally, it is of especial interest that the speech of apes seems on physiological comparison to be a stage in the formation of articulate human speech. Among living apes there is an Indian species which is musical; the *hylobates syndactylus* sings a full octave in perfectly pure, harmonious half - tones. No impartial philologist can hesitate any longer to admit that our elaborate rational language has been slowly and gradually developed out of the imperfect speech of our Pliocene simian ancestors.

CHAPTER IV

OUR EMBRYONIC DEVELOPMENT

The Older Embryology—The Theory of Preformation—The Theory of Scatulation: Haller and Leibnitz—The Theory of Epigenesis: C. F. Wolff—The Theory of Germinal Layers: Carl Ernst Baer—Discovery of the Human Ovum: Remak, Kölliker—The Egg-Cell and the Sperm-Cell—The Theory of the Gastræa—Protozoa and Metazoa—The Ova and the Spermatozoa: Oscar Hertwig — Conception — Embryonic Development in Man—Uniformity of the Vertebrate Embryo—The Germinal Membranes in Man—The Amnion, the Serolemma, and the Allantois—The Formation of the Placenta and the "After-Birth"—The *Decidua* and the *Funiculus Umbilicalis* —The Discoid Placenta of Man and the Ape.

COMPARATIVE ontogeny, or the science of the development of the individual animal, is a child of the nineteenth century in even a truer sense than comparative anatomy and physiology. How is the child formed in the mother's womb? How do animals evolve from ova? How does the plant come forth from the seed? These pregnant questions have occupied the thoughtful mind for thousands of years. Yet it is only seventy years since the embryologist Baer pointed out the correct means and methods for penetrating into the mysteries of embryonic life; it is only forty years since Darwin, by his reform of the theory of descent, gave us the key which should open the long-closed door, and lead to a knowledge of em-

THE RIDDLE OF THE UNIVERSE

bryonic agencies. As I have endeavored to give a complete, popular presentation of this very interesting but difficult study in the first section of my *Anthropogeny*, I will confine myself here to a brief survey and discussion of the most important phenomena. Let us first cast a historical glance at the older ontogeny, and the theory of preformation which is connected with it.

The classical works of Aristotle, the many-sided "father of science," are the oldest known scientific sources of embryology, as we found them to be for comparative anatomy. Not only in his great natural history, but also in a special small work, *Five Books on the Generation and Development of Animals*, the great philosopher gives us a host of interesting facts, adding many observations on their significance; it was not until our own days that many of them were fully appreciated, and, indeed, we may say, discovered afresh. Naturally, many fables and errors are mixed up with them; it was all that was known at that time of the hidden growth of the human germ. Yet during the long space of the next two thousand years the slumbering science made no further progress. It was not until the commencement of the seventeenth century that there was a renewal of activity. In 1600 the Italian anatomist Fabricius ab Aquapendente published at Padua the first pictures and descriptions of the embryos of man and some of the higher animals; in 1687 the famous Marcello Malpighi, of Bologna, a distinguished pioneer alike in zoology and botany, published the first consistent exposition of the growth of the chick in the hatched egg.

All these older scientists were possessed with the idea that the complete body, with all its parts, was

OUR EMBRYONIC DEVELOPMENT

already contained in the ovum of animals, only it was so minute and transparent that it could not be detected; that, therefore, the whole development was nothing more than a *growth*, or an " unfolding," of the parts that were already " infolded " (*involutae*). This erroneous notion, almost universally accepted until the beginning of the present century, is called the " preformation theory "; sometimes it is called the " evolution theory " (in the literal sense of " unfolding "); but the latter title is accepted by modern scientists for the very different theory of " transformation."

Closely connected with the preformation theory, and as a logical consequence of it, there arose in the last century a further theory which keenly interested all thoughtful biologists—the curious " theory of scatulation." As it was thought that the outline of the entire organism, with all its parts, was present in the egg, the ovary of the embryo had to be supposed to contain the ova of the following generation; these, again, the ova of the next, and so on *in infinitum!* On that basis the distinguished physiologist Haller calculated that God had created together, 6000 years ago—on the sixth day of his creatorial labors—the germs of 200,000,000,000 men, and ingeniously packed them all in the ovary of our venerable mother Eve. Even the gifted philosopher Leibnitz fully accepted this conclusion, and embodied it in his monadist theory; and as, on his theory, soul and body are in eternal, inseparable companionship, the consequence had to be accepted for the soul; " the souls of men have existed in organized bodies in their ancestors from Adam downward—that is, from the very beginning of things."

In the month of November, 1759, a young doctor of twenty-six years, Caspar Friedrich Wolff (son of a Berlin tailor), published his dissertation for the degree at Halle, under the title, *Theoria Generationis*. Supported by a series of most laborious and painstaking observations, he proved the entire falsity of the dominant theories of preformation and scatulation. In the hatched egg there is at first no trace of the coming chick and its organs; instead of it we find on top of the yolk a small, circular, white disk. This thin "germinal disk" becomes gradually round, and then breaks up into four folds, lying upon each other, which are the rudiments of the four chief systems of organs—the nervous system above, the muscular system underneath, the vascular system (with the heart), and, finally, the alimentary canal. Thus, as Wolff justly remarked, the embryonic development does not consist in an unfolding of the preformed organs, but in a series of new constructions; it is a true *epigenesis*. One part arises after another, and all make their appearance in a simple form, which is very different from the later structure This only appears after a series of most remarkable formations. Although this great discovery—one of the most important of the eighteenth century—could be directly proved by a verification of the facts Wolff had observed, and although the "theory of generation" which was founded on it was in reality not a theory at all, but a simple fact, it met with no sympathy whatever for half a century. It was particularly retarded by the high authority of Haller, who fought it strenuously with the dogmatic assertion that "there is no such thing as development: no part of the animal body is formed before another; all were created together." Wolff, who had to go to St. Petersburg, was long in his grave before the forgotten facts he had observed were discovered afresh by Oken at Jena, in 1806.

OUR EMBRYONIC DEVELOPMENT

After Wolff's "epigenesis theory" had been established by Oken and Neckel (whose important work on the development of the alimentary canal was translated from Latin into German), a number of young German scientists devoted themselves eagerly to more accurate embryological research. The most important and successful of these was Carl Ernst Baer. His principal work appeared in 1828, with the title, *History of the Development of Animals: Observations and Reflections*. Not only the phenomena of the formation of the germ are clearly illustrated and fully described in it, but it adds a number of very pregnant speculations. In particular, the form of the embryo of man and the mammals is correctly presented, and the vastly different development of the lower invertebrate animals is also considered. The two leaflike layers which appear in the round germ disk of the higher vertebrates first divide, according to Baer, into two further layers, and these four germinal layers are transformed into four tubes, which represent the fundamental organs — the skin layer, the muscular layer, the vascular layer, and the mucous layer. Then, by very complicated evolutionary processes, the later organs arise, in substantially the same manner, in man and all the other vertebrates. The three chief groups of invertebrates, which in their turn differ widely from each other, have a very different development.

One of the most important of Baer's many discoveries was the finding of the human ovum. Up to that time the little vesicles which are found in great numbers in the human ovary and in that of all other mammals had been taken for the ova. Baer was the first to prove, in 1827, that the real ova are enclosed in these vesicles—the "Graafian follicles"—and much smaller, being tiny spheres 1-120th inch in diameter, visible to the naked eye as minute specks under favorable conditions. He discovered likewise that from this tiny ovum of the mammal there develops first a characteristic germ globule, a hollow sphere with liquid contents, the wall of which forms the slender germinal membrane, or blastoderm.

Ten years after Baer had given a firm foundation to embryological science by his theory of germ layers a new task confronted it on the establishment of the cellular theory in 1838. What is the relation of the ovum and the layers which arise from it to the tissues and cells which compose the fully developed organism? The correct answer to this difficult question was given about the middle of this century by two distinguished pupils of Johannes Müller—Robert Remak, of Berlin, and Albert Kölliker, of Würzburg. They showed that the ovum is at first one simple cell, and that the many germinal globules, or granules, which arise from it by repeated segmentation, are also simple cells. From this mulberry-like group of cells are constructed first the germinal layers, and subsequently by differentiation, or division of labor, all the different organs. Kölliker has the further merit of showing that the seminal fluid of male animals is also a mass of microscopic cells. The active pin-shaped " seed-animalcules," or *spermatozoa*, in it are merely ciliated cells, as I first proved in the case of the seed-filaments of the sponge in 1866 Thus it was proved that both the materials of generation, the male sperm and the female ova, fell in with the cellular theory That was a discovery of which the great philosophic significance was not appreciated until a much later date, on a close study of the phenomena of conception in 1875.

OUR EMBRYONIC DEVELOPMENT

All the older studies in embryonic development concern man and the higher vertebrates, especially the embryonic bird, since hens' eggs are the largest and most convenient objects for investigation, and are plentiful enough to facilitate experiment; we can hatch them in the incubator, as well as by the natural function of the hen, and so observe from hour to hour, during the space of three weeks, the whole series of formations, from the simple germ cell to the complete organism. Even Baer had only been able to gather from such observations the fact that the different classes of vertebrates agreed in the characteristic form of the germ layers and the growth of particular organs. In the innumerable classes of invertebrates, on the other hand —that is, in the great majority of animals—the embryonic development seemed to run quite a different course, and most of them seemed to be altogether without true germinal layers. It was not until about the middle of the century that such layers were found in some of the invertebrates. Huxley, for instance, found them in the medusæ in 1849, and Kölliker in the cephalopods in 1844. Particularly important was the discovery of Kowalewsky (1886) that the lowest vertebrate—the lancelot, or amphioxus—is developed in just the same manner (and a very original fashion it is) as an invertebrate, apparently quite remote, tunicate, the sea-squirt, or ascidian. Even in some of the worms, the radiata and the articulata, a similar formation of the germinal layers was pointed out by the same observer. I myself was then (since 1886) occupied with the embryology of the sponges, corals, medusæ, and siphonophoræ, and, as I found the same formation of two primary germ layers everywhere in these lowest classes of multicellular animals, I came to the conclusion that this impor-

59

tant embryonic feature is common to the entire animal world. The circumstance that in the sponges and the cnidaria (polyps, medusæ, etc.) the body consists for a long time, sometimes throughout life, merely of two simple layers of cells, seemed to me especially significant Huxley had already (1849) compared these, in the case of the medusæ, with the two primary germinal layers of the vertebrates. On the ground of these observations and comparisons I then, in 1872, in my *Philosophy of the Calcispongiae*, published the "theory of the gastræa," of which the following are the essential points:

I. The whole animal world falls into two essentially different groups, the unicellular primitive animals (Protozoa) and the multicellular animals with complex tissues (Metazoa). The entire organism of the protozoon (the rhizopods of the infusoria) remains throughout life a single simple cell (or occasionally a loose colony of cells without the formation of tissue, a *coenobium*) The organism of the metazoon, on the contrary, is only unicellular at the commencement, and is subsequently built up of a number of cells which form tissues.

II. Hence the method of reproduction and development is very different in each of these great categories of animals. The protozoa usually multiply by *nonsexual* means, by fission, gemmation, or spores; they have no real ova and no sperm. The metazoa, on the contrary, are divided into male and female sexes, and generally propagate sexually, by means of true ova, which are fertilized by the male sperm.

III. Hence, further, true germinal layers, and the tissues which are formed from them, are found only in the metazoa; they are entirely wanting in the protozoa.

OUR EMBRYONIC DEVELOPMENT

IV. In all the metazoa only two primary layers appear at first, and these have always the same essential significance; from the *outer* layer the external skin and the nervous system are developed; from the *inner* layer are formed the alimentary canal and all the other organs.

V. I called the germ, which always arises first from the impregnated ovum, and which consists of these two primary layers, the "gut-larva," or the *gastrula*; its cup-shaped body with the two layers encloses originally a simple digestive cavity, the primitive gut (the *progaster* or *archenteron*), and its simple opening is the primitive mouth (the *prostoma* or *blastoporus*). These are the earliest organs of the multicellular body, and the two cell layers of its enclosing wall, simple epithelia, are its earliest tissues; all the other organs and tissues are a later and secondary growth from these.

VI. From this similarity, or *homology*, of the gastrula in all classes of compound animals I drew the conclusion, in virtue of the biogenetic law (p. 81), that all the metazoa come originally from one simple ancestral form, the *gastraea*, and that this ancient (Laurentian), long-extinct form had the structure and composition of the actual gastrula, in which it is preserved by heredity.

VII. This phylogenetic conclusion, based on the comparison of ontogenetic facts, is confirmed by the circumstance that there are several of these gastræades still in existence (*gastraemaria, cyemaria, physemaria*, etc.), and also some ancient forms of other animal groups whose organization is very little higher (the *olynthus* of the sponges, the *hydra*, or common freshwater polyp, of the cnidaria, the *convoluta* and other cryptocæla, or worms of the simplest type, of the *platodes*).

THE RIDDLE OF THE UNIVERSE

VIII. In the further development of the various tissue-forming animals from the gastrula we have to distinguish two principal groups The earlier and *lower* types (the *coelenteria* or *acoelomia*) have no body cavity, no vent, and no blood; such is the case with the gastræades, sponges, cnidaria, and platodes The later and *higher* types (the *caelomaria* or *bilateria*), on the other hand, have a true body cavity, and generally blood and a vent; to these we must refer the worms and the higher types of animals which were evolved from these later on, the echinodermata, mollusca, articulata, tunicata, and vertebrata.

Those are the main points of my "gastræa theory"; I have since enlarged the first sketch of it (given in 1872), and have endeavored to substantiate it in a series of "Studies on the gastræa theory" (1873–84). Although it was almost universally rejected at first, and fiercely combated for ten years by many authorities, it is now (and has been for the last fifteen years) accepted by nearly all my colleagues. Let us now see what far-reaching consequences follow from it, and from the evolution of the germ, especially with regard to our great question, "the place of man in nature."

The human ovum, like that of all other animals, is a single cell, and this tiny globular egg cell (about the 120th of an inch in diameter) has just the same characteristic appearance as that of all other viviparous organisms. The little ball of protoplasm is surrounded by a thick, transparent, finely reticulated membrane, called the *zona pellucida*; even the little, g'obular, germinal vesicle (the cell-nucleus), which is enclosed in the protoplasm (the cell-body), is of the same size and the same qualities as in the rest of the mammals. The same applies to the active spermatozoa of the

OUR EMBRYONIC DEVELOPMENT

male, the minute, threadlike, ciliated cells of which millions are found in every drop of the seminal fluid; on account of their lifelike movements they were previously taken to be forms of life, as the name indicates (spermatozoa — sperm animals). Moreover, the origin of both these important sexual cells in their respective organs is the same in man as in the other mammals; both the ova in the ovary of the female and the spermatozoa in the spermarium of the male arise in the same fashion—they always come from cells, which are originally derived from the cœlous epithelium, the layer of cells which clothes the cavity of the body.

The most important moment in the life of every man, as in that of all other complex animals, is the moment in which he begins his individual existence; it is the moment when the sexual cells of both parents meet and coalesce for the formation of a single simple cell. This new cell, the impregnated egg cell, is the individual stem cell (the *cytula*), the continued segmentation of which produces the cells of the germinal layers and the gastrula. With the formation of this cytula, hence in the process of conception itself, the existence of the personality, the independent individual, commences. This ontogenic fact is supremely important, for the most far-reaching conclusions may be drawn from it. In the first place, we have a clear perception that man, like all the other complex animals, inherits all his personal characteristics, bodily and mental, from his parents; and, further, we come to the momentous conclusion that the new personality which arises thus can lay no claim to " immortality."

Hence the minute processes of conception and sexual generation are of the first importance. We are, however, only familiar with their details since 1875, when Oscar Hertwig, my pupil and fellow-traveller at that time, began his researches into the impregnation of the egg of the sea-urchin at Ajaccio, in Corsica. The beautiful capital of the island in which Napoleon the Great was born, in 1769, was also the spot in which the mysteries of animal conception were carefully studied for the first time in their most important aspects. Hertwig found that the one essential element in conception is the coalescence of the two sexual cells and their nuclei. Only one out of the millions of male ciliated cells which press round the ovum penetrates to its nucleus. The nuclei of both cells, of the spermatozoon and of the ovum, drawn together by a mysterious force, which we take to be a chemical sense-activity, related to smell, approach each other and melt into one. Thus, by the sensitive perception of the sexual nuclei, following upon a kind of " erotic chemicotropism," a new cell is formed, which unites in itself the inherited qualities of both parents; the nucleus of the spermatozoon conveys the paternal features, the nucleus of the ovum those of the mother, to the stem cell, from which the child is to be developed. That applies both to the bodily and to the mental characteristics.

The formation of the germinal layers by the repeated division of the stem cell, the growth of the gastrula and of the later germ structures which succeed it, take place in man in just the same manner as in the other higher mammals, under the peculiar conditions which differentiate this group from the lower vertebrates. In the earlier stages of development these special characters of the placentalia are not to be detected. The significant embryonic or larval form of the chordula, which succeeds the gastrula, has substantially the

OUR EMBRYONIC DEVELOPMENT

same structure in all vertebrates; a simple straight rod, the dorsal cord, lies lengthways along the main axis of the shield-shaped body—the "embryonic shield"; above the cord the spinal marrow develops out of the outer germinal layer, while the gut makes its appearance underneath. Then, on both sides, to the right and left of the axial rod, appear the segments of the "pro-vertebræ" and the outlines of the muscular plates, with which the formation of the members of the vertebrate body begins. The gill-clefts appear on either side of the fore-gut; they are the openings of the gullet, through which, in our primitive fish-ancestors, the water which had entered at the mouth for breathing purposes made its exit at the sides of the head. By a tenacious heredity these gill-clefts, which have no meaning except for our fish-like aquatic ancestors, are still preserved in the embryo of man and all the other vertebrates. They disappear after a time. Even after the five vesicles of the embryonic brain appear in the head, and the rudiments of the eyes and ears at the sides, and after the legs sprout out at the base of the fish-like embryo, in the form of two roundish, flat buds, the fœtus is still so like that of other vertebrates that it is indistinguishable from them.

The substantial similarity in outer form and inner structure which characterizes the embryo of man and other vertebrates in this early stage of development is an embryological fact of the first importance; from it, by the fundamental law of biogeny, we may draw the most momentous conclusions. There is but one explanation of it—heredity from a common parent form. When we see that, at a certain stage, the embryos of man and the ape, the dog and the rabbit, the pig and the sheep, although recognizable as higher vertebrates,

THE RIDDLE OF THE UNIVERSE

cannot be distinguished from each other, the fact can only be elucidated by assuming a common parentage. And this explanation is strengthened when we follow the subsequent divergence of these embryonic forms. The nearer two animals are in their bodily structure, and, therefore, in the scheme of nature, so much the longer do we find their embryos to retain this resemblance, and so much the closer do they approach each other in the ancestral tree of their respective group, so much the closer is their genetic relationship. Hence it is that the embryos of man and the anthropoid ape retain the resemblance much later, at an advanced stage of development, when their distinction from the embryos of other mammals can be seen at a glance. I have illustrated this significant fact by a juxtaposition of corresponding stages in the development of a number of different vertebrates in my *Natural History of Creation* and in my *Anthropogeny*.

The great phylogenetic significance of the resemblance we have described is seen, not only in the comparison of the embryos of vertebrates, but also in the comparison of their protective membranes. All vertebrates of the three higher classes—reptiles, birds, and mammals—are distinguished from the lower classes by the possession of certain special fœtal membranes, the amnion and the serolemma. The embryo is enclosed in these membranes, or bags, which are full of water, and is thus protected from pressure or shock. This provident arrangement probably arose during the Permian period, when the oldest reptiles, the *proreptilia*, the common ancestors of all the amniotes (animals with an *amnion*), completely adapted themselves to a life on land. Their direct ancestors, the amphibia, and the fishes are devoid of these fœtal membranes; they

OUR EMBRYONIC DEVELOPMENT

would have been superfluous to these inhabitants of the water. With the inheritance of these protective coverings are closely connected two other changes in the amniotes: firstly, the entire disappearance of the gills (while the gill arches and clefts continue to be inherited as " rudimentary organs "); secondly, the construction of the *allantois*. This vesicular bag, filled with water, grows out of the hind-gut in the embryo of all the amniotes, and is nothing else than an enlargement of the bladder of their amphibious ancestors. From its innermost and inferior section is formed subsequently the permanent bladder of the amniotes, while the larger outer part shrivels up. Usually this has an important part to play for a long time as the respiratory organ of the embryo, a number of large blood-vessels spreading out over its inner surface. The formation of the membranes, the amnion and the serolemma, and of the allantois, is just the same, and is effected by the same complicated process of growth, in man as in all the other amniotes; *man is a true amniote*.

The nourishment of the fœtus in the maternal womb is effected, as is well known, by a peculiar organ, richly supplied with blood at its surface, called the *placenta*. This important nutritive organ is a spongy, round disk, from six to eight inches in diameter, about an inch thick, and one or two pounds in weight; it is separated after the birth of the child, and issues as the " after-birth." The placenta consists of two very different parts, the fœtal and the maternal part. The latter contains highly developed sinuses, which retain the blood conveyed to them by the arteries of the mother. On the other hand, the fœtal placenta is formed by innumerable branching tufts or villi, which grow out of the outer surface of the allantois, and derive their blood from the umbilical vessels. The hollow, blood-filled villi of the fœtal placenta protrude into the sinuses of the maternal placenta, and the slender membrane between the two is so attenuated that it offers no impediment to the direct interchange of material through the nutritive bloodstream (by osmosis).

In the older and lower groups of the placentals the entire surface of the chorion is covered with a number of short villi; these "chorion-villi" take the form of pit-like depressions of the mucous membrane of the mother, and are easily detached at birth. That happens in most of the ungulata (the sow, camel, mare, etc.), the cetacea, and the prosimiæ; these "malloplacentalia" (with a *diffuse* placenta) have been denominated the *indeciduata*. The same formation is present in man and the other placentals in the beginning. It is soon modified, however, as the villi on one part of the chorion are withdrawn; while on the other part they grow proportionately stronger, and unite intimately with the mucous membrane of the womb. It is in consequence of this intimate blending that a portion of the uterus is detached at birth, and carried away with loss of blood. This detachable membrane—the *decidua*—is a characteristic of the higher placentalia, which have, consequently, been grouped under the title of *deciduata ;* to that category belong the carnassia, rodentia, simiæ, and man. In the carnassia and some of the ungulata (the elephant, for instance) the placenta takes the form of a girdle, hence they are known as the *zonoplacentalia;* in the rodentia, the insectivora (the mole and the hedge-hog), the apes, and man, it takes the form of a disk.

Even ten years ago the majority of embryologists thought that man was distinguished by certain pecu-

OUR EMBRYONIC DEVELOPMENT

liarities in the form of the placenta—namely, by the possession of what is called the *decidua reflexa*, and by a special formation of the umbilical chord which unites the *decidua* to the fœtus. It was supposed that the rest of the placentals, including the apes, were without these special embryonic structures. The *funiculus umbilicalis* is a smooth, cylindrical cord, from sixteen to twenty-three inches long, and as thick as the little finger. It forms the connecting link between the fœtus and the maternal placenta, since it conducts the nutritive vessels from the body of the fœtus to the placenta; it comprises, besides, the pedicle of the allantois and the yelk-sac. The yelk-sac in the human case forms the greater portion of the germinal vesicle during the third week of gestation; but it shrivels up afterwards so that it was formerly entirely missed in the mature fœtus. Yet it remains all the time in a rudimentary condition, and may be detected even after birth as the little umbilical vesicle. Moreover, even the vesicular structure of the allantois disappears at an early stage in the human case; with a deflection of the amnion, it gives rise to the pedicle. We cannot enter here into a discussion of the complicated anatomical and embryological relations of these structures. I have described and illustrated them in my *Anthropogeny* (twenty-third chapter).

The opponents of evolution still appealed to these " special features " of human embryology, which were supposed to distinguish man from all the other mammals, even so late as ten years ago. But in 1890 Emil Selenka proved that the same features are found in the anthropoid apes, especially in the orang (*satyrus*), while the lower apes are without them. Thus Huxley's pithecometra thesis was substantiated once more: " The differences between man and the great apes are not so great as are those between the manlike apes and the lower monkeys." The supposed "evidences *against* the near blood-relationship of man and the apes" proved, on a closer examination of the real circumstances, to be strong reasons in favor of it.

Every scientist who penetrates with open eyes into this dark but profoundly interesting labyrinth of our embryonic development, and who is competent to compare it critically with that of the rest of the mammals, will find in it a most important aid towards the elucidation of the descent of our species. For the various stages of our embryonic development, in the character of *palingenetic* phenomena of heredity, cast a brilliant light on the corresponding stages of our ancestral tree, in accordance with the great law of biogeny. But even the *cenogenetic* phenomena of adaptation, the formation of the temporary fœtal organs—the characteristic fœtal membranes, and especially the placenta—gives us sufficiently definite indications of our *close genetic relationship with the primates.*

CHAPTER V

THE HISTORY OF OUR SPECIES

Origin of Man—Mythical History of Creation—Moses and Linné—The Creation of Permanent Species—The Catastrophic Theory: Cuvier — Transformism. Goethe — Theory of Descent: Lamarck—Theory of Selection: Darwin—Evolution (Phylogeny)—Ancestral Trees—General Morphology—Natural History of Creation—Systematic Phylogeny—Fundamental Law of Biogeny—Anthropogeny—Descent of Man from the Ape—Pithecoid Theory—The Fossil Pithecanthropus of Dubois

THE youngest of the great branches of the living tree of biology is the science we call biological evolution, or *phylogeny*. It came into existence much later, and under much more difficult circumstances, than its natural sister, embryonic evolution or *ontogeny*. The object of the latter was to attain a knowledge of the mysterious processes by which the individual organism, plant or animal, developed from the egg. Phylogeny has to answer the much more obscure and difficult question: " What is the origin of the different organic species of plants and animals?"

Ontogeny (embryology and metamorphism) could follow the empirical method of direct observation in the solution of its not remote problem; it needed but to follow, day by day and hour by hour, the visible changes which the fœtus experiences during a brief period in the course of its development from the ovum. Much more difficult was the remote problem of phylogeny; for the slow processes of gradual construction, which effect the rise of new species of animals and plants, go on imperceptibly during thousands and even millions of years. Their direct observation is possible only within very narrow limits; the vast majority of these historical processes can only be known by direct inference—by critical reflection, and by a comparative use of empirical sciences which belong to very different fields of thought, palæontology, ontogeny, and morphology. To this we must add the immense opposition which was everywhere made to biological evolution on account of the close connection between questions of organic creation and supernatural myths and religious dogmas. For these reasons it can easily be understood how it is that the scientific existence of a true theory of origins was only secured, amid fierce controversy, in the course of the last forty years.

Every serious attempt that was made before the beginning of the nineteenth century to solve the problem of the origin of species lost its way in the mythological labyrinth of the supernatural stories of creation. The efforts of a few distinguished thinkers to emancipate themselves from this tyranny and attain to a naturalistic interpretation proved unavailing. A great variety of creation myths arose in connection with their religion in all the ancient civilized nations. During the Middle Ages triumphant Christendom naturally arrogated to itself the sole right of pronouncing on the question; and, the Bible being the basis of the structure of the Christian religion, the whole story of creation was taken from the book of Genesis. Even Carl Linné, the famous Swedish scientist, started from that basis when, in 1735, in his classical *Systema Naturae*, he

THE HISTORY OF OUR SPECIES

made the first attempt at a systematic arrangement, nomenclature, and classification of the innumerable objects in nature. As the best practical aid in that attempt he introduced the well-known double or binary nomenclature; to each kind of animals and plants he gave a particular specific name, and added to it the wider-reaching name of the genus. A *genus* served to unite the nearest related *species*; thus, for instance, Linné grouped under the genus " dog " (*canis*), as different species, the house-dog (*canis familiaris*), the jackal (*canis aureus*), the wolf (*canis lupus*) the fox (*canis vulpes*), etc. This binary nomenclature immediately proved of such great practical assistance that it was universally accepted, and is still always followed in zoological and botanical classification.

But the theoretical dogma which Linné himself connected with his practical idea of species was fraught with the gravest peril to science. The first question which forced itself on the mind of the thoughtful scientist was the question as to the nature of the concept of species, its contents, and its range. And the creator of the idea answered this fundamental question by a naïve appeal to the dominant Mosaic legend of creation: "*Species tot sunt diversae, quot diversas formas ab initio creavit infinitum ens*"—(There are just so many distinct species as there were distinct types created in the beginning by the Infinite). This theosophic dogma cut short all attempt at a natural explanation of the origin of species. Linné was acquainted only with the plant and animal worlds that exist to-day; he had no suspicion of the much more numerous extinct species which had peopled the earth with their varying forms in the earlier period of its development.

It was not until the beginning of the nineteenth century that we were introduced to these fossil animals by Cuvier. In his famous work on the fossil bones of the four-footed vertebrates he gave (1812) the first correct description and true interpretation of many of these fossil remains. He showed, too, that a series of very different animal populations have succeeded each other in the various stages of the earth's history. Since Cuvier held firmly to Linné's idea of the absolute permanency of species, he thought their origin could only be explained by the supposition that a series of great cataclysms and new creations had marked the history of the globe; he imagined that all living creatures were destroyed at the commencement of each of these terrestrial revolutions, and an entirely new population was created at its close. Although this "catastrophic theory" of Cuvier's led to the most absurd consequences, and was nothing more than a bald faith in miracles, it obtained almost universal recognition, and reigned triumphant until the coming of Darwin.

It is easy to understand that these prevalent ideas of the absolute unchangeability and supernatural creation of organic species could not satisfy the more penetrating thinkers. We find several eminent minds already, in the second half of the last century, busy with the attempt to find a natural explanation of the "problem of creation." Pre-eminent among them was the great German poet and philosopher, Wolfgang Goethe, who, by his long and assiduous study of morphology, obtained, more than a hundred years ago, a clear insight into the intimate connection of all organic forms, and a firm conviction of a common natural origin. In his famed *Metamorphosis of Plants* (1790) he derived all the different species of plants from one primitive type, and all their different organs from one primitive

THE HISTORY OF OUR SPECIES

organ—the leaf. In his vertebral theory of the skull he endeavored to prove that the skulls of the vertebrates —including man—were all alike made up of certain groups of bones, arranged in a definite structure, and that these bones are nothing else than transformed vertebræ. It was his penetrating study of comparative osteology that led Goethe to a firm conviction of the unity of the animal organization; he had recognized that the human skeleton is framed on the same fundamental type as that of all other vertebrates—" built on a primitive plan that only deviates more or less to one side or other in its very constant features, and still develops and refashions itself daily." This remodelling, or transformation, is brought about, according to Goethe, by the constant interaction of two powerful constructive forces—a centripetal force within the organism, the " tendency to specification," and a centrifugal force without, the tendency to variation, or the " idea of metamorphosis"; the former corresponds to what we now call heredity, the latter to the modern idea of adaptation. How deeply Goethe had penetrated into their character by these philosophic studies of the " construction and reconstruction of organic natures," and how far, therefore, he must be considered the most important precursor of Darwin and Lamarck,* may be gathered from the interesting passages from his works which I have collected in the fourth chapter of my *Natural History of Creation*. These evolutionary ideas of Goethe, however, like analogous ideas of Kant, Owen, Treviranus, and other philosophers of the commencement of the century (which we have quoted in the above work), did not amount to more than certain

* Cf. E. Haeckel, *The Systems of Darwin, Goethe, and Lamarck.* Lecture given at Eisenach in 1882.

general conclusions. They had not that great lever which the "natural history of creation" needed for its firm foundation on a criticism of the dogma of fixed species; this lever was first supplied by Lamarck.

The first thorough attempt at a scientific establishment of transformism was made at the beginning of the nineteenth century by the great French scientist Jean Lamarck, the chief opponent of his colleague, Cuvier, at Paris. He had already, in 1802, in his *Observations on Living Organisms*, expressed the new ideas as to the mutability and formation of species, which he thoroughly established in 1809 in the two volumes of his profound work, *Philosophie Zoologique*. In this work he first gave expression to the correct idea, in opposition to the prevalent dogma of fixed species, that the organic " species " is an *artificial abstraction*, a concept of only relative value, like the wider-ranging concepts of genus, family, order, and class. He went on to affirm that all species are changeable, and have arisen from older species in the course of very long periods of time. The common parent forms from which they have descended were originally very simple and lowly organisms. The first and oldest of them arose by abiogenesis. While the type is preserved by *heredity* in the succession of generations, *adaptation*, on the other hand, effects a constant modification of the species by change of habits and the exercise of the various organs. Even our human organism has arisen in the same natural manner, by gradual transformation, from a group of pithecoid mammals. For all these phenomena—indeed, for all phenomena both in nature and in the mind—Lamarck takes exclusively mechanical, physical, and chemical activities to be the true efficient causes. His magnificent *Philosophie Zoologique* con-

THE HISTORY OF OUR SPECIES

tains all the elements of a purely monistic system of nature on the basis of evolution. I have fully treated these achievements of Lamarck in the fourth chapter of my *Anthropogeny*, and in the fourth chapter of the *Natural History of Creation*.

Science had now to wait until this great effort to give a scientific foundation to the theory of evolution should shatter the dominant myth of a "specific creation, and open out the path of natural" development. In this respect Lamarck was not more successful in resisting the conservative authority of his great opponent, Cuvier, than was his colleague and sympathizer, Geoffroy St. Hilaire, twenty years later. The famous controversies which he had with Cuvier in the Parisian Academy in 1830 ended with the complete triumph of the latter. I have elsewhere fully described these conflicts, in which Goethe took so lively an interest. The great expansion which the study of biology experienced at that time, the abundance of interesting discoveries in comparative anatomy and physiology, the establishment of the cellular theory, and the progress of ontogeny, gave zoologists and botanists so overwhelming a flood of welcome material to deal with that the difficult and obscure question of the origin of species was easily forgotten for a time. People rested content with the old dogma of creation. Even when Charles Lyell refuted Cuvier's extraordinary "catastrophic theory" in his *Principles of Geology*, in 1830, and vindicated a natural, continuous evolution for the inorganic structure of our planet, his simple principle of continuity found no one to apply it to the inorganic world. The rudiments of a natural phylogeny which were buried in Lamarck's works were as completely forgotten as the germ of a natural ontogeny which Caspar Friedrich

THE RIDDLE OF THE UNIVERSE

Wolff had given fifty years earlier in his *Theory of Generation*. In both cases a full half-century elapsed before the great idea of a natural development won a fitting recognition. Only when Darwin (in 1859) approached the solution of the problem from a different side altogether, and made a happy use of the rich treasures of empirical knowledge which had accumulated in the mean time, did men begin to think once more of Lamarck as his great precursor.

The unparalleled success of Charles Darwin is well known. It shows him to-day, at the close of the century, to have been, if not the greatest, at least the most effective of its distinguished scientists. No other of the many great thinkers of our time has achieved so magnificent, so thorough, and so far-reaching a success with a single classical work as Darwin did in 1859 with his famous *Origin of Species*. It is true that the reform of comparative anatomy and physiology by Johannes Müller had inaugurated a new and fertile epoch for the whole of biology, that the establishment of the cellular theory by Schleiden and Schwann, the reform of ontogeny by Baer, and the formulation of the law of substance by Robert Mayer and Helmholz were scientific facts of the first importance; but no one of them has had so profound an influence on the whole structure of human knowledge as Darwin's theory of the natural origin of species. For it at once gave us the solution of the mystic " problem of creation," the great " question of all questions "—the problem of the true character and origin of man himself.

If we compare the two great founders of transformism, we find in Lamarck a preponderant inclination to *deduction*, and to forming a completely monistic scheme of nature; in Darwin we have a predominant applica-

THE HISTORY OF OUR SPECIES

tion of *induction*, and a prudent concern to establish the different parts of the theory of selection as firmly as possible on a basis of observation and experiment. While the French scientist far outran the then limits of empirical knowledge, and rather sketched the programme of future investigation, the English empiricist was mainly preoccupied about securing a unifying principle of interpretation for a mass of empirical knowledge which had hitherto accumulated without being understood. We can thus understand how it was that the success of Darwin was just as overwhelming as that of Lamarck was evanescent. Darwin, however, had not only the signal merit of bringing all the results of the various biological sciences to a common focus in the principle of descent, and thus giving them a harmonious interpretation, but he also discovered, in the principle of selection, that direct cause of transformation which Lamarck had missed. In applying, as a practical breeder, the experience of artificial selection to organisms in a state of nature, and in recognizing in the " struggle for life " the selective principle of natural selection, Darwin created his momentous " theory of selection," which is what we properly call Darwinism.

One of the most pressing of the many important tasks which Darwin proposed to modern biology was the reform of the zoological and botanical *system*. Since the innumerable species of animals and plants were not created by a supernatural miracle, but evolved by natural processes, their ancestral tree is their " natural system." The first attempt to frame a system in this sense was made by myself in 1866, in my *General Morphology of Organisms*. The first volume of this work (" General Anatomy ") dealt with the " mechani-

cal science of the developed forms"; the second volume
("General Evolution") was occupied with the science
of the "developing forms." The systematic introduction to the latter formed a "genealogical survey of the
natural system of organisms." Until that time the
term "evolution" had been taken to mean exclusively,
both in zoology and botany, the development of individual organisms—embryology, or metamorphic science. I established the opposite view, that this history of the embryo (ontogeny) must be completed by a
second, equally valuable, and closely connected branch
of thought—the history of the race (phylogeny). Both
these branches of evolutionary science are, in my opinion, in the closest causal connection, this arises from
the reciprocal action of the laws of heredity and adaptation; it has a precise and comprehensive expression
in my "fundamental law of biogeny."

As the new views I had put forward in my *General
Morphology* met with very little notice, and still less
acceptance, from my scientific colleagues, in spite of
their severely scientific setting, I thought I would
make the most important of them accessible to a wider
circle of informed readers by a smaller work, written
in a more popular style. This was done in 1868, in
The Natural History of Creation (a series of popular
scientific lectures on evolution in general, and the systems of Darwin, Goethe, and Lamarck in particular).
If the success of my *General Morphology* was far below
my reasonable anticipation, that of *The Natural History of Creation* went far beyond it. In a period of
thirty years nine editions and twelve different translations of it have appeared. In spite of its great defects,
the book has contributed much to the popularization
of the main ideas of modern evolution. Still, I could

only give the barest outlines in it of my chief object, the phylogenetic construction of a natural system. I have, therefore, given the complete proof, which is wanting in the earlier work, of the phylogenetic system in a subsequent larger work, my *Systematic Phylogeny* (outlines of a natural system of organisms on the basis of their specific development). The first volume of it deals with the protists and plants (1894), the second with the invertebrate animals (1896), the third with the vertebrates (1895). The ancestral tree of both the smaller and the larger groups is carried on in this work as far as my knowledge of the three great "ancestral documents"—palæontology, ontogeny, and morphology—qualified me to extend it.

I had already, in my *General Morphology* (at the end of the fifth book), described the close causative connection which exists, in my opinion, between the two branches of organic evolution as one of the most important ideas of transformism, and I had framed a precise formula for it in a number of "theses on the causal nexus of biontic and phyletic development": "*Ontogenesis is a brief and rapid recapitulation of phylogenesis*, determined by the physiological functions of heredity (generation) and adaptation (maintenance)." Darwin himself had emphasized the great significance of his theory for the elucidation of embryology in 1859, and Fritz Müller had endeavored to prove it as regards the crustacea in the able little work, *Facts and Arguments for Darwin* (1864). My own task has been to prove the universal application and the fundamental importance of the biogenetic law in a series of works, especially in the *Biology of the Calcispongiae* (1872), and in *Studies on the Gastraea Theory* (1873-1884). The theory of the homology of the germinal layers and of the relations of *palingenesis* to *cenogenesis* which I have exposed in them has been confirmed subsequently by a number of works of other zoologists. That theory makes it possible to follow nature's law of unity in the innumerable variations of animal embryology; it gives us for their ancestral history a common derivation from a simple primitive stem form.

The far-seeing founder of the theory of descent, Lamarck, clearly recognized in 1809 that it was of universal application; that even man himself, the most highly developed of the mammals, is derived from the same stem as all the other mammals; and that this in its turn belongs to the same older branch of the ancestral tree as the rest of the vertebrates. He had even indicated the agencies by which it might be possible to explain man's descent from the apes as the nearest related mammals. Darwin, who was, naturally, of the same conviction, purposely avoided this least acceptable consequence of his theory in his chief work in 1859, and put it forward for the first time in his *Descent of Man* in 1871. In the mean time (1863) Huxley had very ably discussed this most important consequence of evolution in his famous *Place of Man in Nature*. With the aid of comparative anatomy and ontogeny, and the support of the facts of palæontology, Huxley proved that the " descent of man from the ape " is a necessary consequence of Darwinism, and that no other scientific explanation of the origin of the human race is possible. Of the same opinion was Karl Gegenbaur, the most distinguished representative of comparative anatomy, who lifted his science to a higher level by a consistent and ingenious application of the theory of descent.

As a further consequence of the " pithecoid theory "

THE HISTORY OF OUR SPECIES

(the theory of the descent of man from the ape) there now arose the difficult task of investigating, not only the nearest related mammal ancestors of man in the Tertiary epoch, but also the long series of the older animal ancestors which had lived in earlier periods of the earth's history and been developed in the course of countless millions of years. I had made a start with the hypothetical solution of this great historic problem in my *General Morphology;* a further development of it appeared in 1874 in my *Anthropogeny* (first section, Origin of the Individual, second section, Origin of the Race). The fourth, enlarged, edition of this work (1891) contains that theory of the development of man which approaches nearest, in my own opinion, to the still remote truth, in the light of our present knowledge of the documentary evidence. I was especially preoccupied in its composition to use the three empirical "documents"—palæontology, ontogeny, and morphology (or comparative anatomy)—as evenly and harmoniously as possible. It is true that my hypotheses were in many cases supplemented and corrected in detail by later phylogenetic research; yet I am convinced that the ancestral tree of human origin which I have sketched therein is substantially correct. For the historical succession of vertebrate fossils corresponds completely with the morphological evolutionary scale which is revealed to us by comparative anatomy and ontogeny. After the Silurian fishes come the *dipnoi* of the Devonian period—the Carboniferous amphibia, the Permian reptilia, and the Mesozoic mammals. Of these, again, the lowest forms, the monotremes, appear first in the Triassic period, the marsupials in the Jurassic, and then the oldest placentals in the Cretaceous. Of the placentals, in turn, the first to appear in the oldest Tertiary period (the Eocene) are the lowest primates, the prosimiæ, which are followed by the simiæ in the Miocene. Of the catarrhinæ, the cynopitheci precede the anthropomorpha; from one branch of the latter, during the Pliocene period, arises the ape-man without speech (the *pithecanthropus alalus*); and from him descends, finally, speaking man.

The chain of our earlier invertebrate ancestors is much more difficult to investigate and much less safe than this tree of our vertebrate predecessors; we have no fossilized relics of their soft, boneless structures, so palæontology can give us no assistance in this case. The evidence of comparative anatomy and ontogeny, therefore, becomes all the more important. Since the human embryo passes through the same *chordula*-stage as the germs of all other vertebrates, since it evolves, similarly, out of two germinal layers of a *gastrula*, we infer, in virtue of the biogenetic law, the early existence of corresponding ancestral forms—vermalia, gastræada, etc. Most important of all is the fact that the human embryo, like that of all other animals, arises originally from a single cell; for this " stem-cell " (*cytula*)—the impregnated egg cell—points indubitably to a corresponding unicellular ancestor, a primitive, Laurentian protozoon.

For the purpose of our monistic philosophy, however, it is a matter of comparative indifference how the succession of our animal predecessors may be confirmed in detail. Sufficient for us, as an incontestable historical fact, is the important thesis that man descends immediately from the ape, and secondarily from a long series of lower vertebrates. I have laid stress on the logical proof of this " pithecometra-thesis " in the seventh book of the *General Morphology:* " The thesis

THE HISTORY OF OUR SPECIES

that man has been evolved from lower vertebrates, and immediately from the *simiae*, is a special inference which results with absolute necessity from the general inductive law of the theory of descent."

For the definitive proof and establishment of this fundamental pithecometra-thesis the palæontological discoveries of the last thirty years are of the greatest importance; in particular, the astonishing discoveries of a number of extinct mammals of the Tertiary period have enabled us to draw up clearly in its main outlines the evolutionary history of this most important class of animals, from the lowest oviparous monotremes up to man. The four chief groups of the placentals, the heterogeneous legions of the carnassia, the rodentia, the ungulata, and the primates, seem to be separated by profound gulfs, when we confine our attention to their representatives of to-day. But these gulfs are completely bridged, and the sharp distinctions of the four legions are entirely lost, when we compare their extinct predecessors of the Tertiary period, and when we go back into the Eocene twilight of history, in the oldest part of the Tertiary period—at least three million years ago. There we find the great subclass of the placentals, which to-day comprises more than two thousand five hundred species, represented by only a small number of little, insignificant "proplacentals"; and in these *prochoriata* the characters of the four divergent legions are so intermingled and toned down that we cannot in reason do other than consider them as the precursors of those features. The oldest carnassia (the *ictopsales*), the oldest rodentia (the *esthonychales*), the oldest ungulata (the *condylarthrales*) and the oldest primates (the *lemuravales*), all have the same fundamental skeletal structure, and the same typ-

THE RIDDLE OF THE UNIVERSE

ical dentition of the primitive placentals, consisting of forty-four teeth (three incisors, one canine, four premolars, and three molars in each half of the jaw); all are characterized by the small size and the imperfect structure of the brain (especially of its chief part, the cortex, which does not become a true "organ of thought" until later on in the Miocene and Pliocene representatives); they have all short legs and five-toed, flat-soled feet (*plantigrada*). In many cases among these oldest placentals of the Eocene period it was very difficult to say at first whether they should be classed with the carnassia, rodentia, ungulata, or primates; so very closely, even to confusion, do these four groups of the placentals, which diverge so widely afterwards, approach each other at that time. Their common origin from a single ancestral group follows incontestably. These *prochoriata* lived in the preceding Cretaceous period (more than three million years ago), and were probably developed in the Jurassic period from a group of insectivorous marsupials (*amphitheria*) by the formation of a primitive *placenta diffusa*, a placenta of the simplest type.

But the most important of all the recent palæontological discoveries which have served to elucidate the origin of the placentals relate to our own stem, the legion of primates. Formerly fossil remains of the primates were very scarce. Even Cuvier, the great founder of palæontology, maintained until his last day (1832) that there were no fossilized primates; he had himself, it is true, described the skull of an Eocene prosimiæ (*adapis*), but he had wrongly classed it with the ungulata. However, during the last twenty years a fair number of well-preserved fossilized skeletons of prosimiæ and simiæ have been discovered; in them we find all the chief intermediate members which complete the connecting chain of ancestors from the oldest prosimiæ to man.

The most famous and most interesting of these discoveries is the fossil ape-man of Java, the much-talked-of *pithecanthropus erectus*, found by a Dutch military doctor, Eugen Dubois, in 1894. It is in truth the much-sought "missing link," supposed to be wanting in the chain of primates, which stretches unbroken from the lowest catarrhinæ to the highest-developed man. I have dealt exhaustively with the significance of this discovery in the paper which I read on August 26, 1898, at the Fourth International Zoological Congress at Cambridge.* The palæontologist, who knows the conditions of the formation and preservation of fossils, will think the discovery of the pithecanthropus an unusually lucky accident. The apes, being arboreal, seldom came into the circumstances (unless they happened to fall into the water) which would secure the preservation and petrifaction of their skeleton. Thus, by the discovery of this fossil man-monkey of Java the descent of man from the ape has become just as clear and certain from the palæontological side as it was previously from the evidence of comparative anatomy and ontogeny. We now have all the principal documents which tell the history of our race.

* *Vide* the translation of Dr. Hans Gadow: *The Last Link*. (A. & C. Black.)

CHAPTER VI

THE NATURE OF THE SOUL

Fundamental Importance of Psychology—Its Definition and Methods—Divergence of Views Thereon—Dualistic and Monistic Psychology—Relation to the Law of Substance—Confusion of Ideas — Psychological Metamorphoses: Kant, Virchow, Du Bois-Reymond—Methods of Research of Psychic Science—Introspective Method (Self-Observation)—Exact Method (Psycho-Physics)—Comparative Method (Animal Psychology)—Psychological Change of Principles: Wundt—Folk-Psychology and Ethnography: Bastian—Ontogenetic Psychology: Preyer—Phylogenetic Psychology: Darwin, Romanes

THE phenomena which are comprised under the title of the "life of the soul," or the psychic activity, are, on the one hand, the most important and interesting, on the other the most intricate and problematical, of all the phenomena we are acquainted with. As the knowledge of nature, the object of the present philosophic study, is itself a part of the life of the soul, and as anthropology, and even cosmology, presuppose a correct knowledge of the "psyche," we may regard psychology, the scientific study of the soul, both as the foundation and the postulate of all other sciences. From another point of view it is itself a part of philosophy, or physiology, or anthropology.

The great difficulty of establishing it on a naturalistic basis arises from the fact that psychology, in turn,

THE NATURE OF THE SOUL

presupposes a correct acquaintance with the human organism, especially the brain, the chief organ of psychic activity. The great majority of "psychologists" have little or no acquaintance with these anatomical foundations of the soul, and thus it happens that in no other science do we find such contradictions and untenable notions as to its proper meaning and its essential object as are current in psychology. This confusion has become more and more palpable during the last thirty years, in proportion as the immense progress of anatomy and physiology has increased our knowledge of the structure and the functions of the chief psychic organ.

What we call the soul is, in my opinion, a natural phenomenon; I therefore consider psychology to be a branch of natural science—a section of physiology. Consequently, I must emphatically assert from the commencement that we have no different methods of research for that science than for any of the others; we have in the first place observation and experiment, in the second place the theory of evolution, and in the third place metaphysical speculation, which seek to penetrate as far as possible into the cryptic nature of the phenomena by inductive and deductive reasoning. However, with a view to a thorough appreciation of the question, we must first of all put clearly before the reader the antithesis of the dualistic and the monistic theories.

The prevailing conception of the psychic activity, which we contest, considers soul and body to be two distinct entities. These two entities can exist independently of each other; there is no intrinsic necessity for their union. The organized body is a mortal, material nature, chemically composed of living protoplasm and its compounds (plasma-products). The soul, on the other hand, is an immortal, immaterial being, a spiritual agent, whose mysterious activity is entirely incomprehensible to us. This trivial conception is, as such, spiritualistic, and its contradictory is, in a certain sense, materialistic. It is, at the same time, supernatural and transcendental, since it affirms the existence of forces which can exist and operate without a material basis; it rests on the assumption that outside of and beyond nature there is a "spiritual," immaterial world, of which we have no experience, and of which we can learn nothing by natural means.

This hypothetical "spirit world," which is supposed to be entirely independent of the material universe, and on the assumption of which the whole artificial structure of the dualistic system is based, is purely a product of poetic imagination; the same must be said of the parallel belief in the "immortality of the soul," the scientific impossibility of which we must prove more fully later on (chap. xi.). If the beliefs which prevail in these credulous circles had a sound foundation, the phenomena they relate to could not be subject to the "law of substance"; moreover, this single exception to the highest law of the cosmos must have appeared very late in the history of the organic world, since it only concerns the "soul" of man and of the higher animals. The dogma of "free will," another essential element of the dualistic psychology, is similarly irreconcilable with the universal law of substance.

Our own naturalistic conception of the psychic activity sees in it a group of vital phenomena, which are dependent on a definite material substratum, like all other phenomena. We shall give to this material basis of all psychic activity, without which it is inconceivable,

THE NATURE OF THE SOUL

the provisional name of "psychoplasm"; and for this good reason—that chemical analysis proves it to be a body of the group we call protoplasmic bodies the albuminoid carbon-combinations which are at the root of all vital processes. In the higher animals, which have a nervous system and sense-organs, "neuroplasm," the nerve-material, has been differentiated out of psychoplasm. Our conception is, in this sense, materialistic. It is at the same time empirical and naturalistic, for our scientific experience has never yet taught us the existence of forces that can dispense with a material substratum, or of a spiritual world over and above the realm of nature.

Like all other natural phenomena, the psychic processes are subject to the supreme, all-ruling law of substance; not even in this province is there a single exception to this highest cosmological law (compare chap. xii.). The phenomena of the lowly psychic life of the unicellular protist and the plant, and of the lowest animal forms—their irritability, their reflex movements, their sensitiveness and instinct of self-preservation—are directly determined by physiological action in the protoplasm of their cells—that is, by physical and chemical changes which are partly due to heredity and partly to adaptation And we must say just the same of the higher psychic activity of the higher animals and man, of the formation of ideas and concepts, of the marvellous phenomena of reason and consciousness; for the latter have been phylogenetically evolved from the former, and it is merely a higher degree of integration or centralization, of association or combination of functions which were formerly isolated, that has elevated them in this manner.

The first task of every science is the clear definition

of the object it has to investigate. In no science, however, is this preliminary task so difficult as in psychology; and this circumstance is the more remarkable since logic, the science of defining, is itself a part of psychology. When we compare all that has been said by the most distinguished philosophers and scientists of all ages on the fundamental idea of psychology, we find ourselves in a perfect chaos of contradictory notions. What, really, is the " soul "? What is its relation to the " mind "? What is the inner meaning of " consciousness "? What is the difference between " sensation " and " sentiment "? What is " instinct "? What is the meaning of " free will "? What is "presentation"? What is the difference between " intellect " and " reason " ? What is the true nature of " emotion "? What is the relation between all these " psychic phenomena " and the " body "? The answers to these and many other cognate questions are infinitely varied; not only are the views of the most eminent thinkers on these questions widely divergent, but even the same scientific authority has often completely changed his views in the course of his psychological development. Indeed, this " psychological metamorphosis " of so many thinkers has contributed not a little to the *colossal confusion of ideas* which prevails in psychology more than in any other branch of knowledge.

The most interesting example of such an entire change of objective and subjective psychological opinions is found in the case of the most influential leader of German philosophy, Immanuel Kant. The young, severely *critical* Kant came to the conclusion that the three great buttresses of mysticism—" God, freedom, and immortality "—were untenable in the light of " pure reason ", the older, *dogmatic* Kant found that these

THE NATURE OF THE SOUL

three great hallucinations were postulates of "practical reason," and were, as such, indispensable. The more the distinguished modern school of "Neokantians" urges a "return to Kant" as the only possible salvation from the frightful jumble of modern metaphysics, the more clearly do we perceive the undeniable and fatal contradiction between the fundamental opinions of the young and the older Kant. We shall return to this point later on.

Other interesting examples of this change of views are found in two of the most famous living scientists, R. Virchow and E. du Bois-Reymond; the metamorphoses of their fundamental views on psychology cannot be overlooked, as both these Berlin biologists have played a most important part at Germany's greatest university for more than forty years, and have, therefore, directly and indirectly, had a most profound influence on the modern mind. Rudolph Virchow, the eminent founder of cellular pathology, was a *pure monist* in the best days of his scientific activity, about the middle of the century; he passed at that time as one of the most distinguished representatives of the newly awakened *materialism*, which appeared in 1855, especially through two famous works, almost contemporaneous in appearance—Ludwig Büchner's *Matter and Force* and Carl Vogt's *Superstition and Science*. Virchow published his general biological views on the vital processes in man—which he takes to be purely mechanical natural phenomena — in a series of distinguished papers in the first volumes of the *Archiv für pathologische Anatomie*, which he founded. The most important of these articles, and the one in which he most clearly expresses his monistic views of that period, is that on "The Tendencies Towards Unity

THE RIDDLE OF THE UNIVERSE

in Scientific Medicine" (1849). It was certainly not without careful thought, and a conviction of its philosophic value, that Virchow put this "medical confession of faith" at the head of his *Collected Essays on Scientific Medicine* in 1856. He defended in it, clearly and definitely, the fundamental principles of monism, which I am presenting here with a view to the solution of the world-problem; he vindicated the exclusive title of empirical science, of which the only reliable sources are sense and brain activity; he vigorously attacked anthropological dualism, the alleged "revelation," and the transcendental philosophy, with their two methods—"faith and anthropomorphism." Above all, he emphasized the monistic character of anthropology, the inseparable connection of spirit and body, of force and matter. "I am convinced," he exclaims, at the end of his preface, "that I shall never find myself compelled to deny the thesis of *the unity* of human nature." Unhappily, this "conviction" proved to be a grave error. Twenty-eight years afterwards Virchow represented the diametrically opposite view; it is to be found in the famous speech on "The Liberty of Science in Modern States," which he delivered at the Scientific Congress at Munich in 1877, and which contains attacks that I have repelled in my *Free Science and Free Teaching* (1878).

In Emil du Bois-Reymond we find similar contradictions with regard to the most important and fundamental theses of philosophy. The more completely the distinguished orator of the Berlin Academy had defended the main principles of the monistic philosophy, the more he had contributed to the refutation of vitalism and the transcendental view of life, so much the louder was the triumphant cry of our opponents

THE NATURE OF THE SOUL

when in 1872, in his famous *Ignorabimus-Speech*, he spoke of consciousness as an insoluble problem, and opposed it to the other functions of the brain as a supernatural phenomenon. I return to the point in the tenth chapter.

The peculiar character of many of the psychic phenomena, especially of consciousness, necessitates certain modifications of our ordinary scientific methods. We have, for instance, to associate with the customary *objective*, external observation, the *introspective* method, the *subjective*, internal observation which scrutinizes our own personality in the mirror of consciousness. The majority of psychologists have started from this "certainty of the ego": "*Cogito ergo sum*," as Descartes said—I think, therefore I am. Let us first cast a glance at this way of inquiry, and then deal with the second, complementary, method.

By far the greater part of the theories of the soul which have been put forward during the last two thousand years or more are based on introspective inquiry—that is, on "self-observation," and on the conclusions which we draw from the association and criticism of these subjective experiences. Introspection is the only possible method of inquiry for an important section of psychology, especially for the study of consciousness. Hence this cerebral function occupies a special position, and has been a more prolific source of philosophic error than any of the others (cf. chap. x.). It is, however, most unsatisfactory, and it leads to entirely false or incomplete notions, to take this self-observation of the mind to be the chief, or, especially, to be the only source of mental science, as has happened in the case of many and distinguished philosophers. A great number of the principal psychic phenomena, particularly the activity of the senses and speech, can only be studied in the same way as every other vital function of the organism—that is, firstly, by a thorough anatomical study of their organs, and, secondly, by an exact physiological analysis of the functions which depend on them. In order, however, to complete this external study of the mental life, and to supplement the results of *internal* observation, one needs a thorough knowledge of human anatomy, histology, ontogeny, and physiology. Most of our so-called " psychologists " have little or no knowledge of these indispensable foundations of anthropology; they are, therefore, incompetent to pronounce on the character even of their own " soul." It must be remembered, too, that the distinguished personality of one of these psychologists usually offers a specimen of an educated mind of the highest civilized races; it is the last link of a long ancestral chain, and the innumerable older and inferior links are indispensable for its proper understanding. Hence it is that most of the psychological literature of the day is so much waste paper. The introspective method is certainly extremely valuable and indispensable, still it needs the constant co-operation and assistance of the other methods.

In proportion as the various branches of the human tree of knowledge have developed during the century, and the methods of the different sciences have been perfected, the desire has grown to make them *exact ;* that is, to make the study of phenomena as purely empirical as possible, and to formulate the laws that result as clearly as the circumstances permit—if possible, *mathematically.* The latter is, however, only feasible in a small province of human knowledge, especially in those sciences in which there is question of measurable

THE NATURE OF THE SOUL

quantities; in mathematics, in the first place, and to a greater or less extent in astronomy, mechanics, and a great part of physics and chemistry Hence these studies are called "exact sciences" in the narrower sense It is, however, productive only of error to call all the physical sciences *exact*, and oppose them to the historical, mental, and moral sciences. The greater part of physical science can no more be treated as an *exact* science than history can; this is especially true of biology and of its subsidiary branch, psychology. As psychology is a part of physiology, it must, as a general rule, follow the chief methods of that science. It must establish the facts of psychic activity by empirical methods as much as possible, by observation and experiment, and it must then gather the laws of the mind by inductive and deductive inferences from its observations, and formulate them with the utmost distinctness. But, for obvious reasons, it is rarely possible to formulate them mathematically. Such a procedure is only profitable in one section of the physiology of the senses; it is not practicable in the greater part of cerebral physiology.

One small section of physiology, which seems amenable to the "exact" method of investigation, has been carefully studied for the last twenty years and raised to the position of a separate science under the title of *psycho-physics*. Its founders, the physiologists Theodor Fechner and Ernst Heinrich Weber, first of all closely investigated the dependence of sensations on the external stimuli that act on the organs of sense, and particularly the quantitative relation between the strength of the stimulus and the intensity of the sensation. They found that a certain minimum strength of stimulus is requisite for the excitement of a sensation, and that a

THE RIDDLE OF THE UNIVERSE

given stimulus must be varied to a definite amount before there is any perceptible change in the sensation. For the highest sensations (of sight, hearing, and pressure) the law holds good that their variations are proportionate to the changes in the strength of the stimulus. From this empirical "law of Weber" Fechner inferred, by mathematical operations, his "fundamental law of psycho-physics," according to which the intensity of a sensation increases in arithmetical progression, the strength of the stimulus in geometrical progression. However, Fechner's law and other psycho-physical laws are frequently contested, and their "exactness" is called into question. In any case modern psycho-physics has fallen far short of the great hopes with which it was greeted twenty years ago; the field of its applicability is extremely limited. One important result of its work is that it has proved the application of physical laws in one, if only a small, branch of the life of the "soul"—an application which was long ago postulated on principle by the materialist psychology for the whole province of mental life. In this, as in many other branches of physiology, the "exact" method has proved inadequate and of little service. It is the ideal to aim at everywhere, but it is unattainable in most cases. Much more profitable are the comparative and genetic methods.

The striking resemblance of man's psychic activity to that of the higher animals—especially our nearest relatives among the mammals—is a familiar fact. Most uncivilized races still make no material distinction between the two sets of mental processes, as the well-known animal fables, the old legends, and the idea of the transmigration of souls prove. Even most of the philosophers of classical antiquity shared the

THE NATURE OF THE SOUL

same conviction, and discovered no essential qualitative difference, but merely a quantitative one, between the soul of man and that of the brute. Plato himself, who was the first to draw a fundamental distinction between soul and body, made one and the same soul (or " idea ") pass through a number of animal and human bodies in his theory of metempsychosis. It was Christianity, intimately connecting faith in immortality with faith in God, that emphasized the essential difference of the immortal soul of man from the mortal soul of the brute. In the dualistic philosophy the idea prevailed principally through the influence of Descartes (1643); he contended that man alone had a true " soul," and, consequently, sensation and free will, and that the animals were mere automata, or machines, without will or sensibility. Ever since the majority of psychologists—including even Kant—have entirely neglected the mental life of the brute, and restricted psychological research to man: human psychology, mainly introspective, dispensed with the fruitful comparative method, and so remained at that lower point of view which human morphology took before Cuvier raised it to the position of a " philosophic science " by the foundation of comparative anatomy.

Scientific interest in the psychic activity of the brute was revived in the second half of the last century, in connection with the advance of systematic zoology and physiology. A strong impulse was given to it by the work of Reimarus: " General observations on the instincts of animals " (Hamburg, 1760). At the same time a deeper scientific investigation had been facilitated by the thorough reform of physiology by Johannes Müller. This distinguished biologist, having a comprehensive knowledge of the whole field of organic nature, of morphology, and of physiology, introduced the " exact methods " of observation and experiment into the whole province of physiology, and, with consummate skill, combined them with the comparative methods. He applied them, not only to mental life in the broader sense (to speech, senses, and brain-action), but to all the other phenomena of life. The sixth book of his *Manual of Human Physiology* treats specially of the life of the soul, and contains eighty pages of important psychological observations.

During the last forty years a great number of works on comparative animal psychology have appeared, principally occasioned by the great impulse which Darwin gave in 1859 by his work on *The Origin of Species*, and by the application of the idea of evolution to the province of psychology. The more impotant of these works we owe to Romanes and Sir J. Lubbock, in England; to W. Wundt, L. Büchner, G. Schneider, Fritz Schultze, and Karl Groos, in Germany; to Alfred Espinas and E. Jourdan, in France; and to Tito Vignoli, in Italy.

In Germany, Wilhelm Wundt, of Leipzig, is considered to be the ablest living psychologist; he has the inestimable advantage over most other philosophers of a thorough zoological, anatomical, and physiological education. Formerly assistant and pupil of Helmholz, Wundt had early accustomed himself to follow the application of the laws of physics and chemistry through the whole field of physiology, and, consequently, in the sense of Johannes Müller, in *psychology*, as a subsection of the latter. Starting from this point of view, Wundt published his valuable " Lectures on human and animal psychology " in 1863. He proved, as he himself tells us in the preface, that the theatre of the

THE NATURE OF THE SOUL

most important psychic processes is in the " unconscious soul," and he affords us " a view of the mechanism which, in the unconscious background of the soul, manipulates the impressions which arise from the external stimuli." What seems to me, however, of special importance and value in Wundt's work is that he " extends the law of the persistence of force for the first time to the psychic world, and makes use of a series of facts of electro-physiology by way of demonstration."

Thirty years afterwards (1892) Wundt published a second, much abridged and entirely modified, edition of his work. The important principles of the first edition are entirely abandoned in the second, and the monistic is exchanged for a purely dualistic stand-point. Wundt himself says in the preface to the second edition that he has emancipated himself from the fundamental errors of the first, and that he " learned many years ago to consider the work a sin of his youth"; it " weighed on him as a kind of crime, from which he longed to free himself as soon as possible." In fact, the most important systems of psychology are completely opposed to each other in the two editions of Wundt's famous *Observations*. In the first edition he is purely monistic and materialistic, in the second edition purely dualistic and spiritualistic. In the one psychology is treated as a *physical* science, on the same laws as the whole of physiology, of which it is only a part; thirty years afterwards he finds psychology to be a *spiritual* science, with principles and objects entirely different from those of physical science. This conversion is most clearly expressed in his principle of psycho-physical parallelism, according to which " every psychic event has a corresponding physical change "; but the two are com-

THE RIDDLE OF THE UNIVERSE

pletely independent, and are not in any natural causal connection. This complete dualism of body and soul, of nature and mind, naturally gave the liveliest satisfaction to the prevailing school-philosophy, and was acclaimed by it as an important advance, especially seeing that it came from a distinguished scientist who had previously adhered to the opposite system of monism. As I myself continue, after more than forty years' study, in this " narrow " position, and have not been able to free myself from it in spite of all my efforts, I must naturally consider the " youthful sin " of the young physiologist Wundt to be a correct knowledge of nature, and energetically defend it against the antagonistic view of the old philosopher Wundt.

This entire change of philosophical principles, which we find in Wundt, as we found it in Kant, Virchow, Du Bois - Reymond, Karl Ernst Baer, and others, is very interesting. In their youth these able and talented scientists embrace the whole field of biological research in a broad survey, and make strenuous efforts to find a unifying, natural basis for their knowledge; in their later years they have found that this is not completely attainable, and so they entirely abandon the idea. In extenuation of these psychological metamorphoses they can, naturally, plead that in their youth they overlooked the difficulties of the great task, and misconceived the true goal; with the maturer judgment of age and the accumulation of experience they were convinced of their errors, and discovered the true path to the source of truth. On the other hand, it is possible to think that great scientists approach their task with less prejudice and more energy in their earlier years—that their vision is clearer and their judgment purer; the experiences of later years sometimes have the effect,

THE NATURE OF THE SOUL

not of enriching, but of disturbing, the mind, and with old age there comes a gradual decay of the brain, just as happens in all other organs. In any case, this change of views is in itself an instructive psychological fact; because, like many other forms of change of opinion, it shows that the highest psychic functions are subject to profound individual changes in the course of life, like all the other vital processes.

For the profitable construction of comparative psychology it is extremely important not to confine the critical comparison to man and the brute in general, but to put side by side the innumerable gradations of their mental activity. Only thus can we attain a clear knowledge of the long scale of psychic development which runs unbroken from the lowest, unicellular forms of life up to the mammals, and to man at their head. But even within the limits of our own race such gradations are very noticeable, and the ramifications of the "psychic ancestral tree" are very numerous. The psychic difference between the crudest savage of the lowest grade and the most perfect specimen of the highest civilization is colossal—much greater than is commonly supposed. By the due appreciation of this fact, especially in the latter half of the century, the "Anthropology of the uncivilized races" (Waitz) has received a strong support, and comparative ethnography has come to be considered extremely important for psychological purposes. Unfortunately, the enormous quantity of raw material of this science has not yet been treated in a satisfactory critical manner What confused and mystic ideas still prevail in this department may be seen, for instance, in the *Volkergedanke* of the famous traveller, Adolf Bastian, who, though a prolific writer,

THE RIDDLE OF THE UNIVERSE

merely turns out a hopeless mass of uncritical compilation and confused speculation.

The most neglected of all psychological methods, even up to the present day, is the evolution of the soul; yet this little-frequented path is precisely the one that leads us most quickly and securely through the gloomy primeval forest of psychological prejudices, dogmas, and errors, to a clear insight into many of the chief psychic problems. As I did in the other branch of organic evolution, I again put before the reader the two great branches of the science which I differentiated in 1866 — ontogeny and phylogeny. The ontogeny, or embryonic development, of the soul, individual or biontic psychogeny, investigates the gradual and hierarchic development of the soul in the individual, and seeks to learn the laws by which it is controlled. For a great part of the life of the mind a good deal has been done in this direction for centuries; rational pedagogy must have set itself the task at an early date of the theoretical study of the gradual development and formative capacity of the young mind that was committed to it for education and formation. Most pedagogues, however, were idealistic or dualistic philosophers, and so they went to work with all the prejudices of the spiritualistic psychology. It is only in the last few decades that this dogmatic tendency has been largely superseded even in the school by scientific methods, we now find a greater concern to apply the chief laws of evolution even in the discussion of the soul of the child. The raw material of the child's soul is already qualitatively determined by *heredity* from parents and ancestors; education has the noble task of bringing it to a perfect maturity by intellectual instruction and moral training —that is, by *adaptation*. Wilhelm Preyer was the first

THE NATURE OF THE SOUL

to lay the foundation of our knowledge of the early psychic development in his interesting work on *The Mind of the Child*. Much is still to be done in the study of the later stages and metamorphoses of the individual soul, and once more the correct, critical application of the biogenetic law is proving a guiding star to the scientific mind.

A new and fertile epoch of higher development dawned for psychology and all other biological sciences when Charles Darwin applied the principles of evolution to them forty years ago. The seventh chapter of his epoch-making work on *The Origin of Species* is devoted to instinct. It contains the valuable proof that the instincts of animals are subject, like all other vital processes, to the general laws of historic development. The special instincts of particular species were formed by *adaptation*, and the modifications thus acquired were handed on to posterity by *heredity;* in their formation and preservation natural selection plays the same part as in the transformation of every other physiological function. Darwin afterwards developed this fundamental thought in a number of works, showing that the same laws of "mental evolution" hold good throughout the entire organic world, not less in man than in the brute, and even in the plant. Hence the unity of the organic world, which is revealed by the common origin of its members, applies also to the entire province of psychic life, from the simplest unicellular organism up to man.

To George Romanes we owe the further development of Darwin's psychology and its special application to the different sections of psychic activity. Unfortunately, his premature decease prevented the completion of the great work which was to reconstruct every section

THE RIDDLE OF THE UNIVERSE

of comparative psychology on the lines of monistic evolution. The two volumes of this work which were completed are among the most valuable productions of psychological literature. For, conformably to the principles of our modern monistic research, his first care was to collect and arrange all the important facts which have been empirically established in the field of comparative psychology in the course of centuries; in the second place, these facts are tested with an *objective criticism*, and systematically distributed; finally, such rational conclusions are drawn from them on the chief general questions of psychology as are in harmony with the fundamental principles of modern monism. The first volume of Romanes's work bears the title of *Mental Evolution in the Animal World*; it presents, in natural connection, the entire length of the chain of psychic evolution in the animal world, from the simplest sensations and instincts of the lowest animals to the elaborate phenomena of consciousness and reason in the highest. It contains also a number of extracts from a manuscript which Darwin left "on instinct," and a complete collection of all that he wrote in the province of psychology.

The second and more important volume of Romanes's work treats of " Mental evolution in man and the origin of human faculties." The distinguished psychologist gives a convincing proof in it "that the psychological barrier between man and the brute has been overcome." Man's power of conceptual thought and of abstraction has been gradually evolved from the non-conceptual stages of thought and ideation in the nearest related mammals. Man's highest mental powers—reason, speech, and conscience—have arisen from the lower stages of the same faculties in our primate ancestors

THE NATURE OF THE SOUL

(the simiæ and prosimiæ). Man has no single mental faculty which is his exclusive prerogative. His whole psychic life differs from that of the nearest related mammals only in degree, and not in kind; quantitatively, not qualitatively.

I recommend those of my readers who are interested in these momentous questions of psychology to study the profound work of Romanes. I am completely at one with him and Darwin in almost all their views and convictions. Wherever an apparent discrepancy is found between these authors and my earlier productions, it is either a case of imperfect expression on my part or an unimportant difference in application of principle. For the rest, it is characteristic of this " science of ideas" that the most eminent philosophers hold entirely antagonistic views on its fundamental notions.

CHAPTER VII

PSYCHIC GRADATIONS

Psychological Unity of Organic Nature—Material Basis of the Soul · Psychoplasm—Scale of Sensation—Scale of Movement —Scale of Reflex Action—Simple and Compound Reflex Action—Reflex Action and Consciousness—Scale of Perception —Unconscious and Conscious Perception—Scale of Memory —Unconscious and Conscious Memory—Association of Perceptions—Instinct—Primary and Secondary Instincts—Scale of Reason—Language—Emotion and Passion—The Will— Freedom of the Will

THE great progress which psychology has made, with the assistance of evolution, in the latter half of the century culminates in the recognition of *the psychological unity of the organic world*. Comparative psychology, in co-operation with the ontogeny and phylogeny of the *psyche*, has enforced the conviction that organic life in all its stages, from the simplest unicellular protozoon up to man, springs from the same elementary forces of nature, from the physiological functions of sensation and movement The future task of scientific psychology, therefore, is not, as it once was, the exclusively subjective and introspective analysis of the highly developed mind of a philosopher, but the objective, comparative study of the long gradation by which man has slowly arisen through a vast series of lower animal conditions. This great task of separat-

PSYCHIC GRADATIONS

ing the different steps in the psychological ladder, and proving their unbroken phylogenetic connection, has only been seriously attempted during the last ten years, especially in the splendid work of Romanes. We must confine ourselves here to a brief discussion of a few of the general questions which that gradation has suggested.

All the phenomena of the psychic life are, without exception, bound up with certain material changes in the living substance of the body, the *protoplasm*. We have given to that part of the protoplasm which seems to be the indispensable substratum of psychic life the name of *psychoplasm* (the " soul-substance," in the monistic sense); in other words, we do not attribute any peculiar " essence" to it, but we consider the *psyche* to be merely *a collective idea of all the psychic functions of protoplasm*. In this sense the "soul" is merely a physiological abstraction like " assimilation" or " generation." In man and the higher animals, in accordance with the division of labor of the organs and tissues, the psychoplasm is a differentiated part of the nervous system, the *neuroplasm* of the ganglionic cells and their fibres. In the lower animals, however, which have no special nerves and organs of sense, and in the plants, the psychoplasm has not yet reached an independent differentiation. Finally, in the unicellular protists, the psychoplasm is identified either with the whole of the living protoplasm of the simple cell or with a portion of it. In all cases, in the lowest as well as the highest stages of the psychological hierarchy, a certain chemical composition and a certain physical activity of the psychoplasm are indispensable before the " soul" can function or act. That is equally true of the elementary psychic function of the plasmatic sen-

THE RIDDLE OF THE UNIVERSE

sation and movement of the protozoa, and of the complex functions of the sense-organs and the brain in the higher animals and man. The activity of the psychoplasm, which we call the "soul," is always connected with metabolism.

All living organisms, without exception, are sensitive; they are influenced by the condition of their environment, and react thereon by certain modifications in their own structure. Light and heat, gravity and electricity, mechanical processes and chemical action in the environment, act as *stimuli* on the sensitive psychoplasm, and effect changes in its molecular composition. We may distinguish the following five chief stages of this sensibility:

I At the lowest stage of organization the *whole psychoplasm*, as such, is sensitive, and reacts on the stimuli from without; that is the case with the lowest protists, with many plants, and with some of the most rudimentary animals

II. At the second stage very simple and undiscriminating *sense-organs* begin to appear on the surface of the organism, in the form of protoplasmic filaments and pigment spots, the forerunners of the nerves of touch and the eyes; these are found in some of the higher protists and in many of the lower animals and plants.

III. At the third stage *specific organs* of sense, each with a peculiar adaptation, have arisen by differentiation out of these rudimentary processes: there are the chemical instruments of smell and taste, and the physical organs of touch, temperature, hearing, and sight. The "specific energy" of these sense-organs is not an original inherent property of theirs, but has been gained by functional adaptation and progressive heredity.

PSYCHIC GRADATIONS

IV. The fourth stage is characterized by the *centralization* or integration of the *nervous system*, and, consequently, of sensation; by the association of the previously isolated or localized sensations presentations arise, though they still remain unconscious. That is the condition of many both of the lower and the higher animals.

V. Finally, at the fifth stage, the highest psychic function, *conscious perception*, is developed by the mirroring of the sensations in a central part of the nervous system, as we find in man and the higher vertebrates, and probably in some of the higher invertebrates, notably the articulata.

All living organisms without exception have the faculty of *spontaneous movement*, in contradistinction to the rigidity and inertia of unorganized substances (*e.g.*, crystals); in other words, certain changes of place of the particles occur in the living psychoplasm from internal causes, which have their source in its own chemical composition. These active vital movements are partly discovered by direct observation and partly only known indirectly, by inference from their effects. We may distinguish five stages of them.

I. At the lowest stage of organic life, in the chromacea, and many protophyta and lower metaphyta, we perceive only those *movements of growth* which are common to all organisms. They are usually so slow that they cannot be directly observed; they have to be inferred from their results—from the change in size and form of the growing organism.

II. Many protists, particularly unicellular algæ of the groups of diatomacea and desmidiacea, accomplish a kind of creeping or swimming motion by *secretion*, by ejecting a slimy substance at one side.

III. Other organisms which float in water—for instance, many of the radiolaria, siphonophora, ktenophora, and others—ascend and descend by altering their *specific gravity*, sometimes by osmosis, sometimes by the separation or squeezing-out of air.

IV. Many plants, especially the sensitive plants (mimosa) and other papilionacea, effect movements of their leaves or other organs by *change of pressure*—that is, they alter the strain of the protoplasm, and, consequently, its pressure on the enclosing elastic walls of the cells.

V. The most important of all organic movements are the *phenomena of contraction*—i.e., changes of form at the surface of the organism, which are dependent on a twofold displacement of their elements; they always involve two different conditions or phases of motion—contraction and expansion. Four different forms of this plasmatic contraction may be enumerated:

- (a) Amœboid movement (in rhizopods, blood-cells, pigment-cells, etc.).
- (b) A similar flow of protoplasm within enclosed cells.
- (c) Vibratory motion (ciliary movements) in infusoria, spermatozoa, ciliated epithelial cells
- (d) Muscular movement (in most animals)

The elementary psychic activity that arises from the combination of sensation and movement is called *reflex* (in the widest sense), reflective function, or *reflex action*. The movement—no matter what kind it is—seems in this case to be the immediate result of the *stimulus* which evoked the sensation; it has, on that account, been called stimulated motion in its simplest form (in the protists). All living protoplasm has this feature of irritability. Any physical or chemical change in

PSYCHIC GRADATIONS

the environment may, in certain circumstances, act as a stimulus on the psychoplasm, and elicit or "release" a movement. We shall see later on how this important physical concept of "releasing" directly connects the simplest organic reflex actions with similar mechanical phenomena of movement in the inorganic world (for instance, in the explosion of powder by a spark, or of dynamite by a blow). We may distinguish the following seven stages in the scale of reflex action:

I. At the lowest stage of organization, in the lowest protists, the stimuli of the outer world (heat, light, electricity, etc.) cause in the indifferent protoplasm only those indispensable movements of growth and nutrition which are common to all organisms, and are absolutely necessary for their preservation That is also the case in most of the plants.

II. In the case of many freely moving protists (especially the amœba, the heliozoon, and the rhizopod) the stimuli from without produce on every spot of the unprotected surface of the unicellular organism external movements which take the form of changes of shape, and sometimes changes of place (amœboid movement, pseudopod formation, the extension and withdrawal of what look like feet) ; these indefinite, variable processes of the protoplasm are not yet permanent organs. In the same way, general organic irritability takes the form of indeterminate reflex action in the sensitive plants and the lowest metazoa; in many multicellular organisms the stimuli may be conducted from one cell to another, as all the cells are connected by fine fibres.

III. Many protists, especially the more highly developed protozoa, produce on their unicellular body two little organs of the simplest character—an organ of touch and an organ of movement. Both these instruments are direct external projections of protoplasm; the stimulus, which alights on the first, is immediately conducted to the other by the psychoplasm of the unicellular body, and causes it to contract. This phenomenon is particularly easy to observe, and even produce experimentally, in many of the stationary infusoria (for instance, the *poteriodendron* among the flagellata, and the *vorticella* among the ciliata). The faintest stimulus that touches the extremely sensitive hairs, or *cilia*, at the free end of the cells, immediately causes a contraction of a thread-like stalk at the other, fixed end. This phenomenon is known as a " simple reflex arch "

IV. These phenomena of the unicellular organism of the infusoria lead on to the interesting mechanism of the neuro-muscular cells, which we find in the multicellular body of many of the lower metazoa, especially in the cnidaria (polyps and corals). Each single neuromuscular cell is a " unicellular reflex organ "; it has on its surface a sensitive spot, and a motor muscular fibre inside at the opposite end; the latter contracts as soon as the former is stimulated.

V. In other cnidaria, notably in the free swimming medusæ—which are closely related to the stationary polyps—the simple neuro-muscular cell becomes two different cells, connected by a filament; an external *sense-cell* (in the outer skin) and an internal *muscular cell* (under the skin). In this *bicellular reflex organ* the one cell is the rudimentary organ of sensation, the other of movement; the connecting bridge of the psychoplasmic filament conducts the stimulus from one to the other.

VI. The most important step in the gradual construction of the reflex mechanism is the division into

PSYCHIC GRADATIONS

three cells; in the place of the simple connecting bridge we spoke of there appears a third independent cell, the *soul-cell*, or ganglionic cell; with it appears also a new psychic function, *unconscious presentation*, which has its seat in this cell. The stimulus is first conducted from the sensitive cell to this intermediate presentative or psychic cell, and then issued from this to the motor muscular cell as a mandate of movement. These *tricellular reflex organs* are preponderantly developed in the great majority of the invertebrates.

VII. Instead of this arrangement we find in most of the vertebrates a *quadricellular reflex organ*, two distinct " soul-cells," instead of one, being inserted between the sensitive cell and the motor cell. The external stimulus, in this case, is first conducted centripetally to the sensitive cell (the sensible psychic cell), from this to the *will-cell* (the motor psychic cell), and from this, finally, to the contractile muscular cell. When many such reflex organs combine and new psychic cells are interposed we have the intricate reflex mechanism of man and the higher vertebrates.

The important distinction which we make, in morphology and physiology, between unicellular and multicellular organisms holds good for their elementary psychic activity, reflex action. In the unicellular protists (both the plasmodomous primitive plants, or *protophyta*, and the plasmophagous primitive animals, or *protozoa*) the whole physical process of reflex action takes place in the protoplasm of one single cell; their "cell-soul" seems to be a unifying function of the psychoplasm of which the various phases only begin to be seen separately when the differentiation of special organs sets in.

The second stage of psychic activity, compound re-

THE RIDDLE OF THE UNIVERSE

flex action, begins with the cenobitic protists (v g., the volvox and the carchesium). The innumerable social cells, which make up this cell-community or cœnobium, are always more or less connected, often directly connected by filamentous bridges of protoplasm. A stimulus that alights on one or more cells of the community is communicated to the rest by means of the connecting fibres, and may produce a general contraction. This connection is found, also, in the tissues of the multicellular animals and plants. It was erroneously believed at one time that the cells of vegetal tissue were completely isolated from each other, but we have now discovered fine filaments of protoplasm throughout, which penetrate the thick membranes of the cells, and maintain a material and psychological communication between their living plasmic contents. That is the explanation of the mimosa: when the tread of the passer-by shakes the root of the plant, the stimulus is immediately conveyed to all the cells, and causes a general contraction of its tender leaves and a drooping of the stems.

An important and universal feature of all reflex phenomena is the absence of consciousness. For reasons which we shall give in the tenth chapter we only admit the presence of consciousness in man and the higher animals, not in plants, the lower animals, and the protists; consequently all stimulated movements in the latter must be regarded as reflex — that is, all movements which are not *spontaneous*, not the outcome of internal causes (impulsive and automatic movements).* It is different with the higher animals which have developed a centralized nervous system and

*Cf. Max Verworn, *Psychophysiologische Protisten-Studien*, pp. 135, 140.

PSYCHIC GRADATIONS

elaborate sense-organs. In these cases consciousness has been gradually evolved from the psychic reflex activity, and now conscious, voluntary action appears, in opposition to the still continuing reflex action below. However, we must distinguish two different processes, as we did in the question of instinct—primary and secondary reflex action. Primary reflex actions are those which have never reached the stage of consciousness in phyletic development, and thus preserve the primitive character (by heredity from lower animal forms). Secondary reflex actions are those which were conscious, voluntary actions in our ancestors, but which afterwards became unconscious from habit or the lapse of consciousness. It is impossible to draw a hard and fast line in such cases between conscious and unconscious psychic function.

Older psychologists (Herbart, for instance) considered "presentation" to be the fundamental psychic phenomenon, from which all the others are derived. Modern comparative psychology endorses this view in so far as it relates to the idea of *unconscious* presentation; but it considers *conscious* presentation to be a secondary phenomenon of mental life, which is entirely wanting in plants and the lower animals, and is only developed in the higher animals. Among the many contradictory definitions which psychologists have given of "presentation," we think the best is that which makes it consist in an internal picture of the external object which is given us in sensation—an "idea," in the broader sense. We may distinguish the following four stages in the rising scale of presentative function:

I. *Cellular presentation.*—At the lowest stages we find presentation to be a general physiological property of psychoplasm; even in the simplest unicellular protist sensations may leave a permanent trace in the psychoplasm, and these may be reproduced by memory. In more than four thousand kinds of radiolaria, which I have described, every single species is distinguished by special, hereditary skeletal structure. The construction of this specific, and often highly elaborate, skeleton by a cell of the simplest description (generally globular) is only intelligible when we attribute the faculty of presentation, and, indeed, of a special reproduction of the plastic "feeling of distance," to the constructive protoplasm—as I have pointed out in my *Psychology of the Radiolaria*.*

II. *Histionic presentation.*—In the cœnobia or cell-colonies of the social protists, and still better in the tissues of plants and lower, nerveless animals (sponges, polyps, etc.), we find the second stage of unconscious presentation, which consists of the common psychic activity of a number of closely connected cells. If a single stimulus may, instead of simply spending itself in the reflex movement of an organ (the leaf of a plant, for instance, or the arm of a polyp), leave a permanent impression, which can be spontaneously reproduced later on, we are bound to assume, in explaining the phenomenon, a histionic presentation, dependent on the psychoplasm of the associated tissue-cells.

III. *Unconscious presentation in the ganglionic cells.*—This third and higher stage of presentation is the commonest form the function takes in the animal world; it seems to be a localization of presentation in definite "soul-cells." In its simplest form it appears at the sixth stage of reflex action, when the tricellular reflex organ arises: the seat of presentation is then the intermediate

* E. Haeckel, "General Natural History of the Radiolaria"; 1887.

PSYCHIC GRADATIONS

psychic cell, which is interposed between the sensitive cell and the muscular cell. With the increasing development of the animal nervous system and its progressive differentiation and integration, this unconscious presentation also rises to higher stages.

IV. *Conscious presentation in the cerebral cells.*—With the highest stage of development of the animal organization consciousness arises, as a special function of a certain central organ of the nervous system. As the presentations are conscious, and as special parts of the brain arise for the association of these conscious presentations, the organism is qualified for those highest psychic functions which we call thought and reflection, intellect and reason. Although the tracing of the phyletic barrier between the older, unconscious, and the younger, conscious, presentation is extremely difficult, we can affirm, with some degree of probability, that the evolution of the latter from the former was *polyphyletic*, because we find conscious and rational thought, not only in the highest forms of the vertebrate stem (man, mammals, birds, and a part of the lower vertebrates), but also in the most highly developed representatives of other animal groups (ants and other insects, spiders and the higher crabs among the articulata, cephalopods among the mollusca).

The evolutionary scale of memory is closely connected with that of presentation; this extremely important function of the psychoplasm—the condition of all further psychic development—consists essentially in the *reproduction of presentations*. The impressions in the bioplasm, which the stimulus produced as sensations, and which became presentations in remaining, are revived by memory; they pass from potentiality to actuality. The latent potential energy of the psychoplasm is transformed into kinetic energy. We may distinguish four stages in the upward development of memory, corresponding to the four stages of presentation.

I. *Cellular memory* —Thirty years ago Ewald Hering showed " memory to be a general property of organized matter" in a thoughtful work, and indicated the great significance of this function, " to which we owe almost all that we are and have." Six years later, in my work on *The Perigenesis of the Plastidule, or the Undulatory Origin of the Parts of Life : an Experiment in the Mechanical Explanation of Elementary Evolutionary Processes*, I developed these ideas, and endeavored to base them on the principles of evolution. I have attempted to show in that work that unconscious memory is a universal and very important function of all *plastidules ;* that is, of those hypothetical molecules, or groups of molecules, which Naegeli has called *micellae*, others *bioplasts*, and so forth. Only *living* plastidules, as individual molecules of the active protoplasm, are reproductive, and so gifted with memory; that is the chief difference between the organic and inorganic worlds. It might be stated thus: " Heredity is the memory of the plastidule, while variability is its comprehension." The elementary memory of the unicellular protist is made up of the molecular memory of the plastidules or *micellae*, of which its living cell-body is constructed As regards the extraordinary performances of unconscious memory in these unicellular protists, nothing could be more instructive than the infinitely varied and regular formation of their defensive apparatus, their shells and skeletons; in particular, the diatomes and cosmaria among the protophytes, and the radiolaria and thalamophora among the protozoa, afford an abundance of most interesting illustrations.

PSYCHIC GRADATIONS

In many thousand species of these protists the specific form which is inherited is *relatively constant,* and proves the fidelity of their unconscious cellular memory.

II. *Histionic memory.*—Equally interesting examples of the second stage of memory, the unconscious memory of tissues, are found in the heredity of the individual organs of plants and the lower, nerveless animals (sponges, etc.). This second stage seems to be *a reproduction of the histionic presentations,* that association of cellular presentations which sets in with the formation of cœnobia in the social protists.

III. In the same way we must regard the third stage, the unconscious memory of those animals which have a nervous system, as a reproduction of the corresponding "unconscious presentations" which are stored up in certain ganglionic cells. In most of the lower animals all memory is unconscious. Moreover, even in man and the higher animals, to whom we must ascribe consciousness, the daily acts of unconscious memory are much more numerous and varied than those of the conscious faculty; we shall easily convince ourselves of that if we make an impartial study of a thousand unconscious acts we perform daily out of habit, and without thinking of them, in walking, speaking, writing, eating, and so forth.

IV. Conscious memory, which is the work of certain brain-cells in man and the higher animals, is an "internal mirroring" of very late development, the highest outcome of the same psychic reproduction of presentations which were mere unconscious processes in the ganglionic cells of our lower animal ancestors.

The concatenation of presentations—usually called the association of ideas—also runs through a long scale, from the lowest to the highest stages. This,

THE RIDDLE OF THE UNIVERSE

too, is originally and predominantly unconscious ("instinct"); only in the higher classes of animals does it gradually become conscious ("reason"). The psychic results of this "association of ideas" are extremely varied, still, a very long, unbroken line of gradual development connects the simplest unconscious association of the lowest protist with the elaborate conscious chain of ideas of the civilized man. The *unity of consciousness* in man is given as its highest consequence (Hume, Condillac). All higher mental activity becomes more perfect in proportion as the normal association extends to more numerous presentations, and in proportion to the order which is imposed on them by the "criticism of pure reason." In dreams, where this criticism is absent, the association of the reproduced impressions often takes the wildest forms. Even in the work of the poetic imagination, which constructs new groups of images by varying the association of the impressions received, and in hallucinations, etc., they are often most unnaturally arranged, and seem to the prosaic observer to be perfectly irrational. This is especially true of supernatural "forms of belief," the apparitions of spiritism, and the fantastic notions of the transcendental dualist philosophy; though it is precisely these *abnormal associations* of "faith" and of "revelation" that have often been deemed the greatest treasures of the human mind (cf. chap. xvi.).

The antiquated psychology of the Middle Ages (which, however, still numbers many adherents) considered the mental life of man and that of the brute to be two entirely different phenomena; the one it attributed to "reason," the other to "instinct." In harmony with the traditional story of creation, it was assumed that each animal species had received a definite, un-

PSYCHIC GRADATIONS

conscious psychic force from the Creator at its formation, and that this instinct of each species was just as unchangeable as its bodily structure. Lamarck proved the untenableness of this error in 1809 by establishing the theory of Descent, and Darwin completely demolished it in 1859. He proved the following important theses with the aid of his theory of selection:

1. The instincts of species show individual differences, and are just as subject to modification under the law of *adaptation* as the morphological features of their bodily structure.

2. These modifications (generally arising from a change of habits) are partly transmitted to offspring by *heredity*, and thus accumulate and are accentuated in the course of generations.

3 *Selection*, both artificial and natural, singles out certain of these inherited modifications of the psychic activity; it preserves the most useful and rejects the least adaptive.

4 The *divergence* of psychic character which thus arises leads, in the course of generations, to the formation of new instincts, just as the divergence of morphological character gives rise to new species.

Darwin's theory of instinct is now accepted by most biologists; Romanes has treated it so ably, and so greatly expanded it in his distinguished work on *Mental Evolution in the Animal World*, that I need merely refer to it here. I will only venture the brief statement that, in my opinion, there are instincts in *all* organisms —in all the protists and plants as well as in all the animals and in man; though in the latter they tend to disappear in proportion as reason makes progress at their expense.

The two chief classes of instincts to be differentiated

are the primary and secondary   Primary instincts are the common lower impulses which are unconscious and inherent in the psychoplasm from the commencement of organic life; especially the impulses to self-preservation (by defence and maintenance) and to the preservation of the species (by generation and the care of the young). Both these fundamental instincts of organic life, *hunger* and *love*, sprang up originally in perfect unconsciousness, without any co-operation of the intellect or reason. It is otherwise with the *secondary* instincts. These were due originally to an intelligent adaptation, to rational thought and resolution, and to purposive conscious action. Gradually, however, they became so automatic that this "other nature" acted unconsciously, and, even through the action of heredity, seemed to be "innate" in subsequent generations. The consciousness and deliberation which originally accompanied these particular instincts of the higher animals and man have died away in the course of the life of the plastidules (as in "abridged heredity"). The unconscious purposive actions of the higher animals (for instance, their mechanical instincts) thus come to appear in the light of innate impulses. We have to explain in the same way the origin of the "*à priori* ideas" of man; they were originally formed empirically by his predecessors.*

In the superficial psychological treatises which ignore the mental activity of animals and attribute to man only a "true soul," we find him credited also with the exclusive possession of reason and consciousness. This is another trivial error (still to be found in many a manual, nevertheless) which the comparative psy-

* *Vide Natural History of Creation*, E. Haeckel.

PSYCHIC GRADATIONS

chology of the last forty years has entirely dissipated. The higher vertebrates (especially those mammals which are most nearly related to man) have just as good a title to "reason" as man himself, and within the limits of the animal world there is the same long chain of the gradual development of reason as in the case of humanity. The difference between the reason of a Goethe, a Kant, a Lamarck, or a Darwin, and that of the lowest savage, a Veddah, an Akka, a native Australian, or a Patagonian, is much greater than the graduated difference between the reason of the latter and that of the most "rational" mammals, the anthropoid apes, or even the papiomorpha, the dog, or the elephant. This important thesis has been convincingly proved by the thoroughly critical comparative work of Romanes and others. We shall not, therefore, attempt to cover that ground here, nor to enlarge on the distinction between the reason and the intellect; as to the meaning and limits of these concepts philosophic experts give the most contradictory definitions, as they do on so many other fundamental questions of psychology. In general it may be said that the process of the formation of concepts, which is common to both these cerebral functions, is confined to the narrower circle of concrete, proximate associations in the intellect, but reaches out to the wider circle of abstract, more comprehensive groups of associations in the work of reason. In the long gradation which connects the reflex actions and the instincts of the lower animals with the reason of the highest, intellect precedes the latter. And there is the fact, of great importance to our whole psychological treatise, that even these highest of our mental faculties are just as much subject to the laws of heredity and adaptation as are their respective organs; Flechsig pointed out in 1894 that the "organs of thought," in man and the higher mammals, are those parts of the cortex of the brain which lie between the four inner sense-centres (cf. chapters x. and xi.).

The higher grade of development of ideas, of intellect and reason, which raises man so much above the brute, is intimately connected with the rise of language. Still here also we have to recognize a long chain of evolution which stretches unbroken from the lowest to the highest stages. Speech is no more an exclusive prerogative of man than reason. In the wider sense, it is a common feature of all the higher gregarious animals, at least of all the articulata and the vertebrates, which live in communities or herds; they need it for the purpose of understanding each other and communicating their impressions. This is effected either by touch or by signs, or by sounds having a definite meaning. The song of the bird or of the anthropoid ape (*hylobates*), the bark of the dog, the neigh of the horse, the chirp of the cricket, the cry of the cicada, are all specimens of animal speech. Only in man, however, has that articulate conceptual speech developed which has enabled his reason to attain such high achievements. Comparative philology, one of the most interesting sciences that has arisen during the century, has shown that the numerous elaborate languages of the different nations have been slowly and gradually evolved from a few simple primitive tongues (Wilhelm Humboldt, Bopp, Schleicher, Steinthal, and others). August Schleicher, of Jena, in particular, has proved that the historical development of language takes place under the same phylogenetic laws as the evolution of other physiological faculties and their organs. Romanes

PSYCHIC GRADATIONS

(1893) has expanded this proof, and amply demonstrated that human speech, also, differs from that of the brute only in *degree* of development, not in essence and kind.

The important group of psychic activities which we embrace under the name of "emotion" plays a conspicuous part both in theoretical and practical psychology. From our point of view they have a peculiar importance from the fact that we clearly see in them the direct connection of cerebral functions with other physiological functions (the beat of the heart, sense-action, muscular movement, etc.); they, therefore, prove the unnatural and untenable character of the philosophy which would essentially dissociate psychology from physiology. All the external expressions of emotional life which we find in man are also present in the higher animals (especially in the anthropoid ape and the dog); however varied their development may be, they are all derived from the two elementary functions of the *psyche*, sensation and motion, and from their combination in reflex action and presentation. To the province of sensation, in a wide sense, we must attribute the feeling of *like* and *dislike* which determines the emotion; while the corresponding *desire* and *aversion* (love and hatred), the effort to attain what is liked and avoid what is disliked, belong to the category of movement. "Attraction" and "repulsion" seem to be the sources of *will*, that momentous element of the soul which determines the character of the individual. The *passions*, which play so important a part in the psychic life of man, are but intensifications of emotion. Romanes has recently shown that these also are common to man and the brute. Even at the lowest stage of organic life we find in all the protists those elementary feelings of like and dislike, revealing themselves in what are called their *tropisms*, in the striving after light and darkness, heat or cold, and in their different relations to positive and negative electricity. On the other hand, we find at the highest stage of psychic life, in civilized man, those finer shades of emotion, of delight and disgust, of love and hatred, which are the mainsprings of civilization and the inexhaustible sources of poetry. Yet a connecting chain of all conceivable gradations unites the most primitive elements of feeling in the psychoplasm of the unicellular protist with the highest forms of passion that rule in the gangliomic cells of the cortex of the human brain. That the latter are absolutely amenable to physical laws was proved long ago by the great Spinoza in his famous *Statics of Emotion*.

The notion of *will* has as many different meanings and definitions as most other psychological notions—presentation, soul, mind, and so forth. Sometimes will is taken in the widest sense as a *cosmic attribute*, as in the "World as will and presentation" of Schopenhauer; sometimes it is taken in its narrowest sense as an *anthropological attribute*, the exclusive prerogative of man—as Descartes taught, for instance, who considered the brute to be a mere machine, without will or sensation. In the ordinary use of the term, *will* is derived from the phenomenon of voluntary movement, and is thus regarded as a psychic attribute of most animals. But when we examine the will in the light of comparative physiology and evolution, we find—as we do in the case of sensation—that it is a universal property of living psychoplasm. The automatic and the reflex movements which we observe everywhere, even in the unicellular protists, seem to be the outcome of inclinations

PSYCHIC GRADATIONS

which are inseparably connected with the very idea of life. Even in the plants and lowest animals these inclinations, or tropisms, seem to be the joint outcome of the inclinations of all the combined individual cells.

But when the "tricellular reflex organ" arises (page 115), and a third independent cell—the "psychic," or "ganglionic," cell—is interposed between the sense-cell and the motor cell, we have an independent elementary organ of will. In the lower animals, however, this will remains *unconscious*. It is only when consciousness arises in the higher animals, as the subjective mirror of the objective, though internal, processes in the neuroplasm of the psychic cells, that the will reaches that highest stage which likens it in character to the human will, and which, in the case of man, assumes in common parlance the predicate of "liberty." Its free dominion and action become more and more deceptive as the muscular system and the sense-organs develop with a free and rapid locomotion, entailing a correlative evolution of the brain and the organs of thought.

The question of the liberty of the will is the one which has more than any other cosmic problem occupied the time of thoughtful humanity, the more so that in this case the great philosophic interest of the question was enhanced by the association of most momentous consequences for practical philosophy—for ethics, education, law, and so forth. Emil du Bois-Reymond, who treats it as the seventh and last of his "seven cosmic problems," rightly says of the question: "Affecting everybody, apparently accessible to everybody, intimately involved in the fundamental conditions of human society, vitally connected with religious belief, this question has been of immeasurable importance in the history of civilization. There is probably no other ob-

THE RIDDLE OF THE UNIVERSE

ject of thought on which the modern library contains so many dusty folios that will never again be opened." The importance of the question is also seen in the fact that Kant put it in the same category with the questions of the immortality of the soul and belief in God. He called these three great questions the indispensable "postulates of practical reason," though he had already clearly shown them to have no reality whatever in the light of *pure* reason.

The most remarkable fact in connection with this fierce and confused struggle over the freedom of the will is, perhaps, that it has been theoretically rejected, not only by the greatest critical philosophers, but even by their extreme opponents, and yet it is still affirmed to be self-evident by the majority of people. Some of the first teachers of the Christian Churches—such as St. Augustine and Calvin—rejected the freedom of the will as decisively as the famous leaders of pure materialism, Holbach in the eighteenth and Büchner in the nineteenth century. Christian theologians deny it, because it is irreconcilable with their belief in the omnipotence of God and in predestination. God, omnipotent and omniscient, saw and willed all things from eternity—he must, consequently, have predetermined the conduct of man. If man, with his free will, were to act otherwise than God had ordained, God would not be all-mighty and all-knowing. In the same sense Leibnitz, too, was an unconditional determinist. The monistic scientists of the last century, especially Laplace, defended determinism as a consequence of their mechanical view of life.

The great struggle between the determinist and the indeterminist, between the opponent and the sustainer of the freedom of the will, has ended to-day, after more

PSYCHIC GRADATIONS

than two thousand years, completely in favor of the determinist. The human will has no more freedom than that of the higher animals, from which it differs only in degree, not in kind. In the last century the dogma of liberty was fought with general philosophic and cosmological arguments. The nineteenth century has given us very different weapons for its definitive destruction—the powerful weapons which we find in the arsenal of comparative physiology and evolution. We now know that each act of the will is as fatally determined by the organization of the individual and as dependent on the momentary condition of his environment as every other psychic activity. The character of the inclination was determined long ago by *heredity* from parents and ancestors; the determination to each particular act is an instance of *adaptation* to the circumstances of the moment wherein the strongest motive prevails, according to the laws which govern the statics of emotion. Ontogeny teaches us to understand the evolution of the will in the individual child. Phylogeny reveals to us the historical development of the will within the ranks of our vertebrate ancestors.

CHAPTER VIII

THE EMBRYOLOGY OF THE SOUL

Importance of Ontogeny to Psychology—Development of the Child-Soul—Commencement of Existence of the Individual Soul—The Storing of the Soul—Mythology of the Origin of the Soul—Physiology of the Origin of the Soul—Elementary Processes in Conception—Coalescence of the Ovum and the Spermatozoon—Cell-Love—Heredity of the Soul from Parents and Ancestors—Its Physiological Nature as the Mechanics of the Protoplasm—Blending of Souls (Psychic Amphigony)—Reversion, Psychological Atavism—The Biogenetic Law in Psychology—Palingenetic Repetition and Cenogenetic Modification—Embryonic and Post-Embryonic Psychogeny.

THE human soul — whatever we may hold as to its nature—undergoes a continual development throughout the life of the individual. This ontogenetic fact is of fundamental importance in our monistic psychology, though the "professional" psychologists pay little or no attention to it. Since the embryology of the individual is, on Baer's principle—and in accordance with the universal belief of modern biologists—the "true torch-bearer for all research into the organic body," it will afford us a reliable light on the momentous problems of its psychic activity.

Although, however, this "embryology of the soul" is so important and interesting, it has hitherto met with the consideration it deserves only within a very narrow circle. Until recently teachers were almost the only

THE EMBRYOLOGY OF THE SOUL

ones to occupy themselves with a part of the problem; since their avocation compelled them to assist and supervise the formation of the psychic activity in the child, they were bound to take a theoretical interest, also, in the psychogenetic facts that came under their notice. However, these teachers, for the most part, both in recent and in earlier times, were dominated by the current dualistic psychology—in so far as they reflected at all; and they were totally ignorant of the important facts of comparative psychology, and unacquainted with the structure and function of the brain. Moreover, their observations only extended to children in their school-days, or in the years immediately preceding. The remarkable phenomena which the individual psychogeny of the child offers in its earliest years, and which are the joy and admiration of all thoughtful parents, were scarcely ever made the subject of serious scientific research Wilhelm Preyer was the pioneer of this study in his interesting work on *The Mind of the Child* (1881). To obtain a perfectly clear knowledge of the matter, however, we must go further back still; we must commence at the first appearance of the soul in the impregnated ovum.

The origin of the human individual—body and soul —was still wrapped in complete mystery at the beginning of the nineteenth century. Caspar Friedrich Wolff had, it is true, discovered the true character of embryonic development in 1759, in his *theoria generationis*, and proved with the confidence of a critical observer that there is a true *epigenesis*—*i.e.*, a series of very remarkable formative processes—in the evolution of the fœtus from the simple ovum. But the physiologists of the time, with the famous Albert Haller at their head, flatly refused to entertain these empirical truths, which

THE RIDDLE OF THE UNIVERSE

may be directly proved by microscopic observation, and clung to the old dogma of "preformation." This theory assumed that in the human ovum—and in the egg of all other animals—the organism was already present, or "preformed," in all its parts; the "evolution" of the embryo consisted literally in an "unfolding" (*evolutio*) of the folded organs. One curious consequence of this error was the theory of *scatulation*, which we have mentioned on p. 55, since the ovary had to be admitted to be present in the embryo of the woman, it was also necessary to suppose that the germs of the next generation were already formed in it, and so on *in infinitum*. Opposed to this dogma of the "Ovulists" was the equally erroneous notion of the "Animalculists"; the latter held that the germ was not really in the female ovum, but in the paternal element, and that the store of succeeding generations was to be sought in the spermatozoa.

Leibnitz consistently applied this theory of scatulation to the human soul; he denied that either soul or body had a real development (*epigenesis*), and said in his *Theodicy* : " Thus I consider that the souls which are destined one day to become human exist in the seed, like those of other species; that they have existed in our ancestors as far back as Adam—that is, since the beginning of the world—in the forms of organized bodies." Similar notions prevailed in biology and philosophy until the third decade of the present century, when the reform of embryology by Baer gave them their death blow. In the province of psychology, however, they still find many adherents; they form one group of the many curious mystical ideas which give us a living illustration of the ontogeny of the soul.

The more accurate knowledge which we have recent-

THE EMBRYOLOGY OF THE SOUL

ly obtained, through comparative ethnology, of the various forms of myths of ancient and modern uncivilized races, is also of great interest in psychogeny. Still, it would take us too far from our purpose if we were to enter into it with any fulness here; we must refer the reader to Adalbert Svoboda's excellent work on *Forms of Faith* (1897). In respect of their scientific and poetical contents, we may arrange all pertinent *psychogenetic myths* in the following five groups:

I. The myth of transmigration.—The soul lived formerly in the body of another animal, and passed from this into a human body. The Egyptian priests, for instance, taught that the human soul wandered through all the species of animals after the death of the body, returning to a human frame after three thousand years of transmigration.

II. The myth of the in-planting of the soul.—The soul existed independently in another place—a psychogenetic store, as it were (in a kind of embryonic slumber or latent life); it was taken out by a bird (sometimes represented as an eagle, generally as a white stork), and implanted in the human body.

III. The myth of the creation of the soul.—God creates the souls, and keeps them stored—sometimes in a pond (living in the form of *plankton*), according to other myths in a tree (where they are conceived as the fruit of a phanerogam); the Creator takes them from the pond or tree, and inserts them in the human germ during the act of conception.

IV. The myth of the scatulation of the soul (the theory of Leibnitz which we have given above).

V. The myth of the division of the soul (the theory of Rudolph Wagner [1855] and of other physiologists). —In the act of procreation a portion is detached from both the (immaterial) souls of the parents; the maternal contribution passes in the ovum, the paternal in the spermatozoa; when these two germinal cells coalesce, the two psychic fragments that accompany them also combine to form a new (immaterial) soul.

Although the poetic fancies we have mentioned as to the origin of the individual human soul are still widely accepted, their purely mythological character is now firmly established. The deeply interesting and remarkable research which has been made in the course of the last twenty-five years into the more minute processes of the impregnation and germination of the ovum has made it clear that these mysterious phenomena belong entirely to the province of cellular physiology (cf. p. 48). Both the female element, the ovum, and the male fertilizing body, the sperma or spermatozoa, are *simple cells*. These living cells possess a certain sum of physiological properties to which we give the title of the "cell-soul," just as we do in the permanently unicellular protist (see p. 48). Both germinal cells have the faculty of movement and sensation. The young ovum, or egg-cell, moves after the manner of an amœba; the minute spermatozoa, of which there are millions in every drop of the seminal fluid, are ciliated cells, and swim about as freely in the sperm, by means of their lashes or *cilia*, as the ordinary ciliated infusoria (the flagellata).

When the two cells meet as a result of copulation, or when they are brought into contact through artificial fertilization (in the fishes, for instance), they attract each other and become firmly attached. The main cause of this cellular attraction is a chemical sensitive action of the protoplasm, allied to smell or taste, which we call "erotic chemicotropism"; it may also

THE EMBRYOLOGY OF THE SOUL

be correctly (both in the chemical and the romantic sense) termed " cellular affinity " or " sexual cell-love." A number of the ciliated cells in the sperm swim rapidly towards the stationary egg-cell and seek to penetrate into it. As Hertwig showed in 1875, as a rule only one of the suitors is fortunate enough to reach the desired goal. As soon as this favored spermatozoon has pierced into the body of the ovum with its head (the nucleus of the cell), a thin mucous layer is detached from the ovum which prevents the further entrance of spermatozoa. The formation of this protective membrane was only prevented when Hertwig kept the ovum stiff with cold by lowering the temperature, or benumbed it with narcotics (chloroform, morphia, nicotine, etc.); then there was "super-impregnation" or "poly-spermy" —a number of sperm-threads pierced into the body of the unconscious ovum. This remarkable fact proved that there is a low degree of "cellular instinct" (or, at least, of specific, lively sensation) in the sexual cells just as effectively as do the important phenomena that immediately follow in their interior. Both nuclei— that of the ovum and of the spermatozoon—attract each other, approach, and, on contact, completely fuse together. Thus from the impregnated ovum arises the important new cell which we call the " stem-cell " (*cytula*), from the repeated segmentation of which the whole polycellular organism is evolved.

The psychological information which is afforded by these remarkable facts of impregnation, which have only been properly observed during the last twenty-five years, is supremely important; its vast significance has hitherto been very far from appreciated. We shall condense the main conclusions of research in the following five theses:

THE RIDDLE OF THE UNIVERSE

I. Each human individual, like every other higher animal, is a single simple cell at the commencement of his existence.

II. This "stem-cell" (cytula) is formed in the same manner in all cases—that is, by the blending or copulation of two separate cells of diverse origin, the female ovum and the male spermatozoon.

III. Each of these sexual cells has its own "cell-soul"—that is, each is distinguished by a peculiar form of sensation and movement.

IV. At the moment of conception or impregnation, not only the protoplasm and the nuclei of the two sexual cells coalesce, but also their "cell-souls"; in other words, the potential energies which are latent in both, and inseparable from the matter of the protoplasm, unite for the formation of a new potential energy, the "germ-soul" of the newly constructed stem-cell.

V. Consequently each personality owes his bodily and spiritual qualities to both parents; by heredity the nucleus of the ovum contributes a portion of the maternal features, while the nucleus of the spermatozoon brings a part of the father's characteristics.

By these empirical facts of conception, moreover, the further fact of extreme importance is established, that every man, like every other animal, *has a beginning of existence ;* the complete copulation of the two sexual cell-nuclei marks the precise moment when not only the body, but also the "soul," of the new stem-cell makes its appearance. This fact suffices of itself to destroy the myth of the immortality of the soul, to which we shall return later on. It suffices, too, for the destruction of the still prevalent superstition that man owes his personal existence to the favor of God. Its origin is rather to be attributed solely to the "eros"

THE EMBRYOLOGY OF THE SOUL

of his parents, to that powerful impulse that is common to all polycellular animals and plants, and leads to their nuptial union. But the essential point in this physiological process is not the " embrace," as was formerly supposed, or the amorousness connected therewith; it is simply the introduction of the spermatozoa into the vagina. This is the sole means, in the land-dwelling animals, by which the fertilizing element can reach the released ova (which usually takes place in the uterus in man). In the case of the lower aquatic animals (fishes, mussels, medusæ, etc.) the mature sexual elements on both sides are simply discharged into the water, and their union is let to chance; they have no real copulation, and so they show none of those higher psychic " erotic " functions which play so conspicuous a part in the life of the higher animals. Hence it is, also, that all the lower, non-copulating animals are wanting in those interesting organs which Darwin has called " secondary sexual characters," and which are the outcome of sexual selection: such are the beard of man, the antlers of the stag, the beautiful plumage of the bird of paradise and of so many other birds, together with other distinctions of the male which are absent in the female.

Among the above theses as to the physiology of conception the inheritance of the psychic qualities of the two parents is of particular importance for psychological purposes. It is well known that every child inherits from both his parents peculiarities of character, temperament, talent, acuteness of sense, and strength of will. It is equally well known that even psychic qualities are often (if not always) transmitted from grandparents by heredity—often, in fact, a man resembles his grandparents more than his parents in certain respects; and that is true both of bodily and mental features. All the chief laws of heredity which I first formulated in my *General Morphology*, and popularized in my *Natural History of Creation*, are just as valid and universal in their application to psychic phenomena as to bodily structure—in fact, they are frequently more striking and conspicuous in the former than in the latter.

However, the great province of heredity, to the inestimable importance of which Darwin first opened our eyes in 1859, is thickly beset with obscure problems and physiological difficulties. We dare not claim, even after forty years of research, that all its aspects are clear to us. Yet we have done so much that we can confidently speak of heredity as a *physiological function* of the organism, which is directly connected with the faculty of generation; and we must reduce it, like all other vital phenomena, to exclusively physical and chemical processes, to the *mechanics of the protoplasm*. We now know accurately enough the process of impregnation itself; we know that in it the nucleus of the spermatozoon contributes the qualities of the male parent, and the nucleus of the ovum gives the qualities of the mother, to the newly born stem-cell. The blending of the two nuclei is the "physiological moment" of heredity; by it the personal features of both body and soul are transmitted to the new individual. These facts of ontogeny are beyond the explanation of the dualistic and mystic psychology which still prevails in the schools; whereas they find a perfectly simple interpretation in our monistic philosophy.

The physiological fact which is most material for a correct appreciation of individual psychogeny is the *continuity* of the *psyche* through the rise and fall of genera-

THE EMBRYOLOGY OF THE SOUL

tions. A new individual comes into existence at the moment of conception; yet it is not an independent entity, either in respect of its mental or its bodily features, but merely the product of the blending of the two parental factors, the maternal egg-cell and paternal sperm-cell. The cell-souls of these two sexual cells combine in the act of conception for the formation of a new cell-soul, just as truly as the two cell-nuclei, which are the material vehicles of this psychic potential energy, unite to form a new nucleus. As we now see that the individuals of one and the same species—even sisters born of the same parents—always show certain differences, however slight, we must assume that these variations were already present in the chemical plasmatic constitution of the generative cells themselves.*

These facts alone would suffice to explain the infinite variety of individual features, of soul and of bodily form, that we find in the organic world. As an extreme, but one-sided, consequence of them, there is the theory of Weismann, which considers the *amphimixis*, or the blending of the germ-plasm in sexual generation, to be the universal and the sole cause of individual variability. This exclusive theory, which is connected with his theory of the continuity of the germ-plasm, is, in my opinion, an exaggeration. I am convinced, on the contrary, that the great laws of *progressive heredity* and of the correlative *functional adaptation* apply to the soul as well as to the body. The new characteristics which the individual has acquired during life may react to some extent on the molecular texture of the germ-plasm in the egg-cell and sperm-cell, and may thus be transferred to the next generation by heredity in

* Law of individual variation. *Vide Natural History of Creation.*

certain conditions (naturally, only in the form of latent energy).

Although in the soul-blending at the moment of conception only the latent forces of the two parent souls are transmitted by the coalescence of the erotic cell-nuclei, still it is possible that the hereditary psychic influence of earlier, and sometimes very much older, generations may be communicated at the same time For the laws of *latent heredity* or atavism apply to the soul just as validly as to the anatomical organization. We find these remarkable phenomena of reversion in a very simple and instructive form in the alternation of generations of the polyps and medusæ. Here we see two very different generations alternate so regularly that the first resembles the third, fifth, and so on ; while the second (very different from the preceding) is like the fourth, sixth, etc. (*Natural History of Creation*). We do not find such alternation of generations in man and the higher animals and plants, in which, owing to continuous heredity, each generation resembles the next ; nevertheless, even in these cases we often meet with phenomena of reversion, which must be reduced to the same law of latent heredity.

Eminent men often take more after their grandparents than their parents even in the finer shades of psychic activity—in the possession of certain artistic talents or inclinations, in force of character, and in warmth of temperament; not infrequently there is a striking feature which neither parents nor grandparents possessed, but which may be traced a long way back to an older branch of the family. Even in these remarkable cases of atavism the same laws of heredity apply to the *psyche* and to the physiognomy, to the personal quality of the sense-organs, muscles, skeleton,

THE EMBRYOLOGY OF THE SOUL

and other parts of the body. We can trace them most clearly in the reigning dynasties and in old families of the nobility, whose conspicuous share in the life of the State has given occasion to a more careful historical picture of the individuals in the chain of generations —for instance, in the Hohenzollerns, the princes of Orange, the Bourbons, etc., and in the Roman Cæsars.

The causal-nexus of *biontic* (individual) and *phyletic* (historical) evolution, which I gave in my *General Morphology* as the supreme law at the root of all biogenetic research, has a universal application to psychology no less than to morphology. I have fully treated the special importance which it has with regard to man, in both respects, in the first chapter of my *Anthropogeny*. In man, as in all other organisms, "the embryonic development is an epitome of the historical development of the species. This condensed and abbreviated recapitulation is the more complete in proportion as the original *epitomized development* (*palingenesis*) is preserved by a constant heredity; on the other hand, it falls off from completeness in proportion as the later *disturbing development* (*cenogenesis*) is accentuated by varying adaptation."

While we apply this law to the evolution of the soul, we must lay special stress on the injunction to keep *both* sides of it critically before us. For, in the case of man, just as in all the higher animals and plants, such appreciable perturbations of type (or *cenogeneses*) have taken place during the millions of years of development that the original simple idea of *palingenesis*, or "epitome of history," has been greatly disturbed and altered. While, on the one side, the *palingenetic* recapitulation is preserved by the laws of like-time and like-place heredity, it is subject to an essential *ceno-*

genetic change, on the other hand, by the laws of abbreviated and simplified heredity. That is clearly seen in the embryonic evolution of the psychic organs, the nervous system, the muscles, and the sense-organs. But it applies in just the same manner to the psychic functions, which are absolutely dependent on the normal construction of these organs. Their evolution is subject to great cenogenetic modification in man and all other viviporous animals, precisely because the complete development of the embryo occupies a longer time within the body of the mother. But we have to distinguish two periods of individual psychogeny: (1) the embryonic, and (2) the post-embryonic development of the soul.

I. *Embryonic Psychogeny.*—The human fœtus, or embryo, normally takes nine months (or two hundred and seventy days) to develop in the uterus During this time it is entirely cut off from the outer world, and protected, not only by the thick muscular wall of the womb, but also by the special fœtal membranes (*embryolemmata*) which are common to all the three higher classes of vertebrates—reptiles, birds, and mammals. In all the classes of amniotes these membranes (the *amnion* and the *serolemma*) develop in just the same fashion. They represent the protective arrangements which were acquired by the earliest reptiles (*proreptilia*), the common parents of all the amniotes, in the Permian period (towards the end of the palæozoic age), when these higher vertebrates accustomed themselves to live on land and breathe the atmosphere. Their ancestors, the amphibia of the Carboniferous period, still lived and breathed in the water, like their earlier predecessors, the fishes.

In the case of these older and lower vertebrates that

lived in the water, the embryonic development had the palingenetic character in a still higher degree, as is the case in most of the fishes and amphibia of the present day. The familiar tadpole and the larva of the salamander or the frog still preserve the structure of their fish-ancestors in the first part of their life in the water; they resemble them, likewise, in their habits of life, in breathing by gills, in the action of their sense-organs, and in other psychic organs. Then, when the interesting metamorphosis of the swimming tadpole takes place, and when it adapts itself to a land-life, the fish-like body changes into that of a four-footed, crawling amphibium; instead of the gill-breathing in the water comes an exclusive breathing of the atmosphere by means of lungs, and, with the changed habits of life, even the psychic apparatus, the nervous system, and the sense-organs reach a higher degree of construction. If we could completely follow the psychogeny of the tadpole from beginning to end, we should be able to apply the biogenetic law in many ways to its psychic evolution. For it develops in direct communication with the changing conditions of the outer world, and so must quickly adapt its sensation and movement to these. The swimming tadpole has not only the structure but the habits of life of a fish, and only acquires those of a frog in its metamorphosis.

It is different with man and all the other amniotes; their embryo is entirely withdrawn from the direct influence of the outer world, and cut off from any reciprocal action therewith, by enclosure in its protective membranes. Besides, the special care of the young on the part of the amniotes gives their embryo much more favorable conditions for the cenogenetic abbreviation of the palingenetic evolution. There is, in the first place, the excellent arrangement for the nourishment of the embryo; in the reptiles, birds, and monotremes (the oviparous mammals) it is effected by the great yellow nutritive yelk, which is associated with the egg; in the rest of the mammals (the marsupials and placentals) it is effected by the mother's blood, which is conducted to the fœtus by the blood-vessels of the yelk-sac and the allantois. In the case of the most highly developed placentals this elaborate nutritive arrangement has reached the highest degree of perfection by the construction of a placenta; hence in these classes the embryo is fully developed before birth. But its soul remains during all this time in a state of embryonic slumber, a state of repose which Preyer has justly compared to the hibernation of animals. We have a similar long sleep in the chrysalis stage of those insects which undergo a complete metamorphosis—butterflies, bees, flies, beetles, and so forth. This sleep of the pupa, during which the most important formations of organs and tissues take place, is the more interesting from the fact that the preceding condition of the free larva (caterpillar, grub, or maggot) included a highly developed psychic activity, and that this is, significantly, lower than the stage which is seen afterwards (when the chrysalis sleep is over) in the perfect, winged, sexually mature insect.

Man's psychic activity, like that of most of the higher animals, runs through a long series of stages of development during the individual life. We may single out the five following as the most important of them:

I. The soul of the new-born infant up to the birth of self-consciousness and the learning of speech.

II. The soul of the boy or girl up to puberty (*i.e.*, until the awakening of the sexual instinct).

THE EMBRYOLOGY OF THE SOUL

III. The soul of the youth or maiden up to the time of sexual intercourse (the " idealist " period).

IV. The soul of the grown man and the mature woman (the period of full maturity and of the founding of families, lasting until about the sixtieth year for the man and the fiftieth for the woman—until *involution* sets in).

V. The soul of the old man or woman (the period of degeneration).

Man's psychic life runs the same evolution—upward progress, full maturity, and downward degeneration—as every other vital activity in his organization.

CHAPTER IX

THE PHYLOGENY OF THE SOUL

Gradual Historical Evolution of the Human Soul from the Animal Soul—Methods of Phylogenetic Psychology—Four Chief Stages in the Phylogeny of the Soul: I. The Cell-Soul (Cytopsyche) of the Protist (Infusoria, Ova, etc.) : Cellular Psychology; II. The Soul of a Colony of Cells, or the Cenobitic Soul (Cœnopsyche) : Psychology of the Morula and Blastula, III. The Soul of the Tissue (Histopsyche): Its Twofold Nature: The Soul of the Plant: The Soul of the Lower, Nerveless Animal · Double Soul of the Siphonophora (Personal and Kormal Soul), IV. The Nerve-Soul (Neuropsyche) of the Higher Animal—Three Sections of its Psychic Apparatus Sense-Organs, Muscles, and Nerves — Typical Formation of the Nerve-Centre in the Various Groups of Animals—Psychic Organ of the Vertebrate: the Brain and the Spinal Cord—Phylogeny of the Mammal Soul.

THE theory of descent, combined with anthropological research, has convinced us of the descent of our human organism from a long series of animal ancestors by a slow and gradual transformation occupying many millions of years. Since, then, we cannot dissever man's psychic life from the rest of his vital functions—we are rather forced to a conviction of the natural evolution of our whole body and mind—it becomes one of the main tasks of the modern monistic psychology to trace the stages of the historical development of the soul of man from the soul of the brute. Our " phylogeny of the soul " seeks to attain this object; it

THE PHYLOGENY OF THE SOUL

may also, as a branch of general psychology, be called *phylogenetic* psychology, or, in contradistinction to *biontic* (individual), *phyletic psychogeny*. And, although this new science has scarcely been taken up in earnest yet, and most of the "professional" psychologists deny its very right to existence, we must claim for it the utmost importance and the deepest interest. For, in our opinion, it is its special province to solve for us the great enigma of the nature and origin of the human soul.

The methods and paths which will lead us to the remote goal of a complete phylogenetic psychology—a goal that is still buried in the mists of the future, and almost imperceptible to many—do not differ from those of other branches of evolutionary research. Comparative anatomy, physiology, and ontogeny are of the first importance. Much support is given also by palæontology, for the order in which the fossil remains of the various classes of vertebrates succeed each other in the course of organic evolution reveals to us, to some extent, the gradual growth of their psychic power as well as their phyletic connection. We must admit that we are here, as we are in every branch of phylogenetic research, driven to the construction of a number of hypotheses in order to fill up the considerable lacunæ of empirical phylogeny. Yet these hypotheses cast so clear and significant a light on the chief stages of historical development that we are afforded a most gratifying insight into their entire course.

The comparative psychology of man and the higher animals enables us to learn from the highest group of the placentals, the primates, the long strides by which the human soul has advanced beyond the *psyche* of the anthropoid ape. The phylogeny of the mammals and of

THE RIDDLE OF THE UNIVERSE

the lower vertebrates acquaints us with the long series of the earlier ancestors of the primates which have arisen within this stem since the Silurian age. All these vertebrates agree in the structure and development of their characteristic psychic organ — the spinal cord. We learn from the comparative anatomy of the vermalia that this spinal cord has been evolved from a dorsal *acroganglion,* or vertical brain, of an invertebrate ancestor. We learn, further, from comparative ontogeny that this simple psychic organ has been evolved from the stratum of cells in the outer germinal layer, the ectoderm, of the platodes. In these earliest flat-worms, which have no specialized nervous system, the outer skin-covering serves as a general sensitive and psychic organ. Finally, comparative embryology teaches us that these simple metazoa have arisen by gastrulation from blastæades, from hollow spheres, the wall of which is merely one simple layer of cells, the *blastoderm;* and the same science, with the aid of the biogenetic law, explains how these protozoic cœnobia originally sprang from the simplest unicellular organisms.

On a critical study of these different embryonic formations, the evolution of which from each other we can directly observe under the microscope, we arrive, by means of the great law of biogeny, at a series of most important conclusions as to the chief stages in the development of our psychic life. We may distinguish eight of these to begin with:

I. Unicellular protozoa with a simple cell-soul: the infusoria.

II. Multicellular protozoa with a communal soul: the catallacta.

III. The earliest metazoa with an epithelial soul: the platodes.

THE PHYLOGENY OF THE SOUL

IV. Invertebrate ancestors with a simple vertical brain: the vermalia.

V. Vertebrates without skull or brain, with a simple spinal cord: the acrania.

VI. Animals with skull and brain (of five vesicles): the craniota.

VII. Mammals with predominant development of the cortex of the brain: the placentals.

VIII. The higher anthropoid apes and man, with organs of thought (in the cerebrum): the anthropomorpha.

Among these eight stages in the development of the human soul we may further distinguish more or less clearly a number of subordinate stages. Naturally, however, in reconstructing them we have to fall back on the same defective evidence of empirical psychology which the comparative anatomy and physiology of the actual fauna affords us. As the craniote animals of the sixth stage—and these are true fishes—are already found fossilized in the Silurian system, we are forced to assume that the five preceding series of ancestors (which were incapable of fossilization) were evolved in an earlier, pre-Silurian age.

I. *The cell-soul* (*or cytopsyche*): first stage of phyletic psychogenesis.—The earliest ancestors of man and all other animals were unicellular protozoa. This fundamental hypothesis of rational phylogeny is based, in virtue of the phylogenetic law, on the familiar embryological fact that every man, like every other metazoon (*i.e.*, every multicellular organism with tissues), begins his personal existence as a simple cell, the stem-cell (*cytula*), or the impregnated egg-cell (see p. 63). As this cell has a "soul" from the commencement, so had also the corresponding unicellular *ancestral forms,* which were represented in the oldest series of man's ancestors by a number of different protozoa.

We learn the character of the psychic activity of these unicellular organisms from the comparative physiology of the protists of to-day. Close observation and careful experiment have opened out to us in this respect, in the second half of the nineteenth century, a new world of the most interesting phenomena. The best description of them was given by Max Verworn in his thoughtful work, based on original research, *Psycho-physiological Studies of the Protists.* The work includes also the few earlier observations of the "psychic life of the protist." Verworn came to the firm conclusion that the psychic processes are unconscious in all the protists, that the phenomena of sensation and movement coincide with the molecular vital processes in their protoplasm, and that their ultimate causes are to be sought in the properties of the protoplasmic molecules (the *plastidules*). " Hence the psychic phenomena of the protists form a bridge that connects the chemical processes of the inorganic world with the psychic life of the highest animals; they represent the germ of the highest psychic phenomena of the metazoa and of man."

The careful observations and many experiments of Verworn, together with those of Wilhelm Engelmann, Wilhelm Preyer, Richard Hertwig, and other more recent students of the protists, afford conlcusive evidence for my "theory of the cell-soul" (1866). On the strength of several years of study of different kinds of protists, especially rhizopods and infusoria, I published a theory thirty-three years ago to the effect that every living cell has psychic properties, and that the

THE PHYLOGENY OF THE SOUL

psychic life of the multicellular animals and plants is merely the sum total of the psychic functions of the cells which build up their structure. In the lower groups (in algæ and sponges, for instance) *all* the cells of the body have an equal share in it (or with very slight differences); in the higher groups, in harmony with the law of the "division of labor," only a select portion of them are involved—the "soul-cells." The important consequences of this "cellular psychology" were partly treated in my work on *The Perigenesis of the Plastidule* (1876), and partly in my speech at Munich, in 1877, on "Modern Evolution in Relation to the Whole of Science." A more popular presentation of them is to be found in my two Vienna papers (1878) on "The Origin and Development of the Sense-Organs" and on "Cell-Souls and Soul-Cells."

Moreover, the cell-soul, even within the limits of the protist world, presents a long series of stages of development, from the most simple and primitive to a comparatively elaborate activity. In the earliest and simplest protists the faculty of sensation and movement is equally distributed over the entire protoplasm of the homogeneous morsel; in the higher forms certain "cell-instruments," or *organella*, appear, as their physiological organs. Motor cell-parts of that character are found in the pseudopodia of the rhizopods, and the vibrating hairs, lashes, or cilia of the infusoria. The cell-nucleus, which is wanting in the earlier and lower protists, is considered to be an internal central organ of the cell-life. It is especially noteworthy, from a physiologico-chemical point of view, that the very earliest protists were plasmodomous, with plant-like nutrition—hence *protophyta*, or primitive plants; from these came as a secondary stage, by metasitism, the first plasmophagi, with animal nutrition—the *protozoa*, or primitive animals.* This metasitism, or circulation of nutritive matter, implies an important psychological advance, with it began the development of those characteristic properties of the animal soul which are wanting in the plant.

We find the highest development of the animal cell-soul in the class of ciliata, or ciliated infusoria. When we compare their activity with the corresponding psychic life of the higher, multicellular animals, we find scarcely any psychological difference; the sensitive and motor *organella* of these protozoa seem to accomplish the same as the sense-organs, nerves, and muscles of the metazoa. Indeed, we have found in the great cell-nucleus (*meganucleus*) of the infusoria a central organ of psychic activity, which plays much the same part in their unicellular organism as the brain does in the psychic life of higher animals. However, it is very difficult to determine how far this comparison is justified; the views of experts diverge considerably over the matter. Some take all spontaneous bodily movement in them to be automatic, or impulsive, and all stimulated movement to be reflex; others are convinced that such movements are partly voluntary and intentional. The latter would attribute to the infusoria a certain degree of consciousness, and even self-consciousness; but this is rejected by the others. However that very difficult question may be settled, it does not alter the fact that these unicellular protozoa give proof of the possession of a highly developed "cell-soul," which is of great interest for a correct decision as to the *psyche* of our earliest unicellular ancestors.

* Cf. E. Haeckel, *Systematic Phylogeny*, vol. i.

THE PHYLOGENY OF THE SOUL

II. *The communal or cenobitic soul* (*coenopsyche*): second stage of phyletic psychogenesis.—Individual development begins, in man and in all other multicellular animals, with the repeated segmentation of one simple cell This *stem-cell*, the impregnated ovum, divides first into two daughter cells, by a process of ordinary indirect segmentation; as the process is repeated there arise (by equal division of the egg) successively four, eight, sixteen, thirty-two, sixty-four such new cells, or "blastomeres." Usually (that is, in the case of the majority of animals) an irregular enlargement sooner or later takes the place of this original regular division of cells. But the result is the same in all cases—the formation of a (generally spherical) cluster of heterogeneous (originally homogeneous) cells. This stage is called the *morula* ("mulberry," which it somewhat resembles in shape). Then, as a rule, a fluid gathers in the interior of this aggregate of cells; it changes into a spherical vesicle; all the cells go to its surface, and arrange themselves in one simple layer—the *blastoderm*. The hollow sphere which is thus formed is the important stage of the "germinal vesicle," the *blastula*, or blastosphere.

The psychological phenomena which we directly observe in the formation of the blastula are partly sensations, partly movements, of this community of cells. The movements may be divided into two groups: (1) the inner movements, which are always repeated in substantially the same manner in the process of ordinary (indirect) segmentation of cells (formation of the axis of the nucleus, mitosis, karyokinesis, etc.); (2) the outer movements, which are seen in the regular change of position of the social cells and their grouping for the construction of the blastoderm.

THE RIDDLE OF THE UNIVERSE

We assume that these movements are hereditary and unconscious, because they are always determined in the same fashion by heredity from the earlier protist ancestors. The sensations also fall into two groups: (1) the sensations of the individual cells, which reveal themselves in the assertion of their individual independence and their relation to neighboring cells (with which they are in contact, and partly in direct combination, by means of protoplasmic fibres); (2) the common sensation of the entire community of cells, which is seen in the individual formation of the *blastula* as a hollow vesicle.

The causal interpretation of the formation of the blastula is given us by the biogenetic law, which explains the phenomena we directly observe to be the outcome of heredity, and relates them to corresponding historical processes which took place long ago in the origin of the earliest protist-cœnobia, the blastæads. But we get a physiological and psychological insight into these important phenomena of the earliest cell-communities by observation and experiment on their modern representatives. Such permanent cell-communities or colonies are still found in great numbers both among the plasmodomous primitive plants (for instance, the paulotomacea, diatomacea, volvocinæ, etc.) and the plasmophagous primitive animals (the infusoria and rhizopods). In all these cœnobia we can easily distinguish two different grades of psychic activity: (1) the cell-soul of the individual cells (the " elementary organisms ") and (2) the communal soul of the entire colony.

III. *The tissue-soul (histopsyche)*: third stage of phyletic psychogenesis.—In all multicellular, tissue-forming plants (*metaphyta*) and in the lowest, nerve-

THE PHYLOGENY OF THE SOUL

less classes of tissue-forming animals (*metazoa*) we have to distinguish two different forms of psychic activity—namely: (1) the *psyche* of the individual cells which compose the tissue, and (2) the *psyche* of the tissue itself, or of the "cell-state" which is made up of the tissues. This "tissue-soul" is the higher psychological function which gives physiological individuality to the compound multicellular organism as a true "cell-commonwealth." It controls all the separate "cell-souls" of the social cells—the mutually dependent "citizens" which constitute the community. This fundamental twofold character of the *psyche* in the metaphyta and the lower, nerveless metazoa is very important. It may be verified by unprejudiced observation and suitable experiment. In the first place, each single cell has its own sensation and movement, and, in addition, each tissue and each organ, composed of a number of homogeneous cells, has its special irritability and psychic unity (*e g*, the pollen and stamens).

A. *The plant-soul* (*phytopsyche*) is, in our view, the summary of the entire psychic activity of the tissue-forming, multicellular plant (the *metaphyton*, as distinct from the unicellular *protophyton*); it is, however, the subject of the most diverse opinions even at the present day. It was once customary to draw an essential distinction between the plant and the animal, on the ground that the latter had a "soul" and the plant had none. However, an unprejudiced comparison of the irritability and movements of various higher plants and lower animals convinced many observers, even at the beginning of the century, that there must be a "soul" on both sides. At a later date Fechner, Leitgeb, and others strongly contended for the plant-soul. But a profounder knowledge of the subject was obtained when the similarity of the elementary structure of the plant and of the animal was proved by the cellular theory, and especially when the similarity of conduct of the active, living protoplasm in both was shown in the plasma theory of Max Schultze (1859). Modern comparative physiology has shown that the physiological attitude towards various stimuli (light, heat, electricity, gravity, friction, chemical action, etc) of the "sensitive" portions of many plants and animals is exactly the same, and that the reflex movements which the stimuli elicit take place in precisely the same manner on both sides. Hence, if it was necessary to attribute this activity to a "soul" in the lower, nerveless metazoa (sponges, polyps, etc.), it was also necessary in the case of many (if not all) metaphyta, at least in the very sensitive *mimosa*, the " fly-traps " (*dionaea* and *drosera*), and the numerous kinds of climbing plants.

It is true that modern vegetal physiology has given a purely physical explanation of many of these stimulated movements, or tropisms, by special features of growth, variations of pressure, etc. Yet these mechanical causes are neither more nor less *psychophysical* than the similar " reflex movements " of the sponges, polyps, and other nerveless metazoa, even though their mechanism is entirely different. The character of the tissue-soul reveals itself in the same way in both cases—the cells of the tissue (the regular, orderly structure of cells) transmit the stimuli they have received in one part, and thus provoke movements of other parts, or of the whole organ. This transmission of stimuli has as much title to be called "psychic activity" as its more complete form in the higher animals with nerves; the anatomic explanation of it is that the social cells of the tissue, or cell-community, are not isolated

THE PHYLOGENY OF THE SOUL

from each other (as was formerly supposed), but are connected throughout by fine threads or bridges of protoplasm. When the sensitive mimosa closes its graceful leaves and droops its stalk at contact, or on being shaken; when the irritable fly-trap (the dionæa) swiftly clasps its leaves together at a touch, and captures a fly; the sensation seems to be keener, the transmission of the stimulus more rapid, and the movement more energetic than in the reflex action of the stimulated bath-sponge and many other sponges.

B. *The soul of the nerveless metazoa.*—Of very special interest for comparative psychology in general, and for the phylogeny of the animal soul in particular, is the psychic activity of those lower metazoa which have tissues, and sometimes differentiated organs, but no nerves or specific organs of sense. To this category belong four different groups of the earliest cœlenterates: (*a*) the gastræads, (*b*) the platodaria, (*c*) the sponges, and (*d*) the hydropolyps, the lowest form of cnidaria.

The *gastraeads* (or animals with a primitive gut) form a small group of the lowest cœlenterates, which is of great importance as the common ancestral group of all the metazoa. The body of these little swimming animals looks like a tiny (generally oval) vesicle, which has a simple cavity with one opening—the primitive gut and the primitive mouth. The wall of the digestive cavity is formed of two simple layers of cells, or epithelium, the inner of which—the gut-layer—is responsible for the vegetal activity of nourishment, while the outer, or skin-layer, discharges the animal functions of movement and sensation. The homogeneous sensitive cells of the skin-layer bear long, slender hairs or lashes (*cilia*), by the vibration of which the swimming motion is effected   The few surviving forms of gastræads, the gastræmaria (*trichoplacidae*) and cyemaria (*orthonectidae*), are extremely interesting, from the fact that they remain throughout life at a stage of structure which is passed by all the other metazoa (from the sponge to man) at the commencement of their embryonic development.   As I have shown in my *Theory of the Gastraea* (1872), a very characteristic embryonic form, the *gastrula*, is immediately developed from the *blastula* in all the tissue animals.   The germinal membrane (blastoderm), which represents the wall of the hollow vesicle, forms a depression at one side, and this soon sinks in so deep that the inner cavity of the vesicle disappears.   The half of the membrane which bends in is thus laid on, and inside, the other half; the latter forms the *skin-layer*, or outer germinal layer (ectoderm or epiblast), and the former becomes the *gut-layer*, or inner germinal layer (endoderm or hypoblast). The new cavity of the cup-shaped body is the digestive stomach cavity (the *progaste*), and its opening is the primitive mouth (or *prostoma*).*   The skin-layer, or ectoderm, is the primitive psychic organ in the metazoa; from it, in all the nerve animals, not only the external skin and the organs of sense, but also the nervous system, are developed.   In the gastræads, which have no nerves, all the cells which compose the simple epithelium of the ectoderm are equally organs of sensation and of movement; we have here the tissue-soul in its simplest form.

The platodaria, the earliest and simplest form of the platodes, seem to be of the same primitive construction. Some of these cryptocœla—the *convoluta*, etc.—have

* Cf. *Anthropogeny* and *Natural History of Creation*.

THE PHYLOGENY OF THE SOUL

no specific nervous system, while their nearest relatives, the turbellaria, have already differentiated one, and even developed a vertical brain.

The *sponges* form a peculiar group in the animal world, which differs widely in organization from all the other metazoa. The innumerable kinds of sponges grow, as a rule, at the bottom of the sea. The simplest form of sponge, the *olynthus,* is in reality nothing more than a *gastraea,* the body-wall of which is perforated like a sieve, with fine pores, in order to permit the entrance of the nourishing stream of water. In the majority of sponges—even in the most familiar one, the bath-sponge —the bulbous organism constructs a kind of stem or tree, which is made up of thousands of these gastræads, and permeated by a nutritive system of canals. Sensation and movement are only developed in the faintest degree in the sponges; they have no nerves, muscles, or organs of sense. It was therefore quite natural that such stationary, shapeless, insensitive animals should have been commonly taken to be plants in earlier years. Their psychic life—for which no special organs have been differentiated—is far inferior to that of the mimosa and other sensitive plants.

The soul of the cnidaria is of the utmost importance in comparative and phylogenetic psychology; for in this numerous group of the cœlenterates the historical evolution of the *nerve-soul* out of the *tissue-soul* is repeated before our eyes. To this group belong the innumerable classes of stationary polyps and corals, and of swimming medusæ and siphonophora. As the common ancestor of all the cnidaria we can safely assign a very simple polyp, which is substantially the same in structure as the common, still surviving, fresh-water polyp—the hydra. Yet the hydræ, and the stationary, closely related *hydropolyps*, have no nerves or higher sense-organs, although they are extremely sensitive On the other hand, the free-swimming medusæ, which are developed from them—and are still connected with them by alternation of generations—have an independent nervous system and specific sense-organs. Here, also, we may directly observe the ontogenetic evolution of the nerve-soul (*neuropsyche*) out of the tissue-soul (*histopsyche*), and thus learn its phylogenetic origin. This is the more interesting as such phenomena are *polyphyletic*—that is, they have occurred several times—more than once, at least—quite independently. As I have shown elsewhere, the hydromedusæ have arisen from the hydropolyps in a different manner from that of the evolution of the scyphomedusæ from the scyphopolyps; the gemmation is terminal in the case of the latter, and lateral with the former. In addition, both groups have characteristic hereditary differences in the more minute structure of their psychic organs. The class of siphonophora is also very interesting to the psychologist. In these pretty, free-swimming organisms, which come from the hydromedusæ we can observe a double soul: the *personal soul* of the numerous individualities which compose them, and the common, harmoniously acting psyche of the entire colony.

IV. *The nerve-soul* (*neuropsyche*): fourth stage of phyletic psychogeny.—The psychic life of all the higher animals is conducted, as in man, by means of a more or less complicated "psychic apparatus." This apparatus is always composed of three chief sections: the *organs of sense* are responsible for the various sensations; the *muscles* effect the movements; the *nerves* form the connection between the two by means of a special central organ, the brain or ganglion. The arrangement

THE PHYLOGENY OF THE SOUL

and action of this psychic mechanism have been frequently compared with those of a telegraphic system: the nerves are the wires, the brain the central, and the sense-organs subordinate stations. The motor nerves conduct the commands of the will centrifugally from the nerve-centre to the muscles, by the contraction of which they produce the movements: the sensitive nerves transmit the various sensations centripetally—that is, from the peripheral sense-organs to the brain, and thus render an account of the impressions they receive from the outer world. The ganglionic cells, or "psychic cells," which compose the central nervous organ, are the most perfect of all organic elements; they not only conduct the commerce between the muscles and the organs of sense, but they also effect the highest performances of the animal soul, the formation of ideas and thoughts, and especially consciousness.

The great progress of anatomy, physiology, histology, and ontogeny has recently added a wealth of interesting discoveries to our knowledge of the mechanism of the soul. If speculative philosophy assimilated only the most important of these significant results of empirical biology, it would have a very different character from that it unfortunately presents. As I have not space for an exhaustive treatment of them here, I will confine myself to a relation of the chief facts.

Each of the higher animal species has a characteristic psychic organ; the central nervous system of each has certain peculiarities of shape, position, and composition. The medusæ, among the radiating cnidaria, have a ring of nervous matter at the border of the fringe, generally provided with four or eight ganglia. The mouth of the five-rayed cnidarion is girt with a nerve-ring, from which proceed five branches. The bi-symmetrical *platodes* and the *vermalia* have a vertical brain, or acroganglion, composed of two dorsal ganglia, lying above the mouth; from these "upper ganglia" two branch nerves proceed to the skin and the muscles. In some of the vermalia and in the mollusca a pair of ventral "lower ganglia" are added, which are connected with the former by a ring round the gullet. This ring is found also in the *articulata*; but in these it is continued on the belly side of the long body as a ventral medulla, a double fibre like a rope-ladder, which expands into a double ganglion in each member. The vertebrates have an entirely different formation of the psychic organ; they have always a spinal medulla developed at the back of the body; and from an expansion of its fore part there arises subsequently the characteristic vesicular brain.*

Although the psychic organs of the higher species of animals differ very materially in position, form, and composition, nevertheless comparative anatomy is in a position to prove a common origin for most of them —namely, from the vertical brain of the platodes and vermalia; they have all, moreover, had their origin in the outermost layer of the embryo, the *ectoderm*, or outer skin-layer. Hence we find the same typical structure in all varieties of the central nervous organ— a combination of ganglionic cells, or "psychic cells" (the real active elementary organs of the soul), and of nerve-fibres, which effect the connection and transmission of the action.

The first fact we meet in the comparative psychology of the vertebrates, and which should be the em-

* Cf. *Natural History of Creation.*

THE PHYLOGENY OF THE SOUL

pirical starting-point of all scientific human psychology, is the characteristic structure of the central nervous system. This central psychic organ has a particular position, shape, and texture in the vertebrate as it has in all the higher species. In every case we find a spinal medulla, a strong cylindrical nervous cord, which runs down the middle of the back, in the upper part of the vertebral column (or the cord which represents it). In every case a number of nerves branch off from this medulla in regular division, one pair to each segment or vertebra. In every case this medullary cord arises in the same way in the fœtus; a fine groove appears in the middle axis of the skin at the back; then the parallel borders of this medullary groove are lifted up a little, bend over towards each other, and form into a kind of tube.

The long dorsal cylindrical medullary tube which is thus formed is thoroughly characteristic of the vertebrates; it is always the same in the early embryonic sketch of the organism, and it is always the chief feature of the different kinds of psychic organ which evolve from it in time. Only one single group of invertebrates has a similar structure — the rare, marine *tunicata*, copelata, ascidia, and thalidiæ. These animals have other important peculiarities of structure (especially in the chorda and the gut) which show a striking divergence from the other invertebrates and resemblance to the vertebrates. The inference we draw is that both these groups, the vertebrates and the tunicates, have arisen from a common ancestral group of the vermalia, the *prochordonia*.* Still, there is a great difference between the two classes in the fact that the body of the

---
* See chaps. xvi. and xvii. of my *Anthropogeny*.

THE RIDDLE OF THE UNIVERSE

tunicate does not articulate, or form members, and has a very simple organization (most of them subsequently attach themselves to the bottom of the sea and degenerate). The vertebrate, on the other hand, is characterized by an early development of internal members, and the formation of pro-vertebræ (*vertebratio*). This prepares the way for the much higher development of their organism, which finally attains perfection in man. This is easily seen in the finer structure of his spinal cord, and in the development of a number of segmental pairs of nerves, the spinal nerves, which proceed to the various parts of the body.

The long ancestral history of our "vertebrate soul" commences with the formation of the most rudimentary spinal cord in the earliest acrania; slowly and gradually, through a period of many millions of years, it conducts to that marvellous structure of the human brain which seems to entitle the highest primate form to quite an exceptional position in nature. Since a clear conception of this slow and steady progress of our phyletic psychogeny is indispensable for a true psychology, we must divide that vast period into a number of stages or sections: in each of them the perfecting of the structure of the nervous centre has been accompanied by a corresponding evolution of its function, the *psyche*. I distinguish eight of these periods in the phylogeny of the spinal cord, which are characterized by eight different groups of vertebrates: (1) the acrania; (2) the cyclostomata; (3) the fishes; (4) the amphibia; (5) the implacental mammals (monotremes and marsupials); (6) the earlier placental mammals, especially the prosimiæ; (7) the younger primates, the simiæ; and (8) the anthropoid apes and man.

I. First stage—the *acrania*: their only modern

THE PHYLOGENY OF THE SOUL

representative is the lancelot or amphioxus; the psychic organ remains a simple medullary tube, and contains a regularly segmented spinal cord, without brain.

II. Second stage—the *cyclostomata*: the oldest group of the craniota, now only represented by the *petromyzontes* and *myxinoides*: the fore-termination of the cord expands into a vesicle, which then subdivides into five successive parts—the great-brain, intermediate-brain, middle-brain, little-brain, and hind-brain: these five cerebral vesicles form the common type from which the brain of all craniota has evolved, from the lamprey to man.

III. Third stage—the *primitive fishes* (*selachii*): similar to the modern shark: in these oldest fishes, from which all the gnathostomata descend, the more pronounced division of the five cerebral vesicles sets in.

IV. Fourth stage—the *amphibia*. These earliest land animals, making their first appearance in the Carboniferous period, represent the commencement of the characteristic structure of the *tetrapod* and a corresponding development of the fish-brain: it advances still further in their Permian successors, the *reptiles*, the earliest representatives of which, the *tocosauria*, are the common ancestors of all the amniota (reptiles and birds on one side, mammals on the other).

V.-VIII. Fifth to the eighth stages—the *mammals*. I have exhaustively treated, and illustrated with a number of plates, in my *Anthropogeny*, the evolution of our nervous system and the correlative question of the development of the soul. I have now, therefore, merely to refer the reader to that work. It only remains for me to add a few remarks on the last and most interesting class of facts pertaining to this—to the evolution of the soul and its organs within the limits of the class mammalia. In doing so, I must remind the reader that the *monophyletic origin* of this class—that is, the descent of all the mammals from one common ancestral form (of the Triassic period)—is now fully established.

The most important consequence of the monophyletic origin of the mammals is the necessity of deriving the human soul from a long evolutionary series of other mammal souls. A deep anatomical and physiological gulf separated the brain structure and the dependent psychic activity of the higher mammals from those of the lower: this gulf, however, is completely bridged over by a long series of intermediate stages. The period of at least fourteen (more than a hundred, on other estimates) million years, which has elapsed since the commencement of the Triassic period, is amply sufficient to allow even the greatest psychological advance. The following is a summary of the results of investigation in this quarter, which has recently been very penetrating:

I. The brain of the mammal is differentiated from that of the other vertebrates by certain features, which are found in all branches of the class; especially by a preponderant development of the first and fourth vesicles, the cerebrum and cerebellum, while the third vesicle, the middle brain, disappears altogether.

II. The brain development of the lowest and earliest mammals (the monotremes, marsupials, and prochoriates) is closely allied to that of their palæozoic ancestors, the Carboniferous amphibia (the *stegocephala*) and the Permian reptiles (the *tocosauria*).

III. During the Tertiary period commences the typical development of the cerebrum, which distinguishes the younger mammals so strikingly from the older.

IV. The special development (quantitatively and

THE PHYLOGENY OF THE SOUL

qualitatively) of the cerebrum which is so prominent a feature in man, and which is the root of his pre-eminent psychic achievements, is only found, outside humanity, in a small section of the most highly developed mammals of the earlier Tertiary epoch, especially in the anthropoid apes.

V. The differences of brain structure and psychic faculty which separate man from the anthropoid ape are slighter than the corresponding interval between the anthropoid apes and the lower primates (the earliest simiæ and prosimiæ).

VI. Consequently, the historical, gradual evolution of the human soul from a long chain of higher and lower mammal souls must, by application of the universally valid phyletic laws of the theory of descent, be regarded as a *fact* which has been scientifically proved.

CHAPTER X

CONSCIOUSNESS

Consciousness as a Natural Phenomenon—Its Definition—Difficulties of the Problem—Its Relation to the Life of the Soul—Our Human Consciousness—Various Theories. I. Anthropistic Theory (Descartes); II. Neurological Theory (Darwin); III. Animal Theory (Schopenhauer); IV. Biological Theory (Fechner); V. Cellular Theory (Fritz Schultze); VI. Atomistic Theory—Monistic and Dualistic Theories—Transcendental Character of Consciousness — The Ignorabimus Verdict of Du Bois-Reymond — Physiology of Consciousness — Discovery of the Organs of Thought by Flechsig — Pathology—Double and Intermittent Consciousness—Ontogeny of Consciousness: Modifications at Different Ages—Phylogeny of Consciousness—Formation of Concepts

NO phenomenon of the life of the soul is so wonderful and so variously interpreted as consciousness. The most contradictory views are current to-day, as they were two thousand years ago, not only with regard to the nature of this psychic function and its relation to the body, but even as to its diffusion in the organic world and its origin and development. It is more responsible than any other psychic faculty for the erroneous idea of an "immaterial soul" and the belief in "personal immortality"; many of the gravest errors that still dominate even our modern civilization may be traced to it. Hence it is that I have entitled consciousness "the central mystery of psychology", it

CONSCIOUSNESS

is the strong citadel of all mystic and dualistic errors, before whose ramparts the best-equipped efforts of reason threaten to miscarry. This fact would suffice of itself to induce us to make a special critical study of consciousness from our monistic point of view. We shall see that consciousness is simply a natural phenomenon like any other psychic quality, and that it is subject to the law of substance like all other natural phenomena.

Even as to the elementary idea of consciousness, its contents and extension, the views of the most distinguished philosophers and scientists are widely divergent. Perhaps the meaning of consciousness is best conceived as an *internal perception,* and compared with the action of *a mirror.* As its two chief departments we distinguish objective and subjective consciousness —consciousness of the world, the non-ego, and of the ego. By far the greater part of our conscious activity, as Schopenhauer justly remarked, belongs to the consciousness of the outer world, or the non-ego: this *world-consciousness* embraces all possible phenomena of the outer world which are in any sense accessible to our minds. Much more contracted is the sphere of *self-consciousness,* the internal mirror of all our own psychic activity, all our presentations, sensations, and volitions.

Many distinguished thinkers, especially on the physiological side (Wundt and Ziehen, for instance) take the ideas of consciousness and psychic function to be identical—"all psychic action is conscious"; the province of psychic life, they say, is coextensive with that of consciousness. In our opinion, such a definition gives an undue extension to the meaning of consciousness, and occasions many errors and misunderstandings. We share, rather, the view of other philosophers (Romanes, Fritz Schultze, and Paulsen), that even our unconscious presentations, sensations, and volitions pertain to 'our psychic life; indeed, the province of these unconscious psychic actions (reflex action, and so forth) is far more extensive than that of consciousness Moreover, the two provinces are intimately connected, and are separated by no sharp line of demarcation. An unconscious presentation may become conscious at any moment; let our attention be withdrawn from it by some other object, and forthwith it disappears from consciousness once more.

The only source of our knowledge of consciousness is that faculty itself; that is the chief cause of the extraordinary difficulty of subjecting it to scientific research. Subject and object are one and the same in it. the perceptive subject mirrors itself in its own inner nature, which is to be the object of our inquiry. Thus we can never have a complete objective certainty of the consciousness of others; we can only proceed by a comparison of their psychic condition with our own. As long as this comparison is restricted to *normal* people we are justified in drawing certain conclusions as to their consciousness, the validity of which is unchallenged. But when we pass on to consider *abnormal* individuals (the genius, the eccentric, the stupid, or the insane) our conclusions from analogy are either unsafe or entirely erroneous. The same must be said with even greater truth when we attempt to compare human consciousness with that of the animals (even the higher, but especially the lower). In that case such grave difficulties arise that the views of physiologists and philosophers diverge as widely as the

CONSCIOUSNESS

poles on the subject. We shall briefly enumerate the most important of these views.

I. *The anthropistic theory of consciousness.*—It is peculiar to man. To Descartes we must trace the widespread notion that consciousness and thought are man's exclusive prerogative, and that he alone is blessed with an "immortal soul." This famous French philosopher and mathematician (educated in a Jesuit College) established a rigid partition between the psychic activity of man and that of the brute. In his opinion the human soul, a thinking, immaterial being, is completely separated from the body, which is extended and material. Yet it is united to the body at a certain point in the brain (the *glandula pinealis*) for the purpose of receiving impressions from the outer world and effecting muscular movements. The animals, not being endowed with thought, have no soul: they are mere automata, or cleverly constructed machines, whose sensations, presentations, and volitions are purely mechanical, and take place according to the ordinary laws of physics. Hence Descartes was a *dualist* in human psychology, and a *monist* in the psychology of the brute. This open contradiction in so clear and acute a thinker is very striking; in explaining it, it is not unnatural to suppose that he concealed his real opinion, and left the discovery of it to independent scholars. As a pupil of the Jesuits, Descartes had been taught to deny the truth in the face of his better insight; and perhaps he dreaded the power and the fires of the Church. Besides, his sceptical principle, that every sincere effort to attain the truth must start with a doubt of the traditional dogma had already drawn upon him fanatical accusations of scepticism and atheism. The great influence which Descartes had on subsequent philosophy was very remarkable, and entirely in harmony with his "book-keeping by double entry." The *materialists* of the seventeenth and eighteenth centuries appealed to the Cartesian theory of the animal soul and its purely mechanical activity in support of their monistic psychology. The *spiritualists*, on the other hand, asserted that their dogma of the immortality of the soul and its independence of the body was firmly established by Descartes' theory of the human soul. This view is still prevalent in the camp of the theologians and dualistic metaphysicians. The scientific conception of nature, however, which has been built up in the nineteenth century, has, with the aid of empirical progress, in physiological and comparative psychology, completely falsified it.

II. *Neurological theory of consciousness.*—It is present only in man and those higher animals which have a centralized nervous system and organs of sense. The conviction that a large number of animals—at least the higher mammals—are not less endowed than man with a thinking soul and consciousness prevails in modern zoology, exact physiology, and the monistic psychology. The immense progress we have made in the various branches of biology has contributed to bring about a recognition of this important truth. We confine ourselves for the present to the higher vertebrates, and especially the mammals. That these most intelligent specimens of these highly developed vertebrates — apes and dogs, in particular — have a strong resemblance to man in their whole psychic life has been recognized and speculated on for thousands of years. Their faculty of presentation and sensation, of feeling and desire, is so like that of man that we need adduce no proof of our thesis. But even

CONSCIOUSNESS

the higher associational activity of the brain, the formation of judgments and their connection into chains of reasoning, thought, and consciousness in the narrower sense, are developed in them after the same fashion as in man: they differ only in degree, not in kind. Moreover, we learn from comparative anatomy and histology that the intricate structure of the brain (both in general and in detail) is substantially the same in the mammals as it is in man. The same lesson is enforced by comparative ontogeny with regard to the origin of these psychic organs. Comparative physiology teaches us that the various states of consciousness are just the same in these highest placentals as in man; and we learn by experiment that there is the same reaction to external stimuli. The higher animals can be narcotized by alcohol, chloroform, ether, etc., and may be hypnotized by the usual methods, just as in the case of man.

It is, however, impossible to determine mathematically at what stage of animal life consciousness is to be first recognized as such. Some zoologists draw the line very high in the scale, others very low. Darwin, who most accurately distinguishes the various stages of consciousness, intelligence, and emotion in the higher animals, and explains them by progressive evolution, points out how difficult, or even impossible, it is to determine the first beginning of this supreme psychic faculty in the lower animals. Personally, out of the many contradictory theories, I take that to be most probable which holds *the centralization of the nervous system* to be a condition of consciousness; and that is wanting in the lower classes of animals. The presence of a central nervous organ, of highly developed sense-organs, and an elaborate association of groups of presentations, seem to me to be required before the unity of consciousness is possible.

III. *Animal theory of consciousness.*—All animals, and they alone, have consciousness. This theory would draw a sharp distinction between the psychic life of the animal and of the plant. Such a distinction was urged by many of the older writers, and was clearly formulated by Linné in his celebrated *Systema Naturae;* the two great kingdoms of the organic world are, in his opinion, divided by the fact that animals have sensation and consciousness, and the plants are devoid of them. Later on Schopenhauer laid stress on the same distinction: " Consciousness is only known to us as a feature of animal nature. Even though it extend upwards through the whole animal kingdom, even to man and his reason, the unconsciousness of the plant, from which it started, remains as the basic feature. In the lowest animals we have but the dawn of it." The inaccuracy of this view was obvious by about the middle of the present century, when a deeper study was made of the psychic activity of the lower animal forms, especially the cœlenterates (sponges and cnidaria): they are undoubtedly animals, yet there is no more trace of a definite consciousness in them than in most of the plants. The distinction between the two kingdoms was still further obliterated when more careful research was made into their unicellular forms. There is no psychological difference between the plasmophagous protozoa and the plasmodomous protophyta, even in respect of their consciousness.

IV. *Biological theory of consciousness.*—It is found in all organisms, animal or vegetal, but not in lifeless bodies (such as crystals). This opinion is usually associated with the idea that all organisms (as distin-

CONSCIOUSNESS

guished from inorganic substances) have souls: the three ideas — life, soul, and consciousness — are then taken to be coextensive. Another modification of this view holds that, though these fundamental phenomena of organic life are inseparably connected, yet consciousness is only a part of the activity of the soul, and of the vital activity. Fechner, in particular, has endeavored to prove that the plant has a "soul," in the same sense as an animal is said to have one; and many credit the vegetal soul with a consciousness similar to that of the animal soul. In truth, the remarkable stimulated movements of the leaves of the sensitive plants (the mimosa, drosera, and dionæa), the automatic movements of other plants (the clover and wood-sorrel, and especially the hedysarum), the movements of the "sleeping plants" (particularly the *papilionacea*), etc., are strikingly similar to the movements of the lower animal forms: whoever ascribes consciousness to the latter cannot refuse it to such vegetal forms.

V. *Cellular theory of consciousness.*—It is a vital property of every cell. The application of the cellular theory to every branch of biology involved its extension to psychology. Just as we take the living cell to be the "elementary organism" in anatomy and physiology, and derive the whole system of the multicellular animal or plant from it, so, with equal right, we may consider the "cell-soul" to be the psychological unit, and the complex psychic activity of the higher organism to be the result of the combination of the psychic activity of the cells which compose it. I gave the outlines of this *cellular psychology* in my *General Morphology* in 1866, and entered more fully into the subject in my paper on "Cell-Souls and Soul-Cells." I was led to a deeper study of this "elementary psychology" by my protracted research into the unicellular forms of life Many of these tiny (generally microscopic) protists show similar expressions of sensation and will, and similar instincts and movements, to those of higher animals; that is especially true of the very sensitive and lively infusoria. In the relation of these sensitive cell-organisms to their environment, and in many other of their vital expressions (for instance, in the wonderful architecture of the rhizopods, the thalamophoræ, and the infusoria), we seemed to have clear indications of conscious psychic action. If, then, we accept the biological theory of consciousness (No. IV.), and credit every psychic function with a share of that faculty, we shall be compelled to ascribe it to each independent protist cell. In that case its material basis would be either the entire protoplasm of the cell, or its nucleus, or a portion of it. In the "psychade theory" of Fritz Schultze the elementary consciousness of the *psychade* would have the same relation to the individual cells as personal consciousness has to the multicellular organism of the personality in the higher animals and man. It is impossible definitively to disprove this theory, which I held at one time. Still, I now feel compelled to agree with Max Verworn, in his belief that none of the protists have a developed self-consciousness, but that their sensations and movements are of an unconscious character.

VI. *Atomistic theory of consciousness.*—It is an elementary property of all atoms. This atomistic hypothesis goes furthest of all the different views as to the extension of consciousness. It certainly escapes the difficulty which so many philosophers and biologists experience in solving the problem of the first origin of consciousness. It is a phenomenon of so pecu-

CONSCIOUSNESS

liar a character that a derivation of it from other psychic functions seems extremely hazardous. It seemed, therefore, the easiest way out of the difficulty to conceive it as an inherent property of all matter, like gravitation or chemical affinity. On that hypothesis there would be as many forms of this original consciousness as there are chemical elements, each atom of hydrogen would have its hydrogenic consciousness, each atom of carbon its carbonic consciousness, and so forth. There are philosophers, even, who ascribe consciousness to the four elements of Empedocles, the union of which, by "love and hate," produces the totality of things.

Personally, I have never subscribed to this hypothesis of atomic consciousness. I emphasize the point because Emil du Bois-Reymond has attributed it to me. In the controversy I had with him (1880) he violently attacked my "pernicious and false philosophy," and contended that I had, in my paper on "The Perigenesis of the Plastidule," "laid it down as a metaphysical axiom that every atom has its individual consciousness." On the contrary, I explicitly stated that I conceive the elementary psychic qualities of sensation and will, which may be attributed to atoms, to be *unconscious*—just as unconscious as the elementary memory which I, in company with that distinguished physiologist, Ewald Hering, consider to be "a common function of all organized matter"—or, more correctly, "living substance." Du Bois-Reymond curiously confuses "soul" and "consciousness"; whether from oversight or not I cannot say. Since he considers consciousness to be a transcendental phenomenon (as we shall see presently), while denying that character to other psychic functions—the action of the senses, for example—I must infer that he recognizes the difference of the two ideas. Other parts of his eloquent speeches contain quite the opposite view, for the famous orator not infrequently contradicts himself on important questions of principle. However, I repeat that, in my opinion, consciousness is only *part* of the psychic phenomena which we find in man and the higher animals; the great majority of them are unconscious.

However divergent are the different views as to the nature and origin of consciousness, they may, nevertheless, on a clear and logical examination, all be reduced to two fundamental theories—the transcendental (or dualistic) and the physiological (or monistic). I have myself always held the latter view, in the light of my evolutionary principles, and it is now shared by a great number of distinguished scientists, though it is by no means generally accepted. The transcendental theory is the older and much more common; it has recently come once more into prominence, principally through Du Bois-Reymond, and it has acquired a great importance in modern discussions of cosmic problems through his famous "Ignorabimus speech." On account of the extreme importance of this fundamental question we must touch briefly on its main features.

In the celebrated discourse on "The Limits of Natural Science," which E. du Bois-Reymond gave on August 14, 1872, at the Scientific Congress at Leipzig, he spoke of two "absolute limits" to our possible knowledge of nature which the human mind will never transcend in its most advanced science—*never*, as the oft-quoted termination of the address, "Ignorabimus," emphatically pronounces. The first absolutely insoluble "world-enigma" is the "connection of matter and force," and the distinctive character of these fun-

CONSCIOUSNESS

damental natural phenomena; we shall go more fully into this " problem of substance" in the twelfth chapter. The second insuperable difficulty of philosophy is given as the problem of consciousness—the question how our mental activity is to be explained by material conditions, especially movements, how "substance [the substance which underlies matter and force] comes, under certain conditions, to feel, to desire, and to think."

For brevity, and in order to give a characteristic name to the Leipzig discourse, I have called it the " Ignorabimus speech "; this is the more permissible, as E. du Bois-Reymond himself, with a just pride, eight years afterwards, speaking of the extraordinary consequences of his discourse, said: " Criticism sounded every possible note, from friendly praise to the severest censure, and the word 'Ignorabimus,' which was the culmination of my inquiry, was at once transformed into a kind of scientific shibboleth." It is quite true that loud praise and approbation resounded in the halls of the dualistic and spiritualistic philosophy, and especially in the camp of the " Church militant "; even the spiritists and the host of believers, who thought the immortality of their precious souls was saved by the "Ignorabimus," joined in the chorus. The "severest censure " came at first only from a few scientists and philosophers—from the few who had sufficient scientific knowledge and moral courage to oppose the dogmatism of the all-powerful secretary and dictator of the Berlin Academy of Science.

Towards the end, however, the author of the " Ignorabimus speech" briefly alluded to the question whether these two great "world-enigmas," the general problem of substance and the special problem of consciousness, are not two aspects of one and the same problem.

"This idea," he said, "is certainly the simplest, and preferable to the one which makes the world doubly incomprehensible. Such, however, is the nature of things that even here we can obtain no clear knowledge, and it is useless to speak further of the question." The latter sentiment I have always stoutly contested, and have endeavored to prove that the two great questions are not two distinct problems. "The neurological problem of consciousness is but a particular aspect of the all-pervading cosmological problem of substance."

The peculiar phenomenon of consciousness is not, as Du Bois-Reymond and the dualistic school would have us believe, a completely "transcendental" problem; it is, as I showed thirty-three years ago, a *physiological* problem, and, as such, must be reduced to the phenomena of physics and chemistry. I subsequently gave it the more definite title of a *neurological* problem, as I share the view that true consciousness (thought and reason) is only present in those higher animals which have a centralized nervous system and organs of sense of a certain degree of development. Those conditions are certainly found in the higher vertebrates, especially in the placental mammals, the class from which man has sprung. The consciousness of the highest apes, dogs, elephants, etc., differs from that of man in degree only, not in kind, and the graduated interval between the consciousness of these "rational" placentals and that of the lowest races of men (the Veddahs, etc.) is less than the corresponding interval between these uncivilized races and the highest specimens of thoughtful humanity (Spinoza, Goethe, Lamarck, Darwin, etc.). Consciousness is but a part of the higher activity of the soul, and as

CONSCIOUSNESS

such it is dependent on the normal structure of the corresponding psychic organ, the brain.

Physiological observation and experiment determined twenty years ago that the particular portion of the mammal-brain which we call the *seat* (preferably the *organ*) of consciousness is a part of the cerebrum, an area in the late-developed gray bed, or cortex, which is evolved out of the convex dorsal portion of the primary cerebral vesicle, the " fore-brain." Now, the morphological proof of this physiological thesis has been successfully given by the remarkable progress of the microscopic anatomy of the brain, which we owe to the perfect methods of research of modern science (Kölliker, Flechsig, Golgi, Edinger, Weigert, and others).

The most important development is the discovery of the *organs of thought* by Paul Flechsig, of Leipzig; he proved that in the gray bed of the brain are found the four seats of the central sense-organs, or four " inner spheres of sensation "—the sphere of touch in the vertical lobe, the sphere of smell in the frontal lobe, the sphere of sight in the occipital lobe, and the sphere of hearing in the temporal lobe. Between these four " sense-centres " lie the four great " thought-centres," or centres of association, the *real organs of mental life;* they are those highest instruments of psychic activity that produce thought and consciousness. In front we have the frontal brain or centre of association; behind, on top there is the vertical brain, or parietal centre of association, and underneath the principal brain, or " the great occipito-temporal centre of association " (the most important of all); lower down, and internally, the insular brain or the insula of Reil, the insular centre of association. These four " thought-centres," distinguished from the intermediate " sense-centres "

THE RIDDLE OF THE UNIVERSE

by a peculiar and elaborate nerve-structure, are the true and sole organs of thought and consciousness. Flechsig has recently pointed out that, in the case of man, very specific structures are found in one part of them; these structures are wanting in the other mammals, and they, therefore, afford an explanation of the superiority of man's mental powers.

The momentous announcement of modern physiology, that the cerebrum is the organ of consciousness and mental action in man and the higher mammals, is illustrated and confirmed by the pathological study of its diseases. When parts of the cortex are destroyed by disease their respective functions are affected, and thus we are enabled, to some extent, to localize the activities of the brain; when certain parts of the area are diseased, that portion of thought and consciousness disappears which depends on those particular sections. Pathological experiment yields the same result; the decay of some known area (for instance, the centre of speech) extinguishes its function (speech). In fact, there is proof enough in the most familiar phenomena of consciousness of their complete dependence on chemical changes in the substance of the brain. Many beverages (such as coffee and tea) stimulate our powers of thought; others (such as wine and beer) intensify feeling; musk and camphor reanimate the fainting consciousness; ether and chloroform deaden it, and so forth. How would that be possible if consciousness were an immaterial entity, independent of these anatomical organs? And what becomes of the consciousness of the "immortal soul" when it no longer has the use of these organs?

These and other familiar facts prove that man's consciousness — and that of the nearest mammals — is

CONSCIOUSNESS

changeable, and that its activity is always open to modification from inner (alimentation, circulation, etc) and outer causes (lesion of the brain, stimulation, etc). Very instructive, too, are the facts of double and intermittent consciousness, which remind us of " alternate generations of presentations." The same individual has an entirely different consciousness on different days, with a change of circumstances, he does not know to-day what he did yesterday: yesterday he could say, "I am I"; to-day he must say, "I am another being." Such intermittence of consciousness may last not only days, but months, and even years; the change may even become permanent.

As everybody knows, the new-born infant has no consciousness. Preyer has shown that it is only developed after the child has begun to speak; for a long time it speaks of itself in the third person. In the important moment when it first pronounces the word " I," when the feeling of self becomes clear, we have the beginning of self-consciousness, and of the antithesis to the non-ego. The rapid and solid progress in knowledge which the child makes in its first ten years, under the care of parents and teachers, and the slower progress of the second decade, until it reaches complete maturity of mind, are intimately connected with a great advancement in the growth and development of consciousness and of its organ, the brain. But even when the pupil has got his "certificate of maturity" his consciousness is still far from mature; it is then that his "world-consciousness" first begins to develop, in his manifold relations with the outer world. Then, in the third decade, we have the full maturity of rational thought and consciousness, which, in cases of normal development, yield their ripe fruits during the next three decades.

THE RIDDLE OF THE UNIVERSE

The slow, gradual degeneration of the higher mental powers, which characterizes senility, usually sets in at the commencement of the seventh decade—sometimes earlier, sometimes later. Memory, receptiveness, and interest in particular objects gradually decay; though productivity, mature consciousness, and philosophic interest in general truths often remain for many years longer.

The individual development of consciousness in earlier youth proves the universal validity of the *biogenetic law* ; and, indeed, it is still recognizable in many ways during the later years. In any case, the ontogenesis of consciousness makes it perfectly clear that it is not an " immaterial entity," but a physiological function of the brain, and that it is, consequently, no exception to the general law of substance.

From the fact that consciousness, like all other psychic functions, is dependent on the normal development of certain organs, and that it gradually unfolds in the child in proportion to the development of those organs, we may already conclude that it has arisen in the animal kingdom by a gradual historical development. Still, however certain we are of the fact of this natural evolution of consciousness, we are, unfortunately, not yet in a position to enter more deeply into the question and construct special hypotheses in elucidation of it. Palæontology, it is true, gives us a few facts which are not without significance. For instance, the quantitative and qualitative development of the brain of the placental mammals during the Tertiary period is very remarkable. The cavity of many of the fossil skulls of the period has been carefully examined, and has given us a good deal of reliable information as to the size, and, to some extent, as to the

CONSCIOUSNESS

structure, of the brain they enclosed. We find, within the limits of one and the same group (the ungulates, the rodents, or the primates), a marked advance in the later miocene and pliocene specimens as compared with the earlier eocene and oligocene representatives of the same stem; in the former the brain (in proportion to the size of the organism) is six to eight times as large as in the latter.

Moreover, that highest stage of consciousness, which is reached by man alone, has been evolved step by step—even by the very progress of civilization—from a lower condition, as we find illustrated to-day in the case of uncivilized races. That is easily proved by a comparison of their languages, which is closely connected with the comparison of their ideas. The higher the conceptual faculty advances in thoughtful civilized man, the more qualified he is to detect common features amid a multitude of details, and embody them in general concepts, and so much the clearer and deeper does his consciousness become.

CHAPTER XI

THE IMMORTALITY OF THE SOUL

The Citadel of Superstition—Athanatism and Thanatism—Individual Character of Death—Immortality of the Unicellular Organisms (Protists)—Cosmic and Personal Immortality—Primary Thanatism (of Uncivilized Peoples) — Secondary Thanatism (of Ancient and Recent Philosophers)—Athanatism and Religion—Origin of the Belief in Immortality—Christian Athanatism—Eternal Life—The Day of Judgment—Metaphysical Athanatism—Substance of the Soul—Ether Souls and Air Souls ; Fluid Souls and Solid Souls—Immortality of the Animal Soul—Arguments for and Against Athanatism—Athanatist Illusions.

WHEN we turn from the genetic study of the soul to the great question of its immortality, we come to that highest point of superstition which is regarded as the impregnable citadel of all mystical and dualistic notions. For in this crucial question, more than in any other problem, philosophic thought is complicated by the selfish interest of the human personality, who is determined to have a guarantee of his existence beyond the grave at any price. This "higher necessity of feeling" is so powerful that it sweeps aside all the logical arguments of critical reason. Consciously or unconsciously, most men are influenced in all their general views, and, therefore, in their theory of life, by the dogma of personal immortality ; and to this theoretical error must be added practical consequences of

THE IMMORTALITY OF THE SOUL

the most far-reaching character. It is our task, therefore, to submit every aspect of this important dogma to a critical examination, and to prove its untenability in the light of the empirical data of modern biology.

In order to have a short and convenient expression for the two opposed opinions on the question, we shall call the belief in man's personal immortality "athanatism" (from *athanes* or *athanatos* = immortal). On the other hand, we give the name of "thanatism" (from *thanatos* = death) to the opinion which holds that at a man's death not only all the other physiological functions are arrested, but his "soul" also disappears—that is, that sum of cerebral functions which psychic dualism regards as a peculiar entity, independent of the other vital processes in the living body.

In approaching this physiological problem of death we must point out the *individual* character of this organic phenomenon. By death we understand simply the definitive cessation of the vital activity of the *individual* organism, no matter to which category or stage of individuality the organism in question belongs. Man is dead when his own personality ceases to exist, whether he has left offspring that they may continue to propagate for many generations or not. In a certain sense we often say that the minds of great men (in a dynasty of eminent rulers, for instance, or a family of talented artists) live for many generations; and in the same way we speak of the "soul" of a noble woman living in her children and children's children. But in these cases we are dealing with intricate phenomena of *heredity*, in which a microscopic cell (the sperm-cell of the father or the egg-cell of the mother) transmits certain features to offspring. The particular personalities who produce those sexual cells in thousands are mortal beings, and at their death their personal psychic activity is extinguished like every other physiological function.

A number of eminent zoologists—Weismann being particularly prominent—have recently defended the opinion that only the lowest unicellular organisms, the protists, are immortal, in contradistinction to the multicellular plants and animals, whose bodies are formed of tissues. This curious theory is especially based on the fact that most of the protists multiply without sexual means, by division or the formation of spores. In such processes the whole body of the unicellular organism breaks up into two or more equal parts (daughter cells), and each of these portions completes itself by further growth until it has the size and form of the mother cell. However, by the very process of division the *individuality* of the unicellular creature has been destroyed; both its physiological and its morphological unity have gone. The view of Weismann is logically inconsistent with the very notion of *individual*—an "indivisible" entity; for it implies a unity which cannot be divided without destroying its nature In this sense the unicellular protophyta and protozoa are throughout life *physiological individuals*, just as much as the multicellular tissue-plants and animals. A sexual propagation by simple division is found in many of the multicellular species (for instance, in many cnidaria, corals, medusæ, etc.); the mother animal, the division of which gives birth to the two daughter animals, ceases to exist with the segmentation. "The protozoa," says Weismann, "have no individuals and no generations in the matazoic sense." I must entirely dissent from his thesis. As I was

THE IMMORTALITY OF THE SOUL

the first to introduce the title of *metazoa,* and oppose these multicellular, tissue-forming animals to the unicellular *protozoa* (infusoria, rhizopods, etc.), and as I was the first to point out the essential difference in the development of the two (the former from germinal layers, and the latter not), I must protest that I consider the *protozoa* to be just as mortal in the physiological (and psychological) sense as the *metazoa ;* neither body nor soul is immortal in either group. The other erroneous consequences of Weismann's notion have been refuted by Moebius (1884), who justly remarks that " every event in the world is periodic," and that " there is no source from which immortal organic individuals might have sprung."

When we take the idea of immortality in the widest sense, and extend it to the totality of the knowable universe, it has a scientific significance; it is then not merely acceptable, but self-evident, to the monistic philosopher. In that sense the thesis of the indestructibility and eternal duration of all that exists is equivalent to our supreme law of nature, the *law of substance* (see chap. xii.). As we intend to discuss this immortality of the cosmos fully later on, in establishing the theory of the persistence of matter and force, we shall not dilate on it at present. We pass on immediately to the criticism of that belief in immortality which is the only sense usually attached to the word, the immortality of the individual soul. We shall first inquire into the extent and the origin of this mystic and dualistic notion, and point out, in particular, the wide acceptance of the contradictory thesis, our monistic, empirically established *thanatism.* I must distinguish two essentially different forms of thanatism—primary and secondary; primary thanatism is the

THE RIDDLE OF THE UNIVERSE

original absence of the dogma of immortality (in the primitive uncivilized races); secondary thanatism is the later outcome of a rational knowledge of nature in the civilized intelligence.

We still find it asserted in philosophic, and especially in theological, works that belief in the personal immortality of the human soul was originally shared by all men—or, at least, by all " rational " men. That is not the case. This dogma is not an original idea of the human mind, nor has it ever found universal acceptance. It has been absolutely proved by modern comparative ethnology that many uncivilized races of the earliest and most primitive stage had no notion either of immortality or of God. That is true, for instance, of the Veddahs of Ceylon, those primitive pygmies whom, on the authority of the able studies of the Sarasins, we consider to be a relic of the earliest inhabitants of India ;* it is also the case in several of the earliest groups of the nearly related Dravidas, the Indian Seelongs, and some native Australian races. Similarly, several of the primitive branches of the American race, in the interior of Brazil, on the upper Amazon, etc., have no knowledge either of gods or immortality. This *primary* absence of belief in immortality and deity is an extremely important fact, it is, obviously, easy to distinguish from the *secondary* absence of such belief, which has come about in the highest civilized races as the result of laborious critico-philosophical study.

Differently from the primary thanatism which originally characterized primitive man, and has always been widely spread, the *secondary* absence of belief

* E. Haeckel, *A Visit to Ceylon.*

THE IMMORTALITY OF THE SOUL

in immortality is only found at a late stage of history: it is the ripe fruit of profound reflection on life and death, the outcome of bold and independent philosophical speculation. We first meet it in some of the Ionic philosophers of the sixth century B.C., then in the founders of the old materialistic philosophy, Democritus and Empedocles, and also in Simonides and Epicurus, Seneca and Plinius, and in an elaborate form in Lucretius Carus. With the spread of Christianity at the decay of classical antiquity, athanatism, one of its chief articles of faith, dominated the world, and so, amid other forms of superstition, the myth of personal immortality came to be invested with a high importance.

Naturally, through the long night of the Dark Ages it was rarely that a brave free-thinker ventured to express an opinion to the contrary: the examples of Galileo, Giordano Bruno, and other independent philosophers, effectually destroyed all freedom of utterance. Heresy only became possible when the Reformation and the Renaissance had broken the power of the papacy. The history of modern philosophy tells of the manifold methods by which the matured mind of man sought to rid itself of the superstition of immortality. Still, the intimate connection of the belief with the Christian dogma invested it with such power, even in the more emancipated sphere of Protestantism, that the majority of convinced free-thinkers kept their sentiments to themselves. From time to time some distinguished scholar ventured to make a frank declaration of his belief in the impossibility of the continued life of the soul after death. This was done in France in the second half of the eighteenth century by Voltaire, Danton, Mirabeau, and others, and by the leaders of the materialistic school of those days, Holbach,

THE RIDDLE OF THE UNIVERSE

Lamettrie, etc. The same opinion was defended by the able friend of the Materialists, the greatest of the Hohenzollerns, the monistic "philosopher of Sans-souci." What would Frederick the Great, the "crowned thanatist and atheist," say, could he compare his monistic views with those of his successor of to-day?

Among thoughtful physicians the conviction that the existence of the soul came to an end at death has been common for centuries: generally, however, they refrained from giving it expression. Moreover, the empirical science of the brain remained so imperfect during the last century that the soul could continue to be regarded as its mysterious inhabitant. It was the gigantic progress of biology in the present century, and especially in the latter half of the century, that finally destroyed the myth. The establishment of the theory of descent and the cellular theory, the astounding discoveries of ontogeny and experimental physiology—above all, the marvellous progress of the microscopic anatomy of the brain, gradually deprived athanatism of every basis; now, indeed, it is rarely that an informed and honorable biologist is found to defend the immortality of the soul. All the monistic philosophers of the century (Strauss, Feuerbach, Büchner, Spencer, etc.) are athanatists.

The dogma of personal immortality owes its great popularity and its high importance to its intimate connection with the teaching of Christianity. This circumstance gave rise to the erroneous and still prevalent belief that the myth is a fundamental element of all the higher religions. That is by no means the case. The higher Oriental religions include no belief whatever in the immortality of the soul; it is not found in Buddhism, the religion that dominates

THE IMMORTALITY OF THE SOUL

thirty per cent. of the entire human race; it is not found in the ancient popular religion of the Chinese, nor in the reformed religion of Confucius which succeeded it; and, what is still more significant, it is not found in the earlier and purer religion of the Jews. Neither in the "five Mosaic books," nor in any of the writings of the Old Testament which were written before the Babylonian Exile, is there any trace of the notion of individual persistence after death.

The mystic notion that the human soul will live forever after death has had a polyphyletic origin. It was unknown to the earliest speaking man (the hypothetical *homo primigenius* of Asia), to his predecessors, of course, the *pithecanthropus* and *prothylobates*, and to the least developed of his modern successors, the Veddahs of Ceylon, the Seelongs of India, and other distant races. With the development of reason and deeper reflection on life and death, sleep and dreams, mystic ideas of a dualistic composition of our nature were evolved—independently of each other—in a number of the earlier races. Very different influences were at work in these polyphyletic creations—worship of ancestors, love of relatives, love of life and desire of its prolongation, hope of better conditions of life beyond the grave, hope of the reward of good and punishment of evil deeds, and so forth. Comparative psychology has recently brought to our knowledge a great variety of myths and legends of that character; they are, for the most part, closely associated with the oldest forms of theistic and religious belief. In most of the modern religions athanatism is intimately connected with theism, the majority of believers transfer their materialistic idea of a "personal God" to their "immortal soul"

That is particularly true of the dominant religion of modern civilized states, Christianity.

As everybody knows, the dogma of the immortality of the soul has long since assumed in the Christian religion that rigid form which it has in the articles of faith: " I believe in the resurrection of the body and in an eternal life " Man will arise on " the last day," as Christ is alleged to have done on Easter morn, and receive a reward according to the tenor of his earthly life. This typically Christian idea is thoroughly materialistic and anthropomorphic; it is very little superior to the corresponding crude legends of uncivilized peoples. The impossibility of " the resurrection of the body " is clear to every man who has some knowledge of anatomy and physiology. The resurrection of Christ, which is celebrated every Easter by millions of Christians, is as purely mythical as " the awakening of the dead," which he is alleged to have taught. These mystic articles of faith are just as untenable in the light of pure reason as the cognate hypothesis of " eternal life."

The fantastic notions which the Christian Church disseminates as to the eternal life of the immortal soul after the dissolution of the body are just as materialistic as the dogma of " the resurrection of the body." In his interesting work on *Religion in the Light of the Darwinian Theory*, Savage justly remarks: " It is one of the standing charges of the Church against science that it is materialistic. I must say, in passing, that the whole ecclesiastical doctrine of a future life has always been, and still is, materialism of the purest type. It teaches that the material body shall rise, and dwell in a material heaven." To prove this one has only to read impartially some of the sermons and ornate discourses in which the glory of the future life is extolled

THE IMMORTALITY OF THE SOUL

as the highest good of the Christian, and belief in it is laid down to be the foundation of morality. According to them, all the joys of the most advanced modern civilization await the pious believer in Paradise, while the "All-loving Father" reserves his eternal fires for the godless materialist.

In opposition to the materialist athanatism, which is dominant in the Christian and Mohammedan Churches, we have, apparently, a purer and higher form of faith in the *metaphysical athanatism*, as taught by most of our dualist and spiritualist philosophers. Plato must be considered its chief creator: in the fourth century before Christ he taught that complete dualism of body and soul which afterwards became one of the most important, theoretically, and one of the most influential, practically, of the Christian articles of faith. The body is mortal, material, physical; the soul is immortal, immaterial, metaphysical. They are only temporarily associated, for the course of the individual life. As Plato postulated an eternal life before as well as after this temporary association, he must be classed as an adherent of " metempsychosis," or transmigration of souls; the soul existed as such, or as an " eternal idea," before it entered into a human body. When it quits one body it seeks such other as is most suited to its character for its habitation. The souls of bloody tyrants pass into the bodies of wolves and vultures, those of virtuous toilers migrate into the bodies of bees and ants, and so forth. The childish naïvety of this Platonic morality is obvious; on closer examination his views are found to be absolutely incompatible with the scientific truth which we owe to modern anatomy, physiology, histology, and ontogeny; we mention them only because, in spite of their absurdity, they have had a profound influence on thought and culture. On the one hand, the mysticism of the Neo-Platonists, which penetrated into Christianity, attaches itself to the psychology of Plato; on the other hand, it became subsequently one of the chief supports of spiritualistic and idealistic philosophy The Platonic "idea" gave way in time to the notion of psychic "substance"; this is just as incomprehensible and metaphysical, though it often assumed a physical appearance.

The conception of the soul as a "substance" is far from clear in many psychologists; sometimes it is regarded as an "immaterial" entity of a peculiar character in an abstract and idealistic sense, sometimes in a concrete and realistic sense, and sometimes as a confused *tertium quid* between the two. If we adhere to the monistic idea of substance, which we develop in chap. xii., and which takes it to be the simplest element of our whole world-system, we find *energy* and *matter* inseparably associated in it. We must, therefore, distinguish in the "substance of the soul" the characteristic psychic *energy* which is all we perceive (sensation, presentation, volition, etc.), and the psychic *matter*, which is the inseparable basis of its activity—that is, the living protoplasm. Thus, in the higher animals the "matter" of the soul is a part of the nervous system; in the lower nerveless animals and plants it is a part of their multicellular protoplasmic body; and in the unicellular protists it is a part of their protoplasmic cell-body. In this way we are brought once more to the psychic organs, and to an appreciation of the fact that these material organs are indispensable for the action of the soul; but the soul itself is *actual*—it is the sum-total of their physiological functions.

However, the idea of a specific "soul-substance"

THE IMMORTALITY OF THE SOUL

found in the dualistic philosophers who admit such a thing is very different from this. They conceive the immortal soul to be material, yet invisible, and essentially different from the visible body which it inhabits.

Thus *invisibility* comes to be regarded as a most important attribute of the soul. Some, in fact, compare the soul with ether, and regard it, like ether, as an extremely subtle, light, and highly elastic material, an imponderable agency, that fills the intervals between the ponderable particles of the living organism, others compare the soul with the wind, and so give it a gaseous nature; and it is this simile which first found favor with primitive peoples, and led in time to the familiar dualistic conception. When a man died, the body remained as a lifeless corpse, but the immortal soul " flew out of it with the last breath."

The comparison of the human soul with physical ether as a qualitatively similar idea has assumed a more concrete shape in recent times through the great progress of optics and electricity (especially in the last decade); for these sciences have taught us a good deal about the energy of ether, and enabled us to formulate certain conclusions as to the material character of this all-pervading agency. As I intend to describe these important discoveries later on (in chap. xii.), I shall do no more at present than briefly point out that they render the notion of an " etheric soul " absolutely untenable. Such an etheric soul — that is a psychic substance—which is similar to physical ether, and which, like ether, passes between the ponderable elements of the living protoplasm or the molecules of the brain, cannot possibly account for the individual life of the soul. Neither the mystic notions of that kind which were warmly discussed about the middle of the century, nor the attempts of modern "Neovitalists" to put their mystical "vital force" on a line with physical ether, call for refutation any longer.

Much more widespread, and still much respected, is the view which ascribes a gaseous nature to the substance of the soul. The comparison of human breath with the wind is a very old one; they were originally considered to be identical, and were both given the same name. The *anemos* and *psyche* of the Greeks, and the *anima* and *spiritus* of the Romans, were originally all names for "a breath of wind"; they were transferred from this to the breath of man. After a time this "living breath" was identified with the "vital force," and finally it came to be regarded as the soul itself, or, in a narrower sense, as its highest manifestation, the "spirit." From that the imagination went on to derive the mystic notion of individual "spirits"; these, also, are still usually conceived as "aëriform beings"—though they are credited with the physiological functions of an organism, and they have been photographed in certain well-known spiritist circles.

Experimental physics has succeeded, during the last decade of the century, in reducing all gaseous bodies to a liquid—most of them, also, to a solid—condition. Nothing more is needed than special apparatus, which exerts a violent pressure on the gases at a very low temperature. By this process not only the atmospheric elements, oxygen, hydrogen, and nitrogen, but even compound gases (such as carbonic-acid gas) and gaseous aggregates (like the atmosphere) have been changed from gaseous to liquid form. In this way the "invisible" substances have become "visible" to all, and in a certain sense "tangible." With

THE IMMORTALITY OF THE SOUL

this transformation the mystic nimbus which formerly veiled the character of the gas in popular estimation—as an invisible body that wrought visible effects—has entirely disappeared. If, then, the substance of the soul were really gaseous, it should be possible to liquefy it by the application of a high pressure at a low temperature. We could then catch the soul as it is "breathed out" at the moment of death, condense it, and exhibit it in a bottle as "immortal fluid" (*Fluidum animae immortale*). By a further lowering of temperature and increase of pressure it might be possible to solidify it—to produce "soul-snow." The experiment has not yet succeeded.

If athanatism were true, if, indeed, the human soul were to live for all eternity, we should have to grant the same privilege to the souls of the higher animals, at least to those of the nearest related mammals (apes, dogs, etc.). For man is not distinguished from them by a special *kind* of soul, or by any peculiar and exclusive psychic function, but only by a higher *degree* of psychic activity, a superior stage of development. In particular, consciousness—the function of the association of ideas, thought, and reason—has reached a higher level in many men (by no means in all) than in most of the animals. Yet this difference is far from being so great as is popularly supposed; and it is much slighter in every respect than the corresponding difference between the higher and the lower animal souls, or even the difference between the highest and the lowest stages of the human soul itself. If we ascribe "personal immortality" to man, we are bound to grant it also to the higher animals.

It is, therefore, quite natural that we should find this belief in the immortality of the animal soul among

THE RIDDLE OF THE UNIVERSE

many ancient and modern peoples; we even meet it sometimes to-day in many thoughtful men who postulate an "immortal life" for themselves, and have, at the same time, a thorough empirical knowledge of the psychic life of the animals. I once knew an old head-forester, who, being left a widower and without children at an early age, had lived alone for more than thirty years in a noble forest of East Prussia. His only companions were one or two servants, with whom he exchanged merely a few necessary words, and a great pack of different kinds of dogs, with which he lived in perfect psychic communion. Through many years of training this keen observer and friend of nature had penetrated deep into the individual souls of his dogs, and he was as convinced of their personal immortality as he was of his own. Some of his most intelligent dogs were, in his impartial and objective estimation, at a higher stage of psychic development than his old, stupid maid and the rough, wrinkled man-servant. Any unprejudiced observer, who will study the conscious and intelligent psychic activity of a fine dog for a year, and follow attentively the physiological processes of its thought, judgment, and reason, will have to admit that it has just as valid a claim to immortality as man himself.

The proofs of the immortality of the soul, which have been adduced for the last two thousand years, and are, indeed, still credited with some validity, have their origin, for the most part, not in an effort to discover the truth, but in an alleged "necessity of emotion"—that is, in imagination and poetic conceit. As Kant puts it, the immortality of the soul is not an object of pure reason, but a "postulate of practical reason." But we must set "practical reason" entirely aside, together

THE IMMORTALITY OF THE SOUL

with all the "exigencies of emotion, or of moral education, etc.," when we enter upon an honest and impartial pursuit of truth; for we shall only attain it by the work of pure reason, starting from empirical data and capable of logical analysis. We have to say the same of athanatism as of theism; both are creations of poetic mysticism and of transcendental "faith," not of rational science.

When we come to analyze all the different proofs that have been urged for the immortality of the soul, we find that not a single one of them is of a scientific character; not a single one is consistent with the truths we have learned in the last few decades from physiological psychology and the theory of descent. The *theological* proof—that a personal creator has breathed an immortal soul (generally regarded as a portion of the divine soul) into man—is a pure myth. The *cosmological* proof—that the "moral order of the world" demands the eternal duration of the human soul—is a baseless dogma. The *teleological* proof—that the "higher destiny" of man involves the perfecting of his defective, earthly soul beyond the grave—rests on a false anthropism. The *moral* proof—that the defects and the unsatisfied desires of earthly existence must be fulfilled by "compensative justice" on the other side of eternity—is nothing more than a pious wish. The *ethnological* proof—that the belief in immortality, like the belief in God, is an innate truth, common to all humanity—is an error in fact. The *ontological* proof—that the soul, being a "simple, immaterial, and indivisible entity," cannot be involved in the corruption of death—is based on an entirely erroneous view of the psychic phenomena; it is a spiritualistic fallacy. All these and similar "proofs of athanatism" are in a parlous condition;

THE RIDDLE OF THE UNIVERSE

they are definitely annulled by the scientific criticism of the last few decades.

The extreme importance of the subject leads us to oppose to these untenable "proofs of immortality" a brief exposition of the sound scientific arguments against it. The *physiological* argument shows that the human soul is not an independent, immaterial substance, but, like the soul of all the higher animals, merely a collective title for the sum-total of man's cerebral functions; and these are just as much determined by physical and chemical processes as any of the other vital functions, and just as amenable to the law of substance. The *histological* argument is based on the extremely complicated microscopic structure of the brain; it shows us the true "elementary organs of the soul" in the ganglionic cells. The *experimental* argument proves that the various functions of the soul are bound up with certain special parts of the brain, and cannot be exercised unless these are in a normal condition; if the areas are destroyed, their function is extinguished; and this is especially applicable to the "organs of thought," the four central instruments of mental activity. The *pathological* argument is the complement of the physiological; when certain parts of the brain (the centres of speech, sight, hearing, etc.) are destroyed by sickness, their activity (speech, vision, hearing, etc.) disappears; in this way nature herself makes the decisive physiological experiment. The *ontogenetic* argument puts before us the facts of the development of the soul in the individual; we see how the child-soul gradually unfolds its various powers; the youth presents them in full bloom, the mature man shows their ripe fruit; in old age we see the gradual decay of the psychic powers, corresponding to the senile

THE IMMORTALITY OF THE SOUL

degeneration of the brain. The *phylogenetic* argument derives its strength from palæontology, and the comparative anatomy and physiology of the brain; co-operating with and completing each other, these sciences prove to the hilt that the human brain (and, consequently, its function—the soul) has been evolved step by step from that of the mammal, and, still further back, from that of the lower vertebrate.

These inquiries, which might be supplemented by many other results of modern science, prove the old dogma of the immortality of the soul to be absolutely untenable; in the twentieth century it will not be regarded as a subject of serious scientific research, but will be left wholly to transcendental "faith." The "critique of pure reason" shows this treasured faith to be a mere *superstition*, like the belief in a personal God which generally accompanies it. Yet even to-day millions of "believers"—not only of the lower, uneducated masses, but even of the most cultured classes—look on this superstition as their dearest possession and their most "priceless treasure." It is, therefore, necessary to enter more deeply into the subject, and—assuming it to be true—to make a critical inquiry into its practical value. It soon becomes apparent to the impartial critic that this value rests, for the most part, on fancy, on the want of clear judgment and consecutive thought. It is my firm and honest conviction that a definitive abandonment of these "athanatist illusions" would involve no painful loss, but an inestimable positive gain for humanity.

Man's "emotional craving" clings to the belief on immortality for two main reasons: firstly, in the hope of better conditions of life beyond the grave; and, secondly, in the hope of seeing once more the dear and loved ones whom death has torn from us. As for the first hope, it corresponds to a natural feeling of the justice of compensation, which is quite correct subjectively, but has no objective validity whatever. We make our claim for an indemnity for the unnumbered defects and sorrows of our earthly existence, without the slightest real prospect or guarantee of receiving it. We long for an eternal life in which we shall meet no sadness and no pain, but an unbounded peace and joy. The pictures that most men form of this blissful existence are extremely curious; the immaterial soul is placed in the midst of grossly material pleasures. The imagination of each believer paints the enduring splendor according to his personal taste. The American Indian, whose athanatism Schiller has so well depicted, trusts to find in his Paradise the finest hunting-grounds with innumerable hordes of buffaloes and bears; the Eskimo looks forward to sun-tipped icebergs with an inexhaustible supply of bears, seals, and other polar animals; the effeminate Cingalese frames his Paradise on the wonderful island-paradise of Ceylon with its noble gardens and forests—adding that there will be unlimited supplies of rice and curry, of cocoanuts and other fruit, always at hand; the Mohammedan Arab believes it will be a place of shady gardens of flowers, watered by cool springs, and filled with lovely maidens; the Catholic fisherman of Sicily looks forward to a daily superabundance of the most valuable fishes and the finest macaroni, and eternal absolution for all his sins, which he can go on committing in his eternal home; the evangelical of North Europe longs for an immense Gothic cathedral, in which he can chant the praises of the Lord of Hosts for all eternity. In a word, each believer really expects his eternal life to be

THE IMMORTALITY OF THE SOUL

a direct continuation of his individual life on earth, only in a " much improved and enlarged edition."

We must lay special stress on the thoroughly materialistic character of *Christian* athanatism, which is closely connected with the absurd dogma of the "resurrection of the body." As thousands of paintings of famous masters inform us, the bodies that have risen again, with the souls that have been born again, walk about in heaven just as they did in this vale of tears; they see God with their eyes, they hear His voice with their ears, they sing hymns to His praise with their larynx, and so forth. In fine, the modern inhabitants of the Christian Paradise have the same dual character of body and soul, the same organs of an earthly body, as our ancient ancestors had in Odin's Hall in Walhalla, as the "immortal" Turks and Arabs have in Mohammed's lovely gardens, as the old Greek demigods and heroes had in the enjoyment of nectar and ambrosia at the table of Zeus.

But, however gloriously we may depict this eternal life in Paradise, it remains *endless* in duration. Do we realize what " eternity " means?—the uninterrupted continuance of our individual life forever! The profound legend of the "wandering Jew," the fruitless search for rest of the unhappy Ahasuerus, should teach us to appreciate such an " eternal life " at its true value. The best we can desire after a courageous life, spent in doing good according to our light, is the eternal peace of the grave. " Lord, give them an eternal rest."

Any impartial scholar who is acquainted with geological calculations of time, and has reflected on the long series of millions of years the organic history of the earth has occupied, must admit that the crude notion of an eternal life is not a *comfort*, but a fearful

THE RIDDLE OF THE UNIVERSE

menace, to the best of men. Only want of clear judgment and consecutive thought can dispute it.

The best and most plausible ground for athanatism is found in the hope that immortality will reunite us to the beloved friends who have been prematurely taken from us by some grim mischance. But even this supposed good fortune proves to be an illusion on closer inquiry; and in any case it would be greatly marred by the prospect of meeting the less agreeable acquaintances and the enemies who have troubled our existence here below. Even the closest family ties would involve many a difficulty. There are plenty of men who would gladly sacrifice all the glories of Paradise if it meant the eternal companionship of their " better half " and their mother-in-law. It is more than questionable whether Henry VIII. would like the prospect of living eternally with his six wives; or Augustus the Strong of Poland, who had a hundred mistresses and three hundred and fifty-two children. As he was on good terms with the Vicar of Christ, he must be assumed to be in Paradise, in spite of his sins, and in spite of the fact that his mad military ventures cost the lives of more than a hundred thousand Saxons.

Another insoluble difficulty faces the athanatist when he asks *in what stage of their individual development* the disembodied souls will spend their eternal life. Will the new-born infant develop its psychic powers in heaven under the same hard conditions of the " struggle for life " which educate man here on earth? Will the talented youth who has fallen in the wholesale murder of war unfold his rich, unused mental powers in Walhalla? Will the feeble, childish old man, who has filled the world with the fame of his deeds in the ripeness of his age, live forever in mental

THE IMMORTALITY OF THE SOUL

decay? Or will he return to an earlier stage of development? If the immortal souls in Olympus are to live in a condition of rejuvenescence and perfectness, then both the stimulus to the formation of, and the interest in, personality disappear for them.

Not less impossible, in the light of pure reason, do we find the anthropistic myth of the "last judgment," and the separation of the souls of men into two great groups, of which one is destined for the eternal joys of Paradise and the other for the eternal torments of hell —and that from a personal God who is called the "Father of Love"! And it is this "Universal Father" who has himself created the conditions of heredity and adaptation, in virtue of which the elect, on the one side, were *bound* to pursue the path towards eternal bliss, and the luckless poor and miserable, on the other hand, were *driven* into the paths of the damned?

A critical comparison of the countless and manifold fantasies which belief in immortality has produced during the last few thousand years in the different races and religions yields a most remarkable picture. An intensely interesting presentation of it, based on most extensive original research, may be found in Adalbert Svoboda's distinguished works, *The Illusion of the Soul* and *Forms of Faith*. However absurd and inconsistent with modern knowledge most of these myths seem to be, they still play an important part, and, as "postulates of practical reason," they exercise a powerful influence on the opinions of individuals and on the destiny of races.

The idealist and spiritualist philosophy of the day will freely grant that these prevalent materialistic forms of belief in immortality are untenable; it will say that the refined idea of an immaterial soul, a Platonic "idea" or a transcendental psychic substance, must be substituted for them. But modern realism can have nothing whatever to do with these incomprehensible notions; they satisfy neither the mind's feeling of causality nor the yearning of our emotions. If we take a comprehensive glance at all that modern anthropology, psychology, and cosmology teach with regard to athanatism, we are forced to this definite conclusion· " The belief in the immortality of the human soul is a dogma which is in hopeless contradiction with the most solid empirical truths of modern science."

CHAPTER XII

THE LAW OF SUBSTANCE

The Fundamental Chemical Law of the Constancy of Matter—The Fundamental Physical Law of the Conservation of Energy—Combination of Both Laws in the Law of Substance—The Kinetic, Pyknotic, and Dualistic Ideas of Substance—Monism of Matter—Ponderable Matter—Atoms and Elements—Affinity of the Elements—The Soul of the Atom (Feeling and Inclination)—Existence and Character of Ether—Ether and Ponderable Matter—Force and Energy—Potential and Actual Force—Unity of Natural Forces—Supremacy of the Law of Substance

THE supreme and all-pervading law of nature, the true and only cosmological law, is, in my opinion, *the law of substance*; its discovery and establishment is the greatest intellectual triumph of the nineteenth century, in the sense that all other known laws of nature are subordinate to it. Under the name of "law of substance" we embrace two supreme laws of different origin and age—the older is the chemical law of the "conservation of matter," and the younger is the physical law of the "conservation of energy."* It will be self-evident to many readers, and it is acknowledged by most of the scientific men of the day, that these two great laws are essentially inseparable. This fundamental thesis, however, is still much contested

* Cf. *Monism*, by Ernst Haeckel.

THE RIDDLE OF THE UNIVERSE

in some quarters, and we must proceed to furnish the proof of it. But we must first devote a few words to each of the two laws.

The *law of the "persistence"* or *"indestructibility of matter,"* established by Lavoisier in 1789, may be formulated thus: The sum of matter, which fills infinite space, is unchangeable. A body has merely changed its form, when it seems to have disappeared. When coal burns, it is changed into carbonic-acid gas by combination with the oxygen of the atmosphere; when a piece of sugar melts in water, it merely passes from the solid to the fluid condition. In the same way, it is merely a question of change of form in the cases where a new body seems to be produced. A shower of rain is the moisture of the atmosphere cast down in the form of drops of water; when a piece of iron rusts, the surface layer of the metal has combined with water and with atmospheric oxygen, and formed a "rust," or oxyhydrate of iron. Nowhere in nature do we find an example of the production, or "creation," of new matter; nowhere does a particle of existing matter pass entirely away. This empirical truth is now the unquestionable foundation of chemistry; it may be directly verified at any moment by means of the balance. To the great French chemist Lavoisier belongs the high merit of first making this experiment with the balance. At the present day the scientist, who is occupied from one end of the year to the other with the study of natural phenomena, is so firmly convinced of the absolute "constancy" of matter that he is no longer able to imagine the contrary state of things.

We may formulate *the " law of the persistence of force"* or *" conservation of energy "* thus: The sum of force, which is at work in infinite space and produces all phe-

THE LAW OF SUBSTANCE

nomena, is unchangeable. When the locomotive rushes along the line, the potential energy of the steam is transformed into the kinetic or actual energy of the mechanical movement, when we hear its shrill whistle, as it speeds along, the sound-waves of the vibrating atmosphere are conveyed through the tympanum and the three bones of the ear into the inner labyrinth, and thence transferred by the auditory nerve to the acoustic ganglionic cells which form the centre of hearing in the temporal lobe of the gray bed of the brain. The whole marvellous panorama of life that spreads over the surface of our globe is, in the last analysis, transformed sunlight. It is well known how the remarkable progress of technical science has made it possible for us to convert the different physical forces from one form to another, heat may be changed into molar movement, or movement of mass; this in turn into light or sound, and then into electricity, and so forth. Accurate measurement of the quantity of force which is used in this metamorphosis has shown that it is "constant" or unchanged. No particle of living energy is ever extinguished; no particle is ever created anew. Friedrich Mohr, of Bonn, was very near to the discovery of this great fact in 1837, but the discovery was actually made by the able Swabian physician, Robert Mayer, of Heilbronn, in 1842. Independently of Mayer, however, the principle was reached almost at the same time by the famous physiologist, Hermann Helmholtz; five years afterwards he pointed out its general application to, and fertility in, every branch of physics. We ought to say to-day that it rules also in the entire province of physiology — that is, of "organic physics"; but on that point we meet a strenuous opposition from the vitalistic biologists and the dualist and spiritualist philosophers. For these the peculiar "spiritual forces" of human nature are a group of "free" forces, not subject to the law of energy; the idea is closely connected with the dogma of the "freedom of the will." We have, however, already seen (p. 204) that the dogma is untenable. Modern physics draws a distinction between "force" and "energy," but our general observations so far have not needed a reference to it.

The conviction that these two great cosmic theorems, the chemical law of the persistence of matter and the physical law of the persistence of force, are fundamentally one, is of the utmost importance in our monistic system. The two theories are just as intimately united as their objects—matter and force or energy. Indeed, this fundamental unity of the two laws is self-evident to many monistic scientists and philosophers, since they merely relate to two different aspects of one and the same object, the *cosmos*. But, however natural the thought may be, it is still very far from being generally accepted. It is stoutly contested by the entire dualistic philosophy, vitalistic biology, and parallelistic psychology; even, in fact, by a few (inconsistent) monists, who think they find a check to it in "consciousness," in the higher mental activity of man, or in other phenomena of our "free mental life."

For my part, I am convinced of the profound importance of the unifying "law of substance," as an expression of the inseparable connection in reality of two laws which are only separated in conception. That they were not originally taken together and their unity recognized from the beginning is merely an accident of the date of their respective discoveries. The earlier and more accessible chemical law of the persistence of matter was detected by Lavoisier in 1789,

THE LAW OF SUBSTANCE

and, after a general application of the balance, became the basis of exact chemistry. On the other hand, the more recondite law of the persistence of force was only discovered by Mayer in 1842, and only laid down as the basis of exact physics by Helmholtz. The unity of the two laws—still much disputed—is expressed by many scientists who are convinced of it in the formula: " Law of the persistence of matter and force." In order to have a briefer and more convenient expression for this fundamental thought, I proposed some time ago to call it the "law of substance" or the "fundamental cosmic law"; it might also be called the "universal law," or the "law of constancy," or the "axiom of the constancy of the universe." In the ultimate analysis it is found to be a necessary consequence of the principle of causality.*

The first thinker to introduce the purely monistic conception of substance into science and appreciate its profound importance was the great philosopher Baruch Spinoza; his chief work appeared shortly after his premature death in 1677, just one hundred years before Lavoisier gave empirical proof of the constancy of matter by means of the chemist's principal instrument, the balance. In his stately pantheistic system the notion of the *world* (the universe, or the cosmos) is identical with the all-pervading notion of *God*; it is at one and the same time the purest and most rational *monism* and the clearest and most abstract *monotheism*. This universal substance, this " divine nature of the world," shows us two different aspects of its being, or two fundamental attributes—matter (infinitely *extended* substance) and spirit (the all-embracing energy of

---

* Cf. *Monism,* by Ernst Haeckel.

thought). All the changes which have since come over the idea of substance are reduced, on a logical analysis, to this supreme thought of Spinoza's; with Goethe I take it to be the loftiest, profoundest, and truest thought of all ages. Every single object in the world which comes within the sphere of our cognizance, all individual forms of existence, are but special transitory forms —*accidents* or *modes*—of substance. These modes are material things when we regard them under the attribute of *extension* (or " occupation of space "), but forces or ideas when we consider them under the attribute of *thought* (or " energy "). To this profound thought of Spinoza our purified monism returns after a lapse of two hundred years; for us, too, matter (space-filling substance) and energy (moving force) are but two inseparable attributes of the one underlying substance.

Among the various modifications which the fundamental idea of substance has undergone in modern physics, in association with the prevalent atomism, we shall select only two of the most divergent theories for a brief discussion, the kinetic and the pyknotic. Both theories agree that we have succeeded in reducing all the different forces of nature to one common original force; gravity and chemical action, electricity and magnetism, light and heat, etc., are only different manifestations, forms, or *dynamodes*, of a single primitive force (*prodynamis*). This fundamental force is generally conceived as a vibratory motion of the smallest particles of matter—a vibration of atoms. The atoms themselves, according to the usual " kinetic theory of substance," are dead, separate particles of matter, which dance to and fro in empty space and act at a distance. The real founder and most distinguished representative

THE LAW OF SUBSTANCE

of the kinetic theory is Newton, the famous discoverer of the law of gravitation. In his great work, the *Philosophiae Naturalis Principia Mathematica* (1687), he showed that throughout the universe the same law of attraction controls the unvarying constancy of gravitation; the attraction of two particles being in direct proportion to their mass and in inverse proportion to the square of their distance. This universal force of gravity is at work in the fall of an apple and the tidal wave no less than in the course of the planets round the sun and the movements of all the heavenly bodies. Newton had the immortal merit of establishing the law of gravitation and embodying it in an indisputable mathematical formula. Yet this *dead mathematical formula*, on which most scientists lay great stress, as so frequently happens, gives us merely the *quantitative* demonstration of the theory; it gives us no insight whatever into the *qualitative* nature of the phenomena. The action at a distance without a medium, which Newton deduced from his law of gravitation, and which became one of the most serious and most dangerous dogmas of later physics, does not afford the slightest explanation of the real causes of attraction; indeed, it long obstructed our way to the real discovery of them. I cannot but suspect that his speculations on this mysterious action at a distance contributed not a little to the leading of the great English mathematician into the obscure labyrinth of mystic dreams and theistic superstition in which he passed the last thirty-four years of his life; we find him, at the end, giving metaphysical hypotheses on the predictions of Daniel and on the paradoxical fantasies of St. John.

In fundamental opposition to the theory of vibration, or the kinetic theory of substance, we have the

THE RIDDLE OF THE UNIVERSE

modern "theory of condensation," or the pyknotic theory of substance. It is most ably established in the suggestive work of J. C. Vogt on *The Nature of Electricity and Magnetism on the Basis of a Simplified Conception of Substance* (1891). Vogt assumes the primitive force of the world, the universal *prodynamis*, to be, not the vibration or oscillation of particles in empty space, but the condensation of a simple primitive substance, which fills the infinity of space in an unbroken continuity. Its sole inherent mechanical form of activity consists in a tendency to condensation or contraction, which produces infinitesimal centres of condensation; these may change their degree of thickness, and, therefore, their volume, but are constant as such. These minute parts of the universal substance, the centres of condensation, which might be called *pyknatoms*, correspond in general to the ultimate separate atoms of the kinetic theory; they differ, however, very considerably in that they are credited with sensation and inclination (or will-movement of the simplest form), *with souls*, in a certain sense—in harmony with the old theory of Empedocles of the "love and hatred of the elements." Moreover, these "atoms with souls" do not float in empty space, but in the continuous, extremely attenuated intermediate substance, which represents the uncondensed portion of the primitive matter. By means of certain "constellations, centres of perturbation, or systems of deformation," great masses of centres of condensation quickly unite in immense proportions, and so obtain a preponderance over the surrounding masses. By that process the primitive substance, which in its original state of quiescence had the same mean consistency throughout, divides or differentiates into two kinds.

THE LAW OF SUBSTANCE

The centres of disturbance, which *positively* exceed the mean consistency in virtue of the *pyknosis* or condensation, form the ponderable matter of bodies; the finer, intermediate substance, which occupies the space between them, and *negatively* falls below the mean consistency, forms the ether, or imponderable matter. As a consequence of this division into mass and ether there ensues a ceaseless struggle between the two antagonistic elements, and this struggle is the source of all physical processes. The positive ponderable matter, the element with the feeling of like or desire, is continually striving to complete the process of condensation, and thus collecting an enormous amount of *potential* energy; the negative, imponderable matter, on the other hand, offers a perpetual and equal resistance to the further increase of its strain and of the feeling of dislike connected therewith, and thus gathers the utmost amount of *actual* energy.

We cannot go any further here into the details of the brilliant theory of J. C. Vogt. The interested reader cannot do better than have recourse to the second volume of the above work for a clear, popular exposition of the difficult problem. I am myself too little informed in physics and mathematics to enter into a critical discussion of its lights and shades; still, I think that this pyknotic theory of substance will prove more acceptable to every biologist who is convinced of the unity of nature than the kinetic theory which prevails in physics to-day. A misunderstanding may easily arise from the fact that Vogt puts his process of condensation in explicit contradiction with the general phenomenon of motion; but it must be remembered that he is speaking of vibratory movement in the sense of the physicist. His hypothetical "condensation" is just as much determined by a movement of substance as is the hypothetical "vibration"; only the kind of movement and the relation of the moving elements are very different in the two hypotheses. Moreover, it is not the whole theory of vibration, but only an important section of it, that is contradicted by the theory of condensation.

Modern physics, for the most part, still firmly adheres to the older theory of vibration, to the idea of an *actio in distans* and the eternal vibration of dead atoms in empty space; it rejects the pyknotic theory Although Vogt's theory may be still far from perfect, and his original speculations may be marred by many errors, yet I think he has rendered a very good service in eliminating the untenable principles of the kinetic theory of substance. As to my own opinion—and that of many other scientists—I must lay down the following theses, which are involved in Vogt's pyknotic theory, as indispensable for a truly monistic view of substance, and one that covers the whole field of organic and inorganic nature:

I. The two fundamental forms of substance, ponderable matter and ether, are not dead and only moved by extrinsic force, but they are endowed with sensation and will (though, naturally, of the lowest grade); they experience an inclination for condensation, a dislike of strain; they strive after the one and struggle against the other.

II. There is no such thing as empty space; that part of space which is not occupied with ponderable atoms is filled with ether.

III. There is no such thing as an action at a distance through perfectly empty space; all action of bodies upon each other is either determined by immediate contact or is effected by the mediation of ether.

THE LAW OF SUBSTANCE

Both the theories of substance which we have just contrasted are *monistic* in principle, since the opposition between the two conditions of substance—mass and ether—is not original; moreover, they involve a continuous immediate contact and reciprocal action of the two elements. It is otherwise with the *dualistic* theories of substance which still obtain in the idealist and spiritualist philosophy, and which have the support of a powerful theology, in so far as theology indulges in such metaphysical speculations. These theories draw a distinction between two entirely different kinds of substance, material and immaterial. Material substance enters into the composition of the bodies which are the object of physics and chemistry; the law of the persistence of matter and force is confined to this world (apart from a belief in its "creation from nothing" and other miracles). Immaterial substance is found in the "spiritual world" to which the law does not extend; in this province the laws of physics and chemistry are either entirely inapplicable or they are subordinated to a "vital force," or a "free will," or a "divine omnipotence," or some other phantom which is beyond the ken of critical science. In truth, these profound errors need no further refutation to-day, for experience has never yet discovered for us a single immaterial substance, a single force which is not dependent on matter, or a single form of energy which is not exerted by material movement, whether it be of mass, or of ether, or of both. Even the most elaborate and most perfect forms of energy that we know—the psychic life of the higher animals, the thought and reason of man—depend on material processes, or changes in the neuroplasm of the ganglionic cells; they are inconceivable apart from such modifications. I have already

THE RIDDLE OF THE UNIVERSE

shown (chap. xi.) that the physiological hypothesis of a special, immaterial "soul-substance" is untenable.

The study of ponderable matter is primarily the concern of chemistry. Few are ignorant of the astonishing theoretical progress which this science has made in the course of the century and the immense practical influence it has had on every aspect of modern life. We shall confine ourselves here to a few remarks on the more important questions which concern the nature of ponderable matter. It is well known that analytical chemistry has succeeded in resolving the immense variety of bodies in nature into a small number of simple elements—that is, simple bodies which are incapable of further analysis. The number of these elements is about seventy. Only fourteen of them are widely distributed on the earth and of much practical importance; the majority are rare elements (principally metals) of little practical moment. The affinity of these groups of elements, and the remarkable proportions of their atomic weights, which Lothar Meyer and Mendelejeff have proved in their *Periodic System of the Elements*, make it extremely probable that they are not *absolute species* of ponderable matter—that is, not eternally unchangeable particles. The seventy elements have in that system been distributed into eight leading groups, and arranged in them according to their atomic weight, so that the elements which have a chemical affinity are formed into families. The relations of the various groups in such a natural system of the elements recall, on the one hand, similar relations of the innumerable compounds of carbon, and, again, the relations of parallel groups in the natural arrangement of the animal and plant species. Since in the latter cases the "af-

THE LAW OF SUBSTANCE

finity" of the related forms is based on descent from a common parent form, it seems very probable that the same holds good of the families and orders of the chemical elements. We may, therefore, conclude that the "empirical elements" we now know are not really simple, ultimate, and unchangeable forms of matter, but compounds of homogeneous, simple, primitive atoms, variously distributed as to number and grouping. The recent speculations of Gustav Wendt, Wilhelm Preyer, Sir W. Crookes, and others, have pointed out how we may conceive the evolution of the elements from a simple primitive material, the *prothyl*.

The modern atomistic theory, which is regarded as an indispensable instrument in chemistry to-day, must be carefully distinguished from the old philosophic atomism which was taught more than two thousand years ago by a group of distinguished thinkers of antiquity—Leucippus, Democritus, and Epicurus: it was considerably developed and modified later on by Descartes, Hobbes, Leibnitz, and other famous philosophers. But it was not until 1808 that modern atomism assumed a definite and acceptable form, and was furnished with an empirical basis by Dalton, who formulated the "law of simple and multiple proportions" in the formation of chemical combinations. He first determined the atomic weight of the different elements, and thus created the solid and exact foundation on which more recent chemical theories are based; these are all *atomistic*, in the sense that they assume the elements to be made up of homogeneous, infinitesimal, distinct particles, which are incapable of further analysis. That does not touch the question of the real nature of the atoms—their form, size, psychology, etc. These atomic qualities are merely hypothetical, while the *chemistry* of the atoms, their "chemical affinity"—that is, the constant proportion in which they combine with the atoms of other elements—is empirical.*

The different relation of the various elements towards each other, which chemistry calls "affinity," is one of the most important properties of ponderable matter; it is manifested in the different relative quantities or proportions of their combination in the intensity of its consummation. Every shade of inclination, from complete indifference to the fiercest passion, is exemplified in the chemical relation of the various elements towards each other, just as we find in the psychology of man, and especially in the life of the sexes. Goethe, in his classical romance, *Affinities*, compared the relations of pairs of lovers with the phenomenon of the same name in the formation of chemical combinations. The irresistible passion that draws Edward to the sympathetic Ottilia, or Paris to Helen, and leaps over all bounds of reason and morality, is the same powerful "unconscious" attractive force which impels the living spermatozoon to force an entrance into the ovum in the fertilization of the egg of the animal or plant—the same impetuous movement which unites two atoms of hydrogen to one atom of oxygen for the formation of a molecule of water. This fundamental *unity of affinity in the whole of nature*, from the simplest chemical process to the most complicated love story, was recognized by the great Greek scientist, Empedocles, in the fifth century B.C., in his theory of "the love and hatred of the elements." It receives empirical confirmation from the interesting progress of cellular psychology, the great significance of which we have only learned to

---

* Cf. *Monism*, by Ernst Haeckel.

THE LAW OF SUBSTANCE

appreciate in the last thirty years. On those phenomena we base our conviction that even the *atom* is not without a rudimentary form of sensation and will, or, as it is better expressed, of feeling (*aesthesis*) and inclination (*tropesis*) — that is, a universal "soul" of the simplest character. The same must be said of the molecules which are composed of two or more atoms. Further combinations of different kinds of these molecules give rise to simple and, subsequently, complex chemical compounds, in the activity of which the same phenomena are repeated in a more complicated form.

The study of ether, or imponderable matter, pertains principally to physics. The existence of an extremely attenuated medium, filling the whole of space outside of ponderable matter, was known and applied to the elucidation of various phenomena (especially light) a long time ago; but it was not until the second half of the nineteenth century that we became more closely acquainted with this remarkable substance, in connection with our astonishing empirical discoveries in the province of electricity, with their experimental detection, their theoretical interpretation, and their practical application. The path was opened in particular by the famous researches of Heinrich Hertz, of Bonn, in 1888. The premature death of a brilliant young physicist of so much promise cannot be sufficiently deplored. Like the premature death of Spinoza, Raphael, Schubert, and many other great men, it is one of those brutal facts of human history which are enough of themselves to destroy the untenable myth of a "wise Providence" and an "All-loving Father in heaven."

The existence of ether (or cosmic ether) as a real element is a *positive fact*, and has been known as such for the last twelve years. We sometimes read even to-day that ether is a "pure hypothesis"; this erroneous assertion comes not only from uninformed philosophers and "popular" writers, but even from certain "prudent and exact physicists." But there would be just as much reason to deny the existence of ponderable matter. As a matter of fact, there are metaphysicians who accomplish even this feat, and whose highest wisdom lies in denying or calling into question the existence of an external universe; according to them only one real entity exists — their own precious personality, or, to be more correct, their immortal soul. Several modern physiologists have embraced this ultra-idealist view, which is to be found in Descartes, Berkeley, Fichte, and others. Their "psycho-monism" affirms: "One thing only exists, and that is my own mind." This audacious spiritualism seems to us to rest on an erroneous inference from Kant's correct critical theory, that we can know the outer world only in the phenomenal aspect which is accessible to our human organs of thought—the brain and the organs of sense. If by those means we can attain only an imperfect and limited knowledge of the material world, that is no reason for denying its existence altogether. In my opinion, the existence of ether is as certain as that of ponderable matter—as certain as my own existence, as I reflect and write on it. As we assure ourselves of the existence of ponderable matter by its mass and weight, by chemical and mechanical experiments, so we prove that of ether by the experiences and experiments of optics and electricity.

Although, however, the existence of ether is now regarded as a positive fact by nearly all physicists, and although many effects of this remarkable substance are familiar to us through an extensive experi-

THE LAW OF SUBSTANCE

ence, especially in the way of optical and electrical experiments, yet we are still far from being clear and confident as to its real character. The views of the most eminent physicists, who have made a special study of it, are extremely divergent; they frequently contradict each other on the most important points. One is, therefore, free to choose among the contradictory hypotheses according to one's knowledge and judgment. I will put in the following eight theses the view which has approved itself to me after mature reflection on the subject, though I am no expert in this department:

I. Ether fills the whole of space, in so far as it is not occupied by ponderable matter, as a *continuous substance;* it fully occupies the space between the atoms of ponderable matter.

II. Ether has probably no chemical quality, and is not composed of atoms. If it be supposed that it consists of minute homogeneous atoms (for instance, indivisible etheric particles of a uniform size), it must be further supposed that there is something else between these atoms, either "empty space" or a third, completely unknown medium, a purely hypothetical "interether"; the question as to the nature of this brings us back to the original difficulty, and so on *in infinitum.*

III. As the idea of an empty space and an action at a distance is scarcely possible in the present condition of our knowledge (at least it does not help to a clear monistic view), I postulate for ether a special structure which is not atomistic, like that of ponderable matter, and which may provisionally be called (without further determination) *etheric* or *dynamic* structure.

IV. The consistency of ether is also peculiar, on

our hypothesis, and different from that of ponderable matter. It is neither gaseous, as some conceive, nor solid, as others suppose; the best idea of it can be formed by comparison with an extremely attenuated, elastic, and light jelly.

V. Ether may be called *imponderable* matter in the sense that we have no means of determining its weight experimentally. If it really has weight, as is very probable, it must be so slight as to be far below the capacity of our most delicate balance. Some physicists have attempted to determine its weight by the energy of the light-waves, and have discovered that it is some fifteen trillion times lighter than atmospheric air; on that hypothesis a sphere of ether of the size of our earth would weigh at least two hundred and fifty pounds(?).

VI. The etheric consistency may probably (in accordance with the pyknotic theory) pass into the gaseous state under certain conditions by progressive condensation, just as a gas may be converted into a fluid, and ultimately into a solid, by lowering its temperature.

VII. Consequently, these three conditions of matter may be arranged (and it is a point of great importance in our monistic cosmogony) in a genetic, continuous order. We may distinguish five stages in it: (1) the etheric, (2) the gaseous, (3) the fluid, (4) the viscous (in the living protoplasm), and (5) the solid state.

VIII Ether is boundless and immeasurable, like the space it occupies. It is in eternal motion; and this specific movement of ether (it is immaterial whether we conceive it as vibration, strain, condensation, etc.), in reciprocal action with mass-movement (or gravitation), is the ultimate cause of all phenomena.

THE LAW OF SUBSTANCE

"The great question of the nature of ether," as Hertz justly calls it, includes the question of its relation to ponderable matter; for these two forms of matter are not only always in the closest external contact, but also in eternal, dynamic, reciprocal action. We may divide the most general phenomena of nature, which are distinguished by physics as natural forces or "functions of matter," into two groups; the first of them may be regarded mainly (though not exclusively) as a function of ether, and the second a function of ponderable matter—as in the following scheme which I take from my *Monism*:

THE WORLD (NATURE, OR THE COSMOS)

ETHER—Imponderable.	MASS—Ponderable.
1. *Consistency:* Etheric (*i.e.*, neither gaseous, nor fluid nor solid).	1. *Consistency:* Not etheric (but gaseous, fluid, or solid).
2. *Structure:* Not atomistic, not made up of separate particles (atoms), but continuous.	2. *Structure:* Atomistic, made up of infinitesimal, distinct particles (atoms) discontinuous.
3. *Chief Functions:* Light, radiant heat, electricity, and magnetism.	3. *Chief Functions:* Gravity, inertia, molecular heat, and chemical affinity.

The two groups of functions of matter, which we have opposed in this table, may, to some extent, be regarded as the outcome of the first "division of labor" in the development of matter, the "primary ergonomy of matter." But this distinction must not be supposed to involve an absolute separation of the two antithetic groups; they always retain their connection, and are in constant reciprocal action. It is well known that the optical and electrical phenomena of ether are closely connected with mechanical and chemical changes in ponderable elements; the radiant heat of ether may be directly converted into the mechanical heat of the mass, gravitation is impossible unless the ether effects the mutual attraction of the separated atoms, because we cannot admit the idea of an *actio in distans*. In like manner, the conversion of one form of energy into another, as indicated in the law of the persistence of force, illustrates the constant reciprocity of the two chief types of substance, ether and mass.

The great law of nature, which, under the title of the "law of substance," we put at the head of all physical considerations, was conceived as the law of "the persistence of force" by Robert Meyer, who first formulated it, and Helmholtz, who continued the work. Another German scientist, Friedrich Mohr, of Bonn, had clearly outlined it in its main features ten years earlier (1837). The old idea of *force* was, after a time, differentiated by modern physics from that of *energy*, which was at first synonymous with it. Hence the law is now usually called the "law of the persistence of energy." However this finer distinction need not enter into the general consideration, to which I must confine myself here, and into the question of the great principle of the "persistence of substance." The interested reader will find a very clear treatment of the question in Tyndall's excellent paper on "The Fundamental Law of Nature," in his *Fragments of Science*. It fully explains the broad significance of this profound cosmic law, and points out its application to the main problems of very different branches of science. We shall confine our attention to the important fact that the "principle of

THE LAW OF SUBSTANCE

energy" and the correlative idea of the unity of natural forces, on the basis of a common origin, are now accepted by all competent physicists, and are regarded as the greatest advance of physics in the nineteenth century. We now know that heat, sound, light, chemical action, electricity, and magnetism are all modes of motion. We can, by a certain apparatus, convert any one of these forces into another, and prove by an accurate measurement that not a single particle of energy is lost in the process.

The sum-total of force or energy in the universe remains constant, no matter what changes take place around us; it is eternal and infinite, like the matter on which it is inseparably dependent. The whole drama of nature apparently consists in an alternation of movement and repose; yet the bodies at rest have an inalienable quantity of force, just as truly as those that are in motion. It is in this movement that the potential energy of the former is converted into the kinetic energy of the latter. "As the principle of the persistence of force takes into account repulsion as well as attraction, it affirms that the mechanical value of the potential energy and the kinetic energy in the material world is a constant quantity. To put it briefly, the force of the universe is divided into two parts, which may be mutually converted, according to a fixed relation of value. The diminution of the one involves the increase of the other; the total value remains unchanged in the universe." The potential energy and the actual, or kinetic, energy are being continually transformed from one condition to the other; but the infinite sum of force in the world at large never suffers the slightest curtailment.

Once modern physics had established the law of substance as far as the simpler relations of inorganic bodies are concerned, physiology took up the story, and proved its application to the entire province of the organic world. It showed that all the vital activities of the organism—without exception—are based on a constant "reciprocity of force" and a correlative change of material, or metabolism, just as much as the simplest processes in "lifeless" bodies. Not only the growth and the nutrition of plants and animals, but even their functions of sensation and movement, their sense-action and psychic life, depend on the conversion of potential into kinetic energy, and *vice versâ*. This supreme law dominates also those elaborate performances of the nervous system which we call, in the higher animals and man, "the action of the mind."

Our monistic view, that the great cosmic law applies throughout the whole of nature, is of the highest moment. For it not only involves, on its positive side, the essential unity of the cosmos and the causal connection of all phenomena that come within our cognizance, but it also, in a negative way, marks the highest intellectual progress, in that it definitely rules out the three central dogmas of metaphysics—God, freedom, and immortality. In assigning mechanical causes to phenomena everywhere, the law of substance comes into line with the universal law of causality.

CHAPTER XIII

THE EVOLUTION OF THE WORLD

The Notion of Creation—Miracles—Creation of the Whole Universe and of its Various Parts—Creation of Substance (Cosmological Creation)—Deism. One Creative Day—Creation of Separate Entities—Five Forms of Ontological Creationism—Theory of Evolution—I. Monistic Cosmogony—Beginning and End of the World—The Infinity and Eternity of the Universe—Space and Time—*Universum perpetuum mobile*—Entropy of the Universe—II. Monistic Geogeny—History of the Inorganic and Organic Worlds—III. Monistic Biogeny—Transformism and the Theory of Descent. Lamarck and Darwin—IV. Monistic Anthropogeny—Origin of Man

THE greatest, vastest, and most difficult of all cosmic problems is that of the origin and development of the world—the "question of creation," in a word. Even to the solution of this most difficult worldriddle the nineteenth century has contributed more than all its predecessors; in a certain sense, indeed, it has found the solution. We have at least attained to a clear view of the fact that all the partial questions of creation are indivisibly connected, that they represent one single, comprehensive "cosmic problem," and that the key to this problem is found in the one magic word—evolution. The great questions of the creation of man, the creation of the animals and plants, the creation of the earth and the sun, etc., are all parts of the general question, What is the origin of the whole world? Has it been *created* by supernatural power, or has it been *evolved* by a natural process? What are the causes and the manner of this evolution? If we succeed in finding the correct answer to one of these questions, we have, according to our monistic conception of the world, cast a brilliant light on the solution of them all, and on the entire cosmic problem.

The current opinion as to the origin of the world in earlier ages was almost a universal belief in creation. This belief has been expressed in thousands of interesting, more or less fabulous, legends, poems, cosmogonies, and myths. A few great philosophers were devoid of it, especially those remarkable free-thinkers of classical antiquity who first conceived the idea of natural evolution. All the creation-myths, on the contrary, were of a supernatural, miraculous, and transcendental character. Incompetent, as it was, to investigate for itself the nature of the world and its origin by natural causes, the undeveloped mind naturally had recourse to the idea of miracle. In most of these creation-myths *anthropism* was blended with the belief in the miraculous. The creator was supposed to have constructed the world on a definite plan, just as man accomplishes his artificial constructions; the conception of the creator was generally completely anthropomorphic, a palpable "anthropistic creationism." The "all-mighty maker of heaven and earth," as he is called in Genesis and the Catechism, is just as humanly conceived as the modern creator of Agassiz and Reinke, or the intelligent "engineer" of other recent biologists.

Entering more fully into the notion of creation, we can distinguish as two entirely different acts the production of the universe as a whole and the partial production of its various parts, in harmony with Spinoza's

THE EVOLUTION OF THE WORLD

idea of *substance* (the universe) and *accidents* (or *modes,* the individual phenomena of substance). This distinction is of great importance, because there are many eminent philosophers who admit the one and reject the other.

According to this creationist theory, then, God has "made the world out of nothing." It is supposed that God (a rational, but immaterial, being) existed by himself for an eternity before he resolved to create the world. Some supporters of the theory restrict God's creative function to one single act; they believe that this extramundane God (the rest of whose life is shrouded in mystery) created the substance of the world in a single moment, endowed it with the faculty of the most extensive evolution, and troubled no further about it This view may be found, for instance, in the English Deists in many forms It approaches very close to our monistic theory of evolution, only abandoning it in the one instant in which God accomplished the creation. Other creationists contend that God did not confine himself to the mere creation of matter, but that he continues to be operative as the "sustainer and ruler of the world" Different modifications of this belief are found, some approaching very close to *pantheism* and others to complete *theism*. All these and similar forms of belief in creation are incompatible with the law of the persistence of matter and force; that law knows nothing of a beginning

It is interesting to note that E. du Bois-Reymond has identified himself with this cosmological creationism in his latest speech (on "Neovitalism," 1894). "It is more consonant with the divine omnipotence," he says, "to assume that it created the whole material of the world in one creative act unthinkable ages ago in such wise that it should be endowed with inviolable laws to control the origin and the progress of living things—that, for instance, here on earth rudimentary organisms should arise from which, without further assistance, the whole of living nature could be evolved, from a primitive bacillus to the graceful palm-wood, from a primitive micrococcus to Solomon's lovely wives or to the brain of Newton. Thus we are content with *one* creative day, and we derive organic nature mechanically, without the aid of either old or new vitalism." Du Bois-Reymond here shows, as in the question of consciousness, the shallow and illogical character of his monistic thought.

According to another still prevalent theory, which may be called "ontological creationism," God not only created the world at large, but also its separate contents. In the Christian world the old Semitic legend of creation, taken from Genesis, is still very widely accepted; even among modern scientists it finds an adherent here and there. I have fully entered into the criticism of it in the first chapter of my *Natural History of Creation*. The following theories may be enumerated as the most interesting modifications of this ontological creationism:

I. *Dualistic creation.*—God restricted his interference to *two* creative acts. First he created the inorganic world, mere dead substance, to which alone the law of energy applies, working blindly and aimlessly in the mechanism of material things and the building of the mountains; then God attained intelligence and communicated it to the purposive intelligent forces which initiate and control organic evolution.*

* Reinke, *Die Welt als That* (1899).

THE EVOLUTION OF THE WORLD

II. *Trialistic creation.*—God made the world in *three* creative acts: (a) the creation of the heavens — the extra-terrestrial world, (b) the creation of the earth (as the centre of the world) and of its living inhabitants, and (c) the creation of man (in the image and likeness of God). This dogma is still widely prevalent among theologians and other "educated" people; it is taught as the truth in many of our schools.

III. *Heptameral creation*; a creation in seven days (*teste* Moses).—Although few educated people really believe in this Mosaic myth now, it is still firmly impressed on our children in the biblical lessons of their earliest years. The numerous attempts that have been made, especially in England, to harmonize it with the modern theory of evolution have entirely failed. It obtained some importance in science when Linné adopted it in the establishment of his system, and based his definition of organic species (which he considered to be unchangeable) on it: "There are as many different species of animals and plants as there were different forms created in the beginning by the Infinite." This dogma was pretty generally held until the time of Darwin (1859), although Lamarck had already proved its untenability in 1809.

IV. *Periodic creation.*—At the beginning of each period of the earth's history the whole population of animals and plants was created anew, and destroyed by a general catastrophe at its close; there were as many general creative acts as there are distinct geological periods (the catastrophic theory of Cuvier [1818] and Louis Agassiz [1858]). Palæontology, which seemed to support this theory in its more imperfect stage, has since completely refuted it.

V. *Individual creation.*—Every single man—and

THE RIDDLE OF THE UNIVERSE

every individual animal and plant—does not arise by a natural process of growth, but is created by the favor of God. This view of creation is still often met with in journals, especially in the "births" column. The special talents and features of our children are often gratefully acknowledged to be "gifts of God"; their hereditary defects fit into another theory.

The error of these creation-legends and the cognate belief in miracles must have been apparent to thoughtful minds at an early period; more than two thousand years ago we find that many attempts were made to replace them by a rational theory, and to explain the origin of the world by natural causes. In the front rank, once more, we must place the leaders of the Ionic school, with Democritus, Heraclitus, Empedocles, Aristotle, Lucretius, and other ancient philosophers. The first imperfect attempts which they made astonish us, in a measure, by the flashes of mental light in which they anticipate modern ideas. It must be remembered that classical antiquity had not that solid groundwork for scientific speculation which has been provided by the countless observations and experiments of modern scientists. During the Middle Ages—especially during the domination of the papacy—scientific work in this direction entirely ceased. The torture and the stake of the Inquisition insured that an unconditional belief in the Hebrew mythology should be the final answer to all the questions of creation. Even the phenomena which led directly to the observation of the *facts* of evolution—the embryology of the plant and the animal, and of man—remained unnoticed, or only excited the interest of an occasional keen observer; but their discoveries were ignored or forgotten. Moreover, the path to a correct knowledge

THE EVOLUTION OF THE WORLD

of natural development was barred by the dominant theory of preformation, the dogma which held that the characteristic form and structure of each animal and plant were already sketched in miniature in the germ (cf. p. 54).

The science which we now call the science of evolution (in the broadest sense) is, both in its general outline and in its separate parts, a child of the nineteenth century; it is one of its most momentous and most brilliant achievements. Almost unknown in the preceding century, this theory has now become the sure foundation of our whole world-system. I have treated it exhaustively in my *General Morphology* (1866), more popularly in my *Natural History of Creation* (1868), and in its special application to man in my *Anthropogeny* (1874). Here I shall restrict myself to a brief survey of the chief advances which the science has made in the course of the century. It falls into four sections, according to the nature of its object; that is, it deals with the natural origin of (1) the cosmos, (2) the earth, (3) terrestrial forms of life, and (4) man.

I.—MONISTIC COSMOGONY

The first attempt to explain the constitution and the mechanical origin of the world in a simple manner by "Newtonian laws"—that is, by mathematical and physical laws—was made by Immanuel Kant in the famous work of his youth (1755), *General History of the Earth and Theory of the Heavens*. Unfortunately, this distinguished and daring work remained almost unknown for ninety years; it was only disinterred in 1845 by Alexander Humboldt in the first volume of his *Cosmos*. In the mean time the great French mathematician, Pierre Laplace, had arrived independently at similar views to those of Kant, and he gave them a mathematical foundation in his *Exposition du Système du Monde* (1796). His chief work, the *Mécanique Céleste*, appeared a hundred years ago. The analogous features of the cosmogony of Kant and Laplace consist, as is well known, in a mechanical explanation of the movements of the planets, and the conclusion which is drawn therefrom, that all the cosmic bodies were formed originally by a condensation of rotating nebulous spheres. This "nebular hypothesis" has been much improved and supplemented since, but it is still the best of all the attempts to explain the origin of the world on monistic and mechanical lines. It has recently been strongly confirmed and enlarged by the theory that this cosmogonic process did not simply take place once, but is periodically repeated. While new cosmic bodies arise and develop out of rotating masses of nebula in some parts of the universe, in other parts old, extinct, frigid suns come into collision, and are once more reduced by the heat generated to the condition of nebulæ.

Nearly all the older and the more recent cosmogonies, including most of those which were inspired by Kant and Laplace, started from the popular idea that the world had had a beginning. Hence, according to a widespread version of the nebular hypothesis, "in the beginning" was made a vast nebula of infinitely attenuated and light material, and at a certain moment ("countless ages ago") a movement of rotation was imparted to this mass. Given this "first beginning" of the cosmogonic movement, it is easy, on mechanical principles, to deduce and mathematically establish the further phenomena of the formation of the cosmic bodies, the separation of the planets, and so forth. This first "origin of movement" is Du Bois-Reymond's second "world-enigma"; he regards it as transcendental. Many other scientists and philosophers are equally helpless before this difficulty; they resign themselves to the notion that we have here a primary " supernatural impetus " to the scheme of things, a " miracle."

In our opinion, this second "world-enigma" is solved by the recognition that movement is as innate and original a property of substance as is sensation. The proof of this monistic assumption is found, first, in the law of substance, and, secondly, in the discoveries which astronomy and physics have made in the latter half of the century. By the spectral analysis of Bunsen and Kirchhoff (1860) we have found, not only that the millions of bodies, which fill the infinity of space, are of the same material as our own sun and earth, but also that they are in various stages of evolution; we have obtained by its aid information as to the movements and distances of the stars, which the telescope would never have given us. Moreover, the telescope itself has been vastly improved, and has, in alliance with photography, made a host of scientific discoveries of which no one dreamed at the beginning of the century. In particular, a closer acquaintance with comets, meteorites, star-clusters, and nebulæ has helped us to realize the great significance of the smaller bodies which are found in millions in the space between the stars.

We now know that the *paths* of the millions of heavenly bodies are *changeable*, and to some extent irregular, whereas the planetary system was formerly thought to be constant, and the rotating spheres were described as pursuing their orbits in eternal regularity. Astrophysics owes much of its triumph to the immense progress of other branches of physics, of optics, and electricity, and especially of the theory of ether. And here, again, our supreme law of substance is found to be one of the most valuable achievements of modern science. We now know that it rules unconditionally in the most distant reaches of space, just as it does in our planetary system, in the most minute particle of the earth as well as in the smallest cell of our human frame. We are, moreover, justified in concluding, if we are not logically compelled to conclude, that the persistence of matter and force has held good throughout all time as it does to-day. Through all eternity the infinite universe has been, and is, subject to the law of substance.

From this great progress of astronomy and physics, which mutually elucidate and supplement each other, we draw a series of most important conclusions with regard to the constitution and evolution of the cosmos, and the persistence and transformation of substance. Let us put them briefly in the following theses:

I. The *extent* of the universe is infinite and unbounded; it is empty in no part, but everywhere filled with substance.

II. The *duration* of the world is equally infinite and unbounded; it has no beginning and no end; it is eternity.

III. Substance is everywhere and always in uninterrupted movement and transformation: nowhere is there perfect repose and rigidity; yet the infinite quantity of matter and of eternally changing force remains constant.

IV. This universal movement of substance in space

THE EVOLUTION OF THE WORLD

takes the form of an eternal cycle or of a periodical process of evolution.

V. The phases of this evolution consist in a periodic change of consistency, of which the first outcome is the primary division into mass and ether—the ergonomy of ponderable and imponderable matter.

VI. This division is effected by a progressive condensation of matter as the formation of countless infinitesimal " centres of condensation," in which the inherent primitive properties of substance—feeling and inclination—are the active causes.

VII. While minute and then larger bodies are being formed by this pyknotic process in one part of space, and the intermediate ether increases its strain, the opposite process—the destruction of cosmic bodies by collision—is taking place in another quarter.

VIII. The immense quantity of heat which is generated in this mechanical process of the collision of swiftly moving bodies represents the new kinetic energy which effects the movement of the resultant nebulæ and the construction of new rotating bodies. The eternal drama begins afresh. Even our mother earth, which was formed of part of the gyrating solar system millions of ages ago, will grow cold and lifeless after the lapse of further millions, and, gradually narrowing its orbit, will fall eventually into the sun.

It seems to me that these modern discoveries as to the periodic decay and re-birth of cosmic bodies, which we owe to the most recent advance of physics and astronomy, associated with the law of substance, are especially important in giving us a clear insight into the universal cosmic process of evolution. In their light our earth shrinks into the slender proportions of a "mote in the sunbeam," of which unnumbered millions chase each other through the vast depths of space. Our own "human nature," which exalted itself into an image of God in its anthropistic illusion, sinks to the level of a placental mammal, which has no more value for the universe at large than the ant, the fly of a summer's day, the microscopic infusorium, or the smallest bacillus. Humanity is but a transitory phase of the evolution of an eternal substance, a particular phenomenal form of matter and energy, the true proportion of which we soon perceive when we set it on the background of infinite space and eternal time.

Since Kant explained space and time to be merely "forms of perception"—space the form of external, time of internal, sensitivity—there has been a keen controversy, which still continues, over this important problem. A large section of modern metaphysicians have persuaded themselves that this "critical fact" possesses a great importance as the starting-point of "a purely idealist theory of knowledge," and that, consequently, the natural opinion of the ordinary healthy mind as to the *reality* of time and space is swept aside. This narrow and ultra-idealist conception of time and space has become a prolific source of error. It overlooks the fact that Kant only touched one side of the problem, the *subjective* side, in that theory, and recognized the equal validity of its *objective* side. "Time and space," he said, "have empirical reality, but transcendental ideality." Our modern monism is quite compatible with this thesis of Kant's, but not with the one-sided exaggeration of the subjective aspect of the problem; the latter leads logically to the absurd idealism that culminates in Berkeley's thesis, "Bodies are but ideas; their essence is in their perception." The thesis should be read thus: "Bodies are only ideas

THE EVOLUTION OF THE WORLD

for my personal consciousness; their existence is just as real as that of my organs of thought, the ganglionic cells in the gray bed of my brain, which receive the impress of bodies on my sense-organs and form those ideas by association of the impressions. It is just as easy to doubt or to deny the reality of my own consciousness as to doubt that of time and space. In the delirium of fever, in hallucinations, in dreams, and in double-consciousness, I take ideas to be true which are merely fancies. I mistake my own personality for another (*vide* p. 185); Descartes' famous *Cogito ergo sum* applies no longer. On the other hand, the reality of time and space is now fully established by that expansion of our philosophy which we owe to the law of substance and to our monistic cosmogony. When we have happily got rid of the untenable idea of "empty space," there remains as the infinite "space-filling"-medium matter, in its two forms of ether and mass. So also we find a "time-filling" event in the eternal movement, or genetic energy, which reveals itself in the uninterrupted evolution of substance, in the *perpetuum mobile* of the universe.

As a body which has been set in motion continues to move as long as no external agency interferes with it, the idea was conceived long ago of constructing an apparatus which should illustrate perpetual motion. The fact was overlooked that every movement meets with external impediments and gradually ceases, unless a new impetus is given to it from without and a new force is introduced to counteract the impediments. Thus, for instance, a pendulum would swing backward and forward for an eternity at the same speed if the resistance of the atmosphere and the friction at the point it hangs from did not gradually deprive it of

THE RIDDLE OF THE UNIVERSE

the mechanical kinetic energy of its motion and convert it into heat. We have to furnish it with fresh mechanical energy by a spring (or, as in the pendulum-clock, by the drag of a weight). Hence it is impossible to construct a machine that would produce, without external aid, a surplus of energy by which it could keep itself going. Every attempt to make such a *perpetuum mobile* must necessarily fail; the discovery of the law of substance showed, in addition, the theoretical impossibility of it.

The case is different, however, when we turn to the world at large, the boundless universe that is in eternal movement. The infinite matter, which fills it objectively, is what we call *space* in our subjective impression of it; *time* is our subjective conception of its eternal movement, which is, objectively, a periodic, cyclic evolution. These two "forms of perception" teach us the infinity and eternity of the universe. That is, moreover, equal to saying that the universe itself is a *perpetuum mobile*. This infinite and eternal "machine of the universe" sustains itself in eternal and uninterrupted movement, because every impediment is compensated by an "equivalence of energy," and the unlimited *sum* of kinetic and potential energy remains always the same. The law of the persistence of force proves also that the idea of a *perpetuum mobile* is just as applicable to, and as significant for, the cosmos as a whole as it is impossible for the isolated action of any part of it. Hence the theory of *entropy* is likewise untenable.

The able founder of the mechanical theory of heat (1850), Clausius, embodied the momentous contents of this important theory in two theses. The first runs: " The energy of the universe is constant "—that is one-

THE EVOLUTION OF THE WORLD

half of our law of substance, the principle of energy (*vide* p. 230). The second thesis is: " The energy of the universe tends towards a maximum." In my opinion this second assertion is just as erroneous as the first is true. In the theory of Clausius the entire energy of the universe is of two kinds, one of which (heat of the higher degree, mechanical, electrical, chemical energy, etc.) is partly convertible into work, but the other is not; the latter energy, already converted into heat and distributed in the cooler masses, is irrevocably lost as far as any further work is concerned. Clausius calls this unconsumed energy, which is no longer available for mechanical work, *entropy* (that is, force that is directed *inward*); it is continually increasing at the cost of the other half. As, therefore, the mechanical energy of the universe is daily being transformed into heat, and this cannot be reconverted into mechanical force, the sum of heat and energy in the universe must continually tend to be reduced and dissipated. All difference of temperature must ultimately disappear, and the completely latent heat must be equally distributed through one inert mass of motionless matter. All organic life and movement must cease when this maximum of *entropy* has been reached. That would be a real " end of the world."

If this theory of entropy were true, we should have a " beginning" corresponding to this assumed " end" of the world—a minimum of entropy, in which the differences in temperature of the various parts of the cosmos would be at a maximum. Both ideas are quite untenable in the light of our monistic and consistent theory of the eternal cosmogenetic process; both contradict the law of substance. There is neither beginning nor end of the world. The universe is infinite,

THE RIDDLE OF THE UNIVERSE

and eternally in motion; the conversion of kinetic into potential energy, and *vicissim*, goes on uninterruptedly; and the sum of this actual and potential energy remains constant. The second thesis of the mechanical theory of heat contradicts the first, and so must be rejected.

The representatives of the theory of entropy are quite correct as long as they confine themselves to distinct processes, in which, *under certain conditions*, the latent heat cannot be reconverted into work. Thus, for instance, in the steam-engine the heat can only be converted into mechanical work when it passes from a warmer body (steam) into a cooler (water); the process cannot be reversed. In the world at large, however, quite other conditions obtain—conditions which permit the reconversion of latent heat into mechanical work. For instance, in the collision of two heavenly bodies, which rush towards each other at inconceivable speed, enormous quantities of heat are liberated, while the pulverized masses are hurled and scattered about space. The eternal drama begins afresh—the rotating mass, the condensation of its parts, the formation of new meteorites, their combination into larger bodies, and so on.

II.—MONISTIC GEOGENY

The history of the earth, of which we are now going to make a brief survey, is only a minute section of the history of the cosmos. Like the latter, it has been the object of philosophic speculation and mythological fantasy for many thousand years. Its true scientific study, however, is much younger; it belongs, for the most part, to the nineteenth century. The fact that the earth is a planet revolving round the sun was deter-

THE EVOLUTION OF THE WORLD

mined by the system of Copernicus (1543); Galilei, Kepler, and other great astronomers, mathematically determined its distance from the sun, the laws of its motion, and so forth. Kant and Laplace indicated, in their cosmogony, the way in which the earth had been developed from the parent sun. But the later history of the earth, the formation of its crust, the origin of its seas and continents, its mountains and deserts, was rarely made the subject of serious scientific research in the eighteenth century, and in the first two decades of the nineteenth. As a rule, men were satisfied with unreliable conjectures or with the traditional story of creation; once more the Mosaic legend barred the way to an independent investigation.

In 1822 an important work appeared, which followed the same method in the scientific investigation of the history of the earth that had already proved the most fertile—the *ontological* method, or the principle of "actualism." It consists in a careful study and manipulation of *actual* phenomena with a view to the elucidation of the analogous historical processes of the past. The Society of Science at Göttingen had offered a prize in 1818 for "the most searching and comprehensive inquiry into the changes in the earth's crust which are historically demonstrable, and the application which may be made of a knowledge of them in the investigation of the terrestrial revolutions which lie beyond the range of history." This prize was obtained by Karl Hoff, of Gotha, for his distinguished work, *History of the Natural Changes in the Crust of the Earth in the Light of Tradition* (1822-34). Sir Charles Lyell then applied this *ontological* or *actualistic* method with great success to the whole province of geology; his *Principles of Geology* (1830) laid the firm foundation on which the fabric of the history of the earth was so happily erected. The important geogenetic research of Alexander Humboldt, Leopold Buch, Gustav Bischof, Edward Süss, and other geologists, were wholly based on the empirical foundation and the speculative principles of Karl Hoff and Charles Lyell. They cleared the way for purely rational science in the field of geology, they removed the obstacles that had been put in the path by mythological fancy and religious tradition, especially by the Bible and its legends. I have already discussed the merits of Lyell, and his relations with his friend Charles Darwin, in the sixteenth and seventeenth chapters of my *Natural History of Creation*, and must refer the reader to the standard works on geology for a further acquaintance with the history of the earth and the great progress which dynamical and historical geology have made during the century.

The first division of the history of the earth must be a separation of inorganic and organic geogeny, the latter begins with the first appearance of living things on our planet. The earlier section, the inorganic history of the earth, ran much the same course as that of the other planets of our system. They were all cast off as rings of nebula at the equator of the rotating solar mass, and gradually condensed into independent bodies. After cooling down a little, the glowing ball of the earth was formed out of the gaseous mass, and eventually, as the heat continued to radiate out into space, there was formed at its surface the thin solid crust on which we live. When the temperature at the surface had gone down to a certain point, the water descended upon it from the environing clouds of steam, and thus the first condition was secured for the rise of organic life. Many million years — certainly more

THE EVOLUTION OF THE WORLD

than a hundred — have passed since this important process of the formation of water took place, introducing the third section of cosmogony, which we call *biogeny*.

III.—MONISTIC BIOGENY

The third phase of the evolution of the world opens with the advent of organisms on our planet, and continues uninterrupted from that point until the present day. The great problems which this most interesting part of the earth's history suggests to us were still thought insoluble at the beginning of the nineteenth century, or, at least, so difficult hat their solution seemed to be extremely remote. Now, at the close of the century, we can affirm with legitimate pride that they have been substantially solved by modern biology and its theory of transformism; indeed, many of the phenomena of the organic world are now interpreted on physical principles as completely as the familiar physical phenomena of inorganic nature. The merit of making the first important step in this difficult path and of pointing out the way to the monistic solution of all the problems of biology must be accorded to the great French scientist, Jean Lamarck, it was in 1809, the year of the birth of Charles Darwin, that he published his famous *Philosophie Zoologique*. In this original work not only is a splendid effort made to interpret all the phenomena of organic life from a monistic and physical point of view, but the path is opened which alone leads to the solution of the greatest enigma of this branch of science—the problem of the natural origin of organic species. Lamarck, who had an equally extensive empirical acquaintance with zoology and botany, drew the first sketch of the theory of descent; he showed

THE RIDDLE OF THE UNIVERSE

that all the countless members of the plant and animal kingdoms have arisen by slow transformation from simple, common ancestral types, and that it is the gradual modification of forms by *adaptation*, in reciprocal action with *heredity*, which has brought about this secular metamorphosis.

I have fully appreciated the merit of Lamarck in the fifth chapter, and of Darwin in the sixth and seventh chapters, of the *Natural History of Creation*. Darwin, fifty years afterwards, not only gave a solid foundation to all the essential parts of the theory of descent, but he filled up the *lacunae* of Lamarck's work by his theory of selection. Darwin reaped abundantly the success that Lamarck had never seen, with all his merit. His epoch-making work on *The Origin of Species by Natural Selection* has transformed modern biology from its very foundations, in the course of the last forty years, and has raised it to a stage of development that yields to no other science in existence Darwin is *the Copernicus of the organic world*, as I said in 1868, and E. du Bois-Reymond repeated fifteen years afterwards.*

IV.—MONISTIC ANTHROPOGENY

The fourth and last phase of the world's history must be for us men that latest period of time which has witnessed the development of our own race. Lamarck (1809) had already recognized that this evolution is only rationally conceivable as the outcome of a natural process, by "descent from the apes," our next of kin among the mammals. Huxley then proved, in his famous essay on *The Place of Man in Nature*, that this

* Cf. *Monism*, by Ernst Haeckel.

THE EVOLUTION OF THE WORLD

momentous thesis is an inevitable consequence of the theory of descent, and is thoroughly established by the facts of anatomy, embryology, and palæontology. He considered this "question of all questions" to be substantially answered. Darwin followed with a brilliant discussion of the question under many aspects in his *Descent of Man* (1871). I had myself devoted a special chapter to this important problem of the science of evolution in my *General Morphology* (1866). In 1874 I published my *Anthropogeny*, which contains the first attempt to trace the descent of man through the entire chain of his ancestry right up to the earliest archigonous monera; the attempt was based equally on the three great "documents" of evolutionary science—anatomy, embryology, and palæontology. The progress we have made in anthropogenetic research during the last few years is described in the paper which I read on "Our Present Knowledge of the Origin of Man" at the International Congress of Zoologists at Cambridge in 1898.*

* *The Last Link*, translated by Dr. Gadow.

CHAPTER XIV

THE UNITY OF NATURE

The Monism of the Cosmos—Essential Unity of Organic and Inorganic Nature—Carbon-Theory—The Hypothesis of Abiogenesis—Mechanical and Purposive Causes—Mechanicism and Teleology in Kant's Works—Design in the Organic and Inorganic Worlds—Vitalism—Neovitalism—Dysteleology (the Moral of the Rudimentary Organs) — Absence of Design in, and Imperfection of, Nature—Telic Action in Organized Bodies—Its Absence in Ontogeny and Phylogeny—The Platonist "Ideas"—No Moral Order Discoverable in the History of the Organic World, of the Vertebrates, or of the Human Race—Prevision—Design and Chance

ONE of the first things to be proved by the law of substance is the basic fact that any natural force can be directly or indirectly converted into any other. Mechanical and chemical energy, sound and heat, light and electricity, are mutually convertible; they seem to be but different modes of one and the same fundamental force or *energy*. Thence follows the important thesis of the unity of all natural forces, or, as it may also be expressed, the "monism of energy." This fundamental principle is now generally recognized in the entire province of physics and chemistry, as far as it applies to inorganic substances.

It seems to be otherwise with the organic world and its wealth of color and form. It is, of course, obvious that a great part of the phenomena of life may be im-

THE UNITY OF NATURE

mediately traced to mechanical and chemical energy, and to the effects of electricity and light. For other vital processes, however, especially for psychic activity and consciousness, such an interpretation is vigorously contested. Yet the modern science of evolution has achieved the task of constructing a bridge between these two apparently irreconcilable provinces. We are now certain that all the phenomena of organic life are subject to the universal law of substance no less than the phenomena of the inorganic universe.

The unity of nature which necessarily follows, and the demolition of the earlier dualism, are certainly among the most valuable results of modern evolution Thirty-three years ago I made an exhaustive effort to establish this "monism of the cosmos" and the essential unity of organic and inorganic nature by a thorough, critical demonstration, and a comparison of the accordance of these two great divisions of nature with regard to matter, form, and force.* A short epitome of the result is given in the fifteenth chapter of my *Natural History of Creation*. The views I put forward are accepted by the majority of modern scientists, but an attempt has been made in many quarters lately to dispute them and to maintain the old antithesis of the two divisions of nature. The ablest of these is to be found in the recent *Welt als That* of the botanist Reinke. It defends *pure cosmological* dualism with admirable lucidity and consistency, and only goes to prove how utterly untenable the teleological system is that is connected therewith. According to the author, physical and chemical forces alone are at work in the entire field of inorganic nature, while in

---

* *General Morphology*, book 2, chap. v.

THE RIDDLE OF THE UNIVERSE

the organic world we find "intelligent forces," regulative or dominant forces. The law of substance is supposed to apply to the one, but not to the other. On the whole, it is a question of the old antithesis of a mechanical and a teleological system. But before we go more fully into it, let us glance briefly at two other theories, which seem to me to be of great importance in the decision of that controversy—the carbon-theory and the theory of spontaneous generation.

Physiological chemistry has, after countless analyses, established the following five facts during the last forty years:

I. No other elements are found in organic bodies than those of the inorganic world.

II. The combinations of elements which are peculiar to organisms, and which are responsible for their vital phenomena, are compound protoplasmic substances, of the group of albuminates.

III. Organic life itself is a chemico-physical process, based on the metabolism (or interchange of material) of these albuminates.

IV. The only element which is capable of building up these compound albuminates, in combination with other elements (oxygen, hydrogen, nitrogen, and sulphur), is carbon.

V. These protoplasmic compounds of carbon are distinguished from most other chemical combinations by their very intricate molecular structure, their instability, and their jelly-like consistency.

On the basis of these five fundamental facts the following "carbon-theory" was erected thirty-three years ago: "The peculiar chemico-physical properties of carbon—especially the fluidity and the facility of decomposition of the most elaborate albuminoid com-

THE UNITY OF NATURE

pounds of carbon—are the sole and the mechanical causes of the specific phenomena of movement, which distinguish organic from inorganic substances, and which are called life, in the usual sense of the word" (see *The Natural History of Creation*). Although this "carbon-theory" is warmly disputed in some quarters, no better monistic theory has yet appeared to replace it. We have now a much better and more thorough knowledge of the physiological relations of cell-life, and of the chemistry and physics of the living protoplasm, than we had thirty-three years ago, and so it is possible to make a more confident and effective defence of the carbon-theory.

The old idea of spontaneous generation is now taken in many different senses. It is owing to this indistinctness of the idea, and its application to so many different hypotheses, that the problem is one of the most contentious and confused of the science of the day. I restrict the idea of spontaneous generation—also called abiogenesis or archigony—to the first development of living protoplasm out of inorganic carbonates, and distinguish two phases in this "beginning of biogenesis": (1) *autogony*, or the rise of the simplest protoplasmic substances in a formative fluid, and (2) *plasmogony*, the differentiation of individual primitive organisms out of these protoplasmic compounds, in the form of *monera*. I have treated this important, though difficult, problem so exhaustively in the fifteenth chapter of my *Natural History of Creation* that I may content myself here with referring to it. There is also a very searching and severely scientific inquiry into it in my *General Morphology* (1866). Naegeli has also treated the hypothesis in quite the same sense in his mechanico-physiological theory of descent (1884), and

THE RIDDLE OF THE UNIVERSE

has represented it to be an indispensable thesis in any natural theory of evolution. I entirely agree with his assertion that "to reject abiogenesis is to admit a miracle."

The hypothesis of spontaneous generation and the allied carbon-theory are of great importance in deciding the long-standing conflict between the *teleological* (dualistic) and the *mechanical* (monistic) interpretation of phenomena. Since Darwin gave us the key to the monistic explanation of organization in his theory of selection forty years ago, it has become possible for us to trace the splendid variety of orderly tendencies of the organic world to mechanical, natural causes, just as we could formerly in the inorganic world alone. Hence the supernatural and telic forces, to which the scientist had had recourse, have been rendered superfluous. Modern metaphysics, however, continues to regard the latter as indispensable and the former as inadequate.

No philosopher has done more than Immanuel Kant in defining the profound distinction between efficient and final causes, with relation to the interpretation of the whole cosmos. In his well-known earlier work on *The General Natural History and Theory of the Heavens* he made a bold attempt "to treat the constitution and the mechanical origin of the entire fabric of the universe according to Newtonian laws." This "cosmological nebular theory" was based entirely on the mechanical phenomena of gravitation. It was expanded and mathematically established later on by Laplace. When the famous French astronomer was asked by Napoleon I. where God, the creator and sustainer of all things, came in in his system, he clearly and honestly replied: "Sire, I have managed with-

THE UNITY OF NATURE

out that hypothesis." That indicated the atheistic character which this mechanical cosmogony shares with all the other inorganic sciences. This is the more noteworthy because the theory of Kant and Laplace is now almost universally accepted; every attempt to supersede it has failed. When atheism is denounced as a grave reproach, as it so often is, it is well to remember that the reproach extends to the whole of modern science, in so far as it gives a purely mechanical interpretation of the inorganic world.

Mechanicism (in the Kantian sense) alone can give us a true explanation of natural phenomena, for it traces them to their real efficient causes, to blind and unconscious agencies, which are determined in their action only by the material constitution of the bodies we are investigating. Kant himself emphatically affirms that "there can be no science without this mechanicism of nature," and that the capacity of human reason to give a mechanical interpretation of phenomena is unlimited. But when he came subsequently to give an elucidation of the complex phenomena of organic nature in his *critique* of the teleological system, he declared that these mechanical causes were inadequate; that in this we must call *final causes* to our assistance. It is true, he said, that even here we must recognize the theoretical faculty of the mind to give a mechanical interpretation, but its actual competence to do so is restricted. He grants it this capacity to some extent; but for the majority of the vital processes (and especially for man's psychic activity) he thinks we are bound to postulate *final* causes. The remarkable §79 of the *critique* of judgment bears the characteristic heading: "On the Necessity for the Subordination of the Mechanical Principle to the Teleological in the Explanation of a Thing as a Natural End." It seemed to Kant so impossible to explain the orderly processes in the living organism without postulating supernatural final causes (that is, a purposive creative force) that he said: "It is quite certain that we cannot even satisfactorily understand, much less elucidate, the nature of an organism and its internal faculty on purely mechanical natural principles; it is so certain, indeed, that we may confidently say, ' It is absurd for a man to conceive the idea even that some day a Newton will arise who can explain the origin of a single blade of grass by natural laws which are uncontrolled by design '— such a hope is entirely forbidden us." Seventy years afterwards this impossible "Newton of the organic world" appeared in the person of Charles Darwin, and achieved the great task that Kant had deemed impracticable.

Since Newton (1682) formulated the law of gravitation, and Kant (1755) established "the constitution and mechanical origin of the entire fabric of the world on Newtonian laws," and Laplace (1796) provided a mathematical foundation for this law of cosmic mechanicism, the whole of the inorganic sciences have become purely *mechanical*, and at the same time purely *atheistic*. Astronomy, cosmogony, geology, meteorology, and inorganic physics and chemistry are now absolutely ruled by mechanical laws on a mathematical foundation The idea of "design" has wholly disappeared from this vast province of science. At the close of the nineteenth century, now that this monistic view has fought its way to general recognition, no scientist ever asks seriously of the "purpose" of any single phenomenon in the whole of this great field. Is any astronomer likely to inquire seriously to-day into the

THE UNITY OF NATURE

purpose of planetary motion, or a mineralogist to seek design in the structure of a crystal? Does the physicist investigate the purpose of electric force, or the chemist that of atomic weight? We may confidently answer in the negative—certainly not, in the sense that God, or a purposive natural force, had at some time created these fundamental laws of the mechanism of the universe with a definite design, and causes them to work daily in accordance with his rational will. The anthropomorphic notion of a deliberate architect and ruler of the world has gone forever from this field; the "eternal, iron laws of nature" have taken his place.

But the idea of design has a very great significance and application in the *organic* world. We do undeniably perceive a purpose in the structure and in the life of an organism. The plant and the animal seem to be controlled by a definite design in the combination of their several parts, just as clearly as we see in the machines which man invents and constructs; as long as life continues the functions of the several organs are directed to definite ends, just as is the operation of the various parts of a machine. Hence it was quite natural that the older naïve study of nature, in explaining the origin and activity of the living being, should postulate a creator who had "arranged all things with wisdom and understanding," and had constructed each plant and animal according to the special purpose of its life. The conception of this "almighty creator of heaven and earth" was usually quite anthropomorphic; he created "everything after its kind." As long as the creator seemed to man to be of human shape, to think with his brain, see with his eyes, and fashion with his hands, it was possible to form a definite picture of this "divine engineer" and his artistic work in the great workshop of creation. This was not so easy when the idea of God became refined, and man saw in his "invisible God" a creator without organs—a gaseous being. Still more unintelligible did these anthropomorphic ideas become when physiology substituted for the conscious, divine architect an unconscious, creative "vital force"—a mysterious, purposive, natural force, which differed from the familiar forces of physics and chemistry, and only took these in part, during life, into its service. This vitalism prevailed until about the middle of the nineteenth century. Johannes Müller, the great Berlin physiologist, was the first to menace it with a destructive dose of facts. It is true that the distinguished biologist had himself (like all others in the first half of the century) been educated in a belief in this vital force, and deemed it indispensable for an elucidation of the ultimate sources of life; nevertheless, in his classical and still unrivalled *Manual of Physiology* (1833) he gave a demonstrative proof that there is really nothing to be said for this vital force. Müller himself, in a long series of remarkable observations and experiments, showed that most of the vital processes in the human organism (and in the other animals) take place according to physical and chemical laws, and that many of them are capable of mathematical determination. That was no less true of the animal functions of the muscles and nerves, and of both the higher and the lower sense-organs, than of the vegetal functions of digestion, assimilation, and circulation. Only two branches of the life of the organism, mental action and reproduction, retained any element of mystery, and seemed inexplicable without assuming a vital force.

THE UNITY OF NATURE

But immediately after Müller's death such important discoveries and advances were made in these two branches that the uneasy "phantom of vital force" was driven from its last refuge. By a very remarkable coincidence Johannes Müller died in the year 1858, which saw the publication of Darwin's first communication concerning his famous theory. The theory of selection solved the great problem that had mastered Müller—the question of the origin of orderly arrangements from purely mechanical causes.

Darwin, as we have often said, had a twofold immortal merit in the field of philosophy—firstly, the reform of Lamarck's theory of descent, and its establishment on the mass of facts accumulated in the course of the half-century; secondly, the conception of the theory of selection, which first revealed to us the true causes of the gradual formation of species. Darwin was the first to point out that the "struggle for life" is the unconscious regulator which controls the reciprocal action of heredity and adaptation in the gradual transformation of species; it is the great "selective divinity" which, by a purely "natural choice," without preconceived design, creates new forms, just as selective man creates new types by an "artificial choice" with a definite design. That gave us the solution of the great philosophic problem: "How can purposive contrivances be produced by purely mechanical processes without design?" Kant held the problem to be insoluble, although Empedocles had pointed out the direction of the solution two thousand years before. His principle of "teleological mechanism" has become more and more accepted of late years, and has furnished a mechanical explanation even of the finest and most recondite processes of organic life by "the func-

THE RIDDLE OF THE UNIVERSE

tional self-production of the purposive structure." Thus have we got rid of the transcendental "design" of the teleological philosophy of the schools, which was the greatest obstacle to the growth of a rational and monistic conception of nature.

Very recently, however, this ancient phantom of a mystic vital force, which seemed to be effectually banished, has put in a fresh appearance; a number of distinguished biologists have attempted to reintroduce it under another name. The clearest presentation of it is to be found in the *Welt als That*, of the Kiel botanist, J. Reinke. He takes upon himself the defence of the notion of miracle, of theism, of the Mosaic story of creation, and of the constancy of species; he calls "vital forces," in opposition to physical forces, the directive or dominant forces. Other neovitalists prefer, in the good old anthropomorphic style, a "supreme" engineer, who has endowed organic substance with a purposive structure, directed to the realization of a definite plan. These curious teleological hypotheses, and the objections to Darwinism which generally accompany them, do not call for serious scientific refutation to-day.

Thirty-three years ago I gave the title of "dysteleology" to the science of those extremely interesting and significant biological facts, which, in the most striking fashion, give a direct contradiction to the teleological idea "of the purposive arrangement of the living organism."[*] This "science of rudimentary, abortive, arrested, distorted, atrophied, and cataplastic individuals" is based on an immense quantity of remarkable phenomena, which were long familiar to zoologists

[*] Cf. *General Morphology*, vol. ii., and *The Natural History of Creation.*

THE UNITY OF NATURE

and botanists, but were not properly interpreted, and their great philosophic significance appreciated, until Darwin.

All the higher animals and plants, or, in general, all organisms which are not entirely simple in structure, but are made up of a number of organs in orderly co-operation, are found, on close examination, to possess a number of useless or inoperative members, sometimes, indeed, hurtful and dangerous. In the flowers of most plants we find, besides the actual sex-leaves that effect reproduction, a number of other leaf-organs which have no use or meaning (arrested or "miscarried" pistils, fruit, corona, and calix-leaves, etc). In the two large and variegated classes of flying animals, birds and insects, there are, besides the forms which make constant use of their wings, a number of species which have undeveloped wings and cannot fly. In nearly every class of the higher animals which have eyes there are certain types that live in the dark; they have eyes, as a rule, but undeveloped and useless for vision. In our own human organism we have similar useless rudimentary structures in the muscles of the ear, in the eye-lid, in the nipple and milk-gland of the male, and in other parts of the body; indeed, the vermiform appendix of our cæcum is not only useless, but extremely dangerous, and inflammation of it is responsible for a number of deaths every year.

Neither the old mystic vitalism nor the new, equally irrational, neovitalism can give any explanation of these and many other purposeless contrivances in the structure of the plant and the animal; but they are very simple in the light of the theory of descent. It shows that these rudimentary organs are atrophied, owing to disuse. Just as our muscles, nerves, and organs of sense are strengthened by exercise and frequent use, so, on the other hand, they are liable to degenerate more or less by disuse or suspended exercise. But, although the development of the organs is promoted by exercise and adaptation, they by no means disappear without leaving a trace after neglect; the force of heredity retains them for many generations, and only permits their gradual disappearance after the lapse of a considerable time The blind "struggle for existence between the organs" determines their historical disappearance, just as it effected their first origin and development. There is no internal "purpose" whatever in the drama.

The life of the animal and the plant bears the same universal character of incompleteness as the life of man. This is directly attributable to the circumstance that nature—organic as well as inorganic—is in a perennial state of evolution, change, and transformation. This evolution seems on the whole—at least as far as we can survey the development of organic life on our planet—to be a progressive improvement, an historical advance from the simple to the complex, the lower to the higher, the imperfect to the perfect. I have proved in my *General Morphology* that this historical progress —or gradual perfecting (*teleosis*)—is the inevitable result of selection, and not the outcome of a preconceived design. That is clear from the fact that no organism is perfect; even if it does perfectly adapt itself to its environment at a given moment, this condition would not last very long; the conditions of existence of the environment are themselves subject to perpetual change and they thus necessitate a continuous adaptation on the part of the organism.

Under the title of *Design in the Living Organism,*

THE UNITY OF NATURE

the famous embryologist, Karl Ernst Baer, published a work in 1876 which, together with the article on Darwinism which accompanied it, proved very acceptable to our opponents, and is still much quoted in opposition to evolution. It was a revival of the old teleological system under a new name, and we must devote a line of criticism to it We must premise that, though Baer was a scientist of the highest order, his original monistic views were gradually marred by a tinge of mysticism with the advance of age, and he eventually became a thorough dualist. In his profound work on "the evolution of animals" (1828), which he himself entitled *Observation and Experiment,* these two methods of investigation are equally applied. By careful observation of the various phenomena of the development of the animal ovum Baer succeeded in giving the first consistent presentation of the remarkable changes which take place in the growth of the vertebrate from a simple egg-cell. At the same time he endeavored, by far-seeing comparison and keen reflection, to learn the causes of the transformation, and to reduce them to general constructive laws. He expressed the general result of his research in the following thesis: " The evolution of the individual is the story of the growth of individuality in every respect." He meant that " the one great thought that controls all the different aspects of animal evolution is the same that gathered the scattered fragments of space into spheres and linked them into solar systems. This thought is no other than life itself, and the words and syllables in which it finds utterance are the varied forms of living things."

Baer, however, did not attain to a deeper knowledge of this great genetic truth and a clearer insight into the real efficient causes of organic evolution, because his attention was exclusively given to one half of evolutionary science, the science of the evolution of the individual, embryology, or, in a wider sense, *ontogeny*. The other half, the science of the evolution of species, *phylogeny*, was not yet in existence, although Lamarck had already pointed out the way to it in 1809. When it was established by Darwin in 1859, the aged Baer was no longer in a position to appreciate it; the fruitless struggle which he led against the theory of selection clearly proved that he understood neither its real meaning nor its philosophic importance. Teleological and, subsequently, theological speculations had incapacitated the ageing scientist from appreciating this greatest reform of biology. The teleological observations which he published against it in his *Species and Studies* in his eighty-fouth year are mere repetitions of errors which the teleology of the dualists has opposed to the mechanical or monistic system for more than two thousand years. The "telic idea" which, according to Baer, controls the entire evolution of the animal from the ovum, is only another expression for the eternal "idea" of Plato and the *entelecheia* of his pupil Aristotle.

Our modern biogeny gives a purely physiological explanation of the facts of embryology, in assigning the functions of heredity and adaptation as their causes. The great biogenetic law, which Baer failed to appreciate, reveals the intimate causal connection between the *ontogenesis* of the individual and the *phylogenesis* of its ancestors; the former seems to be a recapitulation of the latter. Nowhere, however, in the evolution of animals and plants do we find any trace of design, but merely the inevitable outcome of the struggle for existence, the blind controller, instead of the provident

THE UNITY OF NATURE

God, that effects the changes of organic forms by a mutual action of the laws of heredity and adaptation. And there is no more trace of "design" in the embryology of the individual plant, animal, or man. This *ontogeny* is but a brief epitome of *phylogeny*, an abbreviated and condensed recapitulation of it, determined by the physiological laws of heredity.

Baer ended the preface to his classical *Evolution of Animals* (1828) with these words: " The palm will be awarded to the fortunate scientist who succeeds in reducing the constructive forces of the animal body to the general forces or life-processes of the entire world. The tree has not yet been planted which is to make his cradle." The great embryologist erred once more. That very year, 1828, witnessed the arrival of Charles Darwin at Cambridge University (for the purpose of studying theology!) — the "fortunate scientist" who richly earned the palm thirty years afterwards by his theory of selection.

In the philosophy of history—that is, in the general reflections which historians make on the destinies of nations and the complicated course of political evolution—there still prevails the notion of a "moral order of the universe." Historians seek in the vivid drama of history a leading design, an ideal purpose, which has ordained one or other race or state to a special triumph, and to dominion over the others. This teleological view of history has recently become more strongly contrasted with our monistic view in proportion as monism has proved to be the only possible interpretation of inorganic nature. Throughout the whole of astronomy, geology, physics, and chemistry there is no question to-day of a "moral order," or a personal God, whose "hand hath disposed all things in wisdom and understanding." And the same must be said of the entire field of biology, the whole constitution and history of organic nature, if we set aside the question of man for the moment. Darwin has not only proved by his theory of selection that the orderly processes in the life and structure of animals and plants have arisen by mechanical laws without any preconceived design, but he has shown us in the "struggle for life" the powerful natural force which has exerted supreme control over the entire course of organic evolution for millions of years. It may be said that the struggle for life is the "survival of the fittest" or the "victory of the best"; that is only correct when we regard the strongest as the best (in a moral sense). Moreover, the whole history of the organic world goes to prove that, besides the predominant advance towards perfection, there are at all times cases of retrogression to lower stages. Even Baer's notion of "design" has no moral feature whatever.

Do we find a different state of things in the history of peoples, which man, in his anthropocentric presumption, loves to call "the history of the world"? Do we find in every phase of it a lofty moral principle or a wise ruler, guiding the destinies of nations? There can be but one answer in the present advanced stage of natural and human history: No. The fate of those branches of the human family, those nations and races which have struggled for existence and progress for thousands of years, is determined by the same "eternal laws of iron" as the history of the whole organic world which has peopled the earth for millions of years.

Geologists distinguish three great epochs in the organic history of the earth, as far as we can read it in the monuments of the science of fossils—the primary,

THE UNITY OF NATURE

secondary, and tertiary epochs. According to a recent calculation, the first occupied at least thirty-four million, the second eleven million, and the third three million years. The history of the family of vertebrates, from which our own race has sprung, unfolds clearly before our eyes during this long period. Three different stages in the evolution of the vertebrate correspond to the three epochs; the *fishes* characterized the primary (palæozoic) age, the *reptiles* the secondary (mesozoic), and the *mammals* the tertiary (cænozoic). Of the three groups the fishes rank lowest in organization, the reptiles come next, and the mammals take the highest place. We find, on nearer examination of the history of the three classes, that their various orders and families also advanced progressively during the three epochs towards a higher stage of perfection. May we consider this progressive development as the outcome of a conscious design or a moral order of the universe? Certainly not. The theory of selection teaches us that this organic progress, like the earlier organic differentiation, is an inevitable consequence of the struggle for existence. Thousands of beautiful and remarkable species of animals and plants have perished during those forty-eight million years, to give place to stronger competitors, and the victors in this struggle for life were not always the noblest or most perfect forms in a moral sense.

It has been just the same with the history of humanity. The splendid civilization of classical antiquity perished because Christianity, with its faith in a loving God and its hope of a better life beyond the grave, gave a fresh, strong impetus to the soaring human mind. The Papal Church quickly degenerated into a pitiful caricature of real Christianity, and ruthlessly scattered

THE RIDDLE OF THE UNIVERSE

the treasures of knowledge which the Hellenic philosophy had gathered; it gained the dominion of the world through the ignorance of the credulous masses. In time the Reformation broke the chains of this mental slavery, and assisted reason to secure its right once more. But in the new, as in the older, period the great struggle for existence went on in its eternal fluctuation, with no trace of a moral order.

And it is just as impossible for the impartial and critical observer to detect a " wise providence" in the fate of individual human beings as a moral order in the history of peoples. Both are determined with iron necessity by a mechanical causality which connects every single phenomenon with one or more antecedent causes. Even the ancient Greeks recognized *ananke*, the blind *heimarmene*, the fate "that rules gods and men," as the supreme principle of the universe. Christianity replaced it by a conscious Providence, which is not blind, but sees, and which governs the world in patriarchal fashion. The anthropomorphic character of this notion, generally closely connected with belief in a personal God, is quite obvious. Belief in a " loving Father," who unceasingly guides the destinies of one billion five hundred million men on our planet, and is attentive at all times to their millions of contradictory prayers and pious wishes, is absolutely impossible; that is at once perceived on laying aside the colored spectacles of "faith" and reflecting rationally on the subject.

As a rule, this belief in Providence and the tutelage of a "loving Father" is more intense in the modern civilized man—just as in the uncultured savage—when some good fortune has fallen him: an escape from peril of life, recovery from a severe illness, the winning

THE UNITY OF NATURE

of the first prize in a lottery, the birth of a long-delayed child, and so forth. When, on the other hand, a misfortune is met with, or an ardent wish is not fulfilled, "Providence" is forgotten. The wise ruler of the world slumbered—or refused his blessing.

In the extraordinary development of commerce of the nineteenth century the number of catastrophes and accidents has necessarily increased beyond all imagination; of that the journal is a daily witness. Thousands are killed every year by shipwreck, railway accidents, mine accidents, etc. Thousands slay each other every year in war, and the preparation for this wholesale massacre absorbs much the greater part of the revenue in the highest civilized nations, the chief professors of "Christian charity." And among these hundreds of thousands of annual victims of modern civilization strong, industrious, courageous workers predominate. Yet the talk of a "moral order" goes on.

Since impartial study of the evolution of the world teaches us that there is no definite aim and no special purpose to be traced in it, there seems to be no alternative but to leave everything to "blind chance." This reproach has been made to the transformism of Lamarck and Darwin, as it had been to the previous systems of Kant and Laplace; there are a number of dualist philosophers who lay great stress on it. It is, therefore, worth while to make a brief remark upon it.

One group of philosophers affirms, in accordance with its teleological conception, that the whole cosmos is an orderly system, in which every phenomenon has its aim and purpose; there is no such thing as chance. The other group, holding a mechanical theory, expresses itself thus: The development of the universe is a monistic mechanical process, in which we discover no aim or purpose whatever; what we call design in the organic world is a special result of biological agencies; neither in the evolution of the heavenly bodies nor in that of the crust of our earth do we find any trace of a controlling purpose—all is the result of chance. Each party is right—according to its definition of chance. The general law of causality, taken in conjunction with the law of substance, teaches us that every phenomenon has a mechanical cause; in this sense there is no such thing as chance. Yet it is not only lawful, but necessary, to retain the term for the purpose of expressing the simultaneous occurrence of two phenomena, which are not causally related to each other, but of which each has its own mechanical cause, independent of that of the other. Everybody knows that chance, in its monistic sense, plays an important part in the life of man and in the universe at large. That, however, does not prevent us from recognizing in each "chance" event, as we do in the evolution of the entire cosmos, the universal sovereignty of nature's supreme law, *the law of substance.*

CHAPTER XV

GOD AND THE WORLD

The Idea of God in General—Antithesis of God and the World; the Supernatural and Nature—Theism and Pantheism—Chief Forms of Theism—Polytheism—Tritheism—Ampitheism—Monotheism—Religious Statistics—Naturalistic Monotheism—Solarism—Anthropistic Monotheism—The Three Great Mediterranean Religions—Mosaism—Christianity—The Cult of the Madonna and the Saints—Papal Polytheism—Islam—Mixotheism—Nature of Theism—An Extramundane and Anthropomorphic God; a Gaseous Vertebrate—Pantheism—Intramundane God (Nature)—The Hylozoism of the Ionic Monists (Anaximander)—Conflict of Pantheism and Christianity—Spinoza—Modern Monism—Atheism

FOR thousands of years humanity has placed the last and supreme basis of all phenomena in an efficient cause, to which it gives the title of God (*deus, theos*). Like all general ideas, this notion of God has undergone a series of remarkable modifications and transformations in the course of the evolution of reason. Indeed, it may be said that no other idea has had so many metamorphoses; for no other belief affects in so high a degree the chief objects of the mind and of rational science, as well as the deepest interests of the emotion and poetic fancy of the believer.

A comparative criticism of the many different forms of the idea of God would be extremely interesting and instructive; but we have not space for it in the present

THE RIDDLE OF THE UNIVERSE

work. We must be content with a passing glance at the most important forms of the belief and their relation to the modern thought that has been evoked by a sound study of nature. For further information on this interesting question the reader would do well to consult the distinguished work of Adalbert Svoboda, *Forms of Faith* (1897).

When we pass over the finer shades and the variegated clothing of the God-idea and confine our attention to its chief element, we can distribute all the different presentations of it in two groups—the *theistic* and *pantheistic* group. The latter is closely connected with the monistic, or rational, view of things, and the former is associated with dualism and mysticism.

I.—THEISM

In this view God is distinct from, and opposed to, the world as its creator, sustainer, and ruler. He is always conceived in a more or less human form, as an organism which thinks and acts like a man—only on a much higher scale. This anthropomorphic God, polyphyletically evolved by the different races, assumes an infinity of shapes in their imagination, from fetichism to the refined monotheistic religions of the present day. The chief forms of theism are polytheism, triplotheism, amphitheism, and monotheism.

The polytheist peoples the world with a variety of gods and goddesses, which enter into its machinery more or less independently. *Fetichism* sees such subordinate deities in the lifeless body of nature, in rocks, in water, in the air, in human productions of every kind (pictures, statues, etc.). *Demonism* sees gods in living organisms of every species—trees, animals, and

GOD AND THE WORLD

men. This kind of polytheism is found in innumerable forms even in the lowest tribes. It reaches the highest stage in Hellenic polytheism, in the myths of ancient Greece, which still furnish the finest images to the modern poet and artist. At a much lower stage we have Catholic polytheism, in which innumerable " saints " (many of them of very equivocal repute) are venerated as subordinate divinities, and prayed to to exert their mediation with the supreme divinity.

The dogma of the " Trinity," which still comprises three of the chief articles of faith in the creed of Christian peoples, culminates in the notion that the *one* God of Christianity is really made up of *three* different persons: (1) God the Father, the omnipotent creator of heaven and earth (this untenable myth was refuted long ago by scientific cosmogony, astronomy, and geology); (2) Jesus Christ; and (3) the Holy Ghost, a mystical being, over whose incomprehensible relation to the Father and the Son millions of Christian theologians have racked their brains in vain for the last nineteen hundred years. The Gospels, which are the only clear sources of this *triplotheism*, are very obscure as to the relation of these three persons to each other, and do not give a satisfactory answer to the question of their unity. On the other hand, it must be carefully noted what confusion this obscure and mystic dogma of the Trinity must necessarily cause in the minds of our children even in the earlier years of instruction. One morning they learn (in their religious instruction) that three times one are one, and the very next hour they are told in their arithmetic class that three times one are three. I remember well the reflection that this confusion led me to in my early school-days.

For the rest, the " Trinity " is not an original ele-

THE RIDDLE OF THE UNIVERSE

ment in Christianity; like most of the other Christian dogmas, it has been borrowed from earlier religions. Out of the sun-worship of the Chaldean magi was evolved the Trinity of Ilu, the mysterious source of the world; its three manifestations were Anu, primeval chaos, Bel, the architect of the world; and Aa, the heavenly light, the all-enlightening wisdom. In the Brahmanic religion the Trimurti is also conceived as a "divine unity" made up of three persons—Brahma (the creator), Vishnu (the sustainer), and Shiva (the destroyer). It would seem that in this and other ideas of a Trinity the "sacred number, three," as such—as a "symbolical number"—has counted for something. The three first Christian virtues—Faith, Hope, and Charity—form a similar *triad*.

According to the *amphitheists*, the world is ruled by *two* different gods, a good and an evil principle, God and the Devil. They are engaged in a perpetual struggle, like rival emperors, or pope and anti-pope. The condition of the world is the result of this conflict The loving God, or good principle, is the source of all that is good and beautiful, of joy and of peace. The world would be perfect if His work were not continually thwarted by the evil principle, the Devil; this being is the cause of all that is bad and hateful, of contradiction and of pain.

Amphitheism is undoubtedly the most rational of all forms of belief in God, and the one which is least incompatible with a scientific view of the world. Hence we find it elaborated in many ancient peoples thousands of years before Christ. In ancient India Vishnu, the preserver, struggles with Shiva, the destroyer. In ancient Egypt the good Osiris is opposed by the wicked Typhon. The early Hebrews had a similar dualism

GOD AND THE WORLD

of Aschera (or Keturah), the fertile mother-earth, and Elion (Moloch or Sethos), the stern heavenly father. In the Zend religion of the ancient Persians, founded by Zoroaster two thousand years before Christ, there is a perpetual struggle between Ormuzd, the good god of light, and Ahriman, the wicked god of darkness.

In Christian mythology the Devil is scarcely less conspicuous as the adversary of the good deity, the tempter and seducer, the prince of hell, and lord of darkness. A personal devil was still an important element in the belief of most Christians at the beginning of the nineteenth century. Towards the middle of the century he was gradually eliminated by being progressively explained away, or he was restricted to the subordinate *rôle* he plays as Mephistopheles in Goethe's great drama. To-day the majority of educated people look upon "belief in a personal devil" as a mediæval superstition, while "belief in God" (that is, the personal, good, and loving God) is retained as an indispensable element of religion. Yet the one belief is just as much (or as little) justified as the other. In any case, the much-lamented "imperfection of our earthly life," the "struggle for existence," and all that pertains to it, are explained much more simply and naturally by this struggle of a good and an evil god than by any other form of theism.

The dogma of the unity of God may in some respects be regarded as the simplest and most natural type of theism; it is popularly supposed to be the most widely accepted element of religion, and to predominate in the ecclesiastical systems of civilized countries. In reality, that is not the case, because this alleged "monotheism" usually turns out on closer inquiry to be one of the other forms of theism we have examined, a number of subordinate deities being generally introduced besides the supreme one. Most of the religions which took a purely monotheistic standpoint have become more or less polytheistic in the course of time. Modern statistics assure us that of the one billion five hundred million men who people the earth the great majority are monotheists; of these, *nominally*, about six hundred millions are Brahma-Buddhists, five hundred millions are called Christians, two hundred millions are heathens (of various types), one hundred and eighty millions are Mohammedans, ten millions are Jews, and ten millions have no religion at all. However, the vast majority of these nominal monotheists have very confused ideas about the deity, or believe in a number of gods and goddesses besides the chief god —angels, devils, etc.

The different forms which monotheism has assumed in the course of its polyphyletic development may be distributed in two groups—those of *naturalistic* and *anthropistic* monotheism. Naturalistic monotheism finds the embodiment of the deity in some lofty and dominating natural phenomenon. The sun, the deity of light and warmth, on whose influence all organic life insensibly and directly depends, was taken to be such a phenomenon many thousand years ago. Sun-worship (solarism, or heliotheism) seems to the modern scientist to be the best of all forms of theism, and the one which may be most easily reconciled with modern monism. For modern astrophysics and geogeny have taught us that the earth is a fragment detached from the sun, and that it will eventually return to the bosom of its parent. Modern physiology teaches us that the first source of organic life on the earth is the formation of protoplasm, and that this synthesis of simple inor-

GOD AND THE WORLD

ganic substances, water, carbonic acid, and ammonia, only takes place under the influence of sunlight. On the primary evolution of he plasmodomous plants followed, secondarily, that of the plasmophagous animals, which directly or indirectly depend on them for nourishment; and the origin of the human race itself is only a later stage in the development of the animal kingdom Indeed, the whole of our bodily and mental life depends, in the last resort, like all other organic life, on the light and heat rays of the sun. Hence in the light of pure reason, sun-worship, as a form of naturalistic monotheism, seems to have a much better foundation than the anthropistic worship of Christians and of other monotheists who conceive their god in human form. As a matter of fact, the sun-worshippers attained, thousands of years ago, a higher intellectual and moral standard than most of the other theists. When I was in Bombay, in 1881, I watched with the greatest sympathy the elevating rites of the pious Parsees, who, standing on the sea-shore, or kneeling on their prayer-rugs, offered their devotion to the sun at its rise and setting.*

Moon-worship (lunarism and selenotheism) is of much less importance than sun-worship. There are a few uncivilized races that have adored the moon as their only deity, but it has generally been associated with a worship of the stars and the sun.

The humanization of God, or the idea that the "Supreme Being" feels, thinks, and acts like man (though in a higher degree), has played a most important part, as *anthropomorphic monotheism*, in the history of civilization. The most prominent in this respect are the

* *Vide A Visit to Ceylon*, E. Haeckel, translated by C. Bell.

three great religions of the Mediterranean peoples —the old Mosaic religion, the intermediate Christian religion, and the younger Mohammedanism. These three great Mediterranean religions, all three arising on the east coast of the most interesting of all seas, and originating in an imaginative enthusiast of the Semitic race, are intimately connected, not only by this external circumstance of an analogous origin, but by many common features of their internal contents. Just as Christianity borrowed a good deal of its mythology directly from ancient Judaism, so Islam has inherited much from both its predecessors. All the three were originally monotheistic; all three were subsequently overlaid with a great variety of polytheistic features, in proportion as they extended, first along the coast of the Mediterranean with its heterogeneous population, and eventually into every part of the world.

The Hebrew monotheism, as it was founded by Moses (about 1600 B.C.), is usually regarded as the ancient faith which has been of the greatest importance in the ethical and religious development of humanity. This high historical appreciation is certainly valid in the sense that the two other world-conquering Mediterranean religions issued from it; Christ was just as truly a pupil of Moses as Mohammed was afterwards of Christ. So also the New Testament, which has become the foundation of the belief of the highest civilized nations in the short space of nineteen hundred years, rests on the venerable basis of the Old Testament. The Bible, which the two compose, has had a greater influence and a wider circulation than any other book in the world. Even to-day the Bible—in spite of its curious mingling of the best and the worst elements—is in a certain sense the " book of books." Yet when we make an impar-

GOD AND THE WORLD

tial and unprejudiced study of this notable historical source, we find it very different in several important respects from the popular impression. Here again modern criticism and history have come to certain conclusions which destroy the prevalent tradition in its very foundations.

The monotheism which Moses endeavored to establish in the worship of Jehovah, and which the prophets —the philosophers of the Hebrew race—afterwards developed with great success, had at first to sustain a long and severe struggle with the dominant polytheism which was in possession. Jehovah, or Yahveh, was originally derived from the heaven-god, which, under the title of Moloch or Baal, was one of the most popular of the Oriental deities (the Sethos or Typhon of the Egyptians, and the Saturn or Cronos of the Greeks) There were, however, other gods in great favor with the Jewish people, and so the struggle with "idolatry" continued. Still, Jehovah was, in principle, the only God, explicitly claiming, in the first precept of the decalogue: "I am the Lord thy God; thou shalt have no other gods beside me."

Christian monotheism shared the fate of its mother, Mosaism; it was generally only monotheistic in theory, while it degenerated practically into every kind of polytheism. In point of fact, monotheism was logically abandoned in the very dogma of the Trinity, which was adopted as an indispensable foundation of the Christian religion. The three persons, which are distinguished as Father, Son, and Holy Ghost, are three distinct individuals (and, indeed, anthropomorphic persons), just as truly as the three Indian deities of the Trimurti (Brahma, Vishnu, and Shiva) or the Trinity of the ancient Hebrews (Anu, Bel, and Aa).

Moreover, in the most widely distributed form of Christianity the "virgin" mother of Christ plays an important part as a fourth deity; in many Catholic countries she is practically taken to be much more powerful and influential than the three male persons of the celestial administration. The cult of the madonna has been developed to such an extent in these countries that we may oppose it to the usual masculine form of monotheism as one of a feminine type. The "Queen of Heaven" becomes so prominent, as is seen in so many pictures and legends of the madonna, that the three male persons practically disappear.

In addition, the imagination of the pious Christian soon came to increase this celestial administration by a numerous company of "saints" of all kinds, and bands of musical angels, who should see that "eternal life" should not prove too dull. The popes—the greatest charlatans that any religion ever produced—have constantly studied to increase this band of celestial satellites by repeated canonizations This curious company received its most interesting acquisition in 1870, when the Vatican Council pronounced the popes, as the vicars of Christ, to be infallible, and thus raised them to a divine dignity When we add the "personal Devil" that they acknowledge, and the "bad angels" who form his court, we have in modern Catholicism, still the most extensive branch of Christianity, a rich and variegated polytheism that dwarfs the Olympic family of the Greeks.

Islam, or the Mohammedan monotheism, is the youngest and purest form of monotheism. When the young Mohammed (born 570) learned to despise the polytheistic idolatry of his Arabian compatriots, and became acquainted with Nestorian Christianity, he

GOD AND THE WORLD

adopted its chief doctrines in a general way, but he could not bring himself to see anything more than a prophet in Christ, like Moses. He found in the dogma of the Trinity what every emancipated thinker finds on impartial reflection—an absurd legend which is neither reconcilable with the first principles of reason nor of any value whatever for our religious advancement. He justly regarded the worship of the immaculate mother of God as a piece of pure idolatry, like the veneration of pictures and images. The longer he reflected on it, and the more he strove after a purified idea of deity, the clearer did the certitude of his great maxim appear: "God is the only God"—there are no other gods beside him.

Yet Mohammed could not free himself from the anthropomorphism of the God-idea. His one only God was an idealized, almighty man, like the stern, vindictive God of Moses, and the gentle, loving God of Christ. Still, we must admit that the Mohammedan religion has preserved the character of pure monotheism throughout the course of its historical development and its inevitable division much more faithfully than the Mosaic and Christian religions. We see that to-day, even externally, in its forms of prayer and preaching, and in the architecture and adornment of its mosques. When I visited the East for the first time, in 1873, and admired the noble mosques of Cairo, Smyrna, Brussa, and Constantinople, I was inspired with a feeling of real devotion by the simple and tasteful decoration of the interior, and the lofty and beautiful architectural work of the exterior. How noble and inspiring do these mosques appear in comparison with the majority of Catholic churches, which are covered internally with gaudy pictures and gilt, and are outwardly disfigured by an immoderate crowd of human and animal figures! Not less elevated are the silent prayers and the simple devotional acts of the Koran when compared with the loud, unintelligible verbosity of the Catholic Mass and the blatant music of their theatrical processions.

Under the title of *mixotheism* we may embrace all the forms of theistic belief which contain mixtures of religious notions of different, sometimes contradictory, kinds. In theory this most widely diffused type of religion is not recognized at all; in the concrete it is the most important and most notable of all The vast majority of men who have religious opinions have always been, and still are, *mixotheists;* their idea of God is picturesquely compounded from the impressions received in childhood from their own sect, and a number of other impressions which are received later on, from contact with members of other religions, and which modify the earlier notions. In educated people there is also sometimes the modifying influence of philosophic studies in maturer years, and especially the unprejudiced study of natural phenomena, which reveals the futility of the theistic idea. The conflict of these contradictory impressions, which is very painful to a sensitive soul, and which often remains undecided throughout life, clearly shows the immense power of the *heredity* of ancient myths on the one hand and the early *adaptation* to erroneous dogmas on the other. The particular faith in which the child has been brought up generally remains in power, unless a "conversion" takes place subsequently, owing to the stronger influence of some other religion. But even in this supersession of one faith by another the new name, like the old one, proves to be merely an outward label covering a

GOD AND THE WORLD

mixture of the most diverse opinions and errors. The greater part of those who call themselves Christians are not monotheists (as they think), but amphitheists, triplotheists, or polytheists. And the same must be said of Islam and Mosaism, and other monotheistic religions. Everywhere we find associated with the original idea of a "sole and triune God" later beliefs in a number of subordinate deities — angels, devils, saints, etc.—a picturesque assortment of the most diverse theistic forms.

All the above forms of theism, in the proper sense of the word—whether the belief assumes a naturalistic or an anthropistic form—represent God to be an extramundane or a supernatural being. He is always opposed to the world, or nature, as an independent being; generally as its creator, sustainer, and ruler. In most religions he has the additional character of personality, or, to put it more definitely still, God as a person is likened to man. "In his gods man paints himself." This anthropomorphic conception of God as one who thinks, feels, and acts like man prevails with the great majority of theists, sometimes in a cruder and more naïve form, sometimes in a more refined and abstract degree. In any case the form of theosophy we have described is sure to affirm that God, the supreme being, is infinite in perfection, and therefore far removed from the imperfection of humanity. Yet, when we examine closely, we always find the same psychic or mental activity in the two. God feels, thinks, and acts as man does, although it be in an infinitely more perfect form.

The *personal anthropism* of God has become so natural to the majority of believers that they experience no shock when they find God personified in human

THE RIDDLE OF THE UNIVERSE

form in pictures and statues, and in the varied images of the poet, in which God takes human form—that is, is changed into a vertebrate. In some myths, even, God takes the form of other mammals (an ape, lion, bull, etc.), and more rarely of a bird (eagle, dove, or stork), or of some lower vertebrate (serpent, crocodile, dragon, etc.).

In the higher and more abstract forms of religion this idea of bodily appearance is entirely abandoned, and God is adored as a "pure spirit" without a body. "God is a spirit, and they who worship him must worship him in spirit and in truth." Nevertheless, the psychic activity of this "pure spirit" remains just the same as that of the anthropomorphic God. In reality, even this immaterial spirit is not conceived to be incorporeal, but merely invisible, gaseous. We thus arrive at the paradoxical conception of God as a *gaseous vertebrate*.

II.—PANTHEISM

Pantheism teaches that God and the world are one. The idea of God is identical with that of nature or substance. This pantheistic view is sharply opposed in principle to all the systems we have described, and to all possible forms of theism although there have been many attempts made from both sides to bridge over the deep chasm that separates the two. There is always this fundamental contradiction between them, that in theism God is opposed to nature as an *extramundane* being, as creating and sustaining the world, and acting upon it from without, while in pantheism God, as an *intramundane* being, is everywhere identical with nature itself, and is operative *within* the world as "force" or "energy." The latter view alone is com-

GOD AND THE WORLD

patible with our supreme law—the law of substance. It follows necessarily that pantheism is *the world-system of the modern scientist*. There are, it is true, still a few men of science who contest this, and think it possible to reconcile the old theistic theory of human nature with the pantheistic truth of the law of substance. All these efforts rest on confusion or sophistry —when they are honest.

As pantheism is a result of an advanced conception of nature in the civilized mind, it is naturally much younger than theism, the crudest forms of which are found in great variety in the uncivilized races of ten thousand years ago. We do, indeed, find the germs of pantheism in different religions at the very dawn of philosophy in the earliest civilized peoples (in India, Egypt, China, and Japan), several thousand years before the time of Christ; still, we do not meet a definite philosophical expression of it until the hylozoism of the Ionic philosophers, in the first half of the sixth century before Christ. All the great thinkers of this flourishing period of Hellenic thought are surpassed by the famous Anaximander, of Miletus, who conceived the essential unity of the infinite universe (*apeiron*) more profoundly and more clearly than his master, Thales, or his pupil, Anaximenes. Not only the great thought of the original unity of the cosmos and the development of all phenomena out of the all-pervading primitive matter found expression in Anaximander, but he even enunciated the bold idea of countless worlds in a periodic alternation of birth and death.

Many other great philosophers of classical antiquity, especially Democritus, Heraclitus, and Empedocles, had, in the same or an analogous sense, a profound conception of this unity of nature and God, of body and spirit, which has obtained its highest expression in the law of substance of our modern monism. The famous Roman poet and philosopher, Lucretius Carus, has presented it in a highly poetic form in his poem "De Rerum Natura." However, this true pantheistic monism was soon entirely displaced by the mystic dualism of Plato, and especially by the powerful influence which the idealistic philosophy obtained by its blending with Christian dogmas. When the papacy attained to its spiritual despotism over the world, pantheism was hopelessly crushed; Giordano Bruno, its most gifted defender, was burned alive by the "Vicar of Christ" in the Campo dei Fiori at Rome on February 17, 1600.

It was not until the middle of the seventeenth century that pantheism was exhibited in its purest form by the great Baruch Spinoza; he gave for the totality of things a definition of substance in which God and the world are inseparably united. The clearness, confidence, and consistency of Spinoza's monistic system are the more remarkable when we remember that this gifted thinker of two hundred and fifty years ago was without the support of all those sound empirical bases which have been obtained in the second half of the nineteenth century. We have already spoken, in the first chapter, of Spinoza's relation to the materialism of the eighteenth and the monism of the nineteenth century. The propagation of his views, especially in Germany, is due, above all, to the immortal works of our greatest poet and thinker, Wolfgang Goethe. His splendid *God and the World, Prometheus, Faust*, etc., embody the great thoughts of pantheism in the most perfect poetic creations.

Atheism affirms that there are no gods or goddesses,

GOD AND THE WORLD

assuming that god means a personal, extramundane entity. This "godless world-system" substantially agrees with the monism or pantheism of the modern scientist; it is only another expression for it, emphasizing its negative aspect, the non-existence of any supernatural deity. In this sense Schopenhauer justly remarks: "Pantheism is only a polite form of atheism. The truth of pantheism lies in its destruction of the dualist antithesis of God and the world, in its recognition that the world exists in virtue of its own inherent forces. The maxim of the pantheist, 'God and the world are one,' is merely a polite way of giving the Lord God his *congé*."

During the whole of the Middle Ages, under the bloody despotism of the popes, atheism was persecuted with fire and sword as a most pernicious system. As the "godless" man is plainly identified with the "wicked" in the Gospel, and is threatened—simply on account of his "want of faith"—with the eternal fires of hell, it was very natural that every good Christian should be anxious to avoid the suspicion of atheism. Unfortunately, the idea still prevails very widely. The atheistic scientist who devotes his strength and his life to the search for the truth, is freely credited with all that is evil; the theistic church-goer, who thoughtlessly follows the empty ceremonies of Catholic worship, is at once assumed to be a good citizen, even if there be no meaning whatever in his faith and his morality be deplorable. This error will only be destroyed when, in the twentieth century, the prevalent superstition gives place to rational knowledge and to a monistic conception of the unity of God and the world.

CHAPTER XVI

KNOWLEDGE AND BELIEF

The Knowledge of the Truth and Its Sources: the Activity of the Senses and the Association of Presentations—Organs of Sense and Organs of Thought—Sense-Organs and their Specific Energy—Their Evolution—The Philosophy of Sensibility—Inestimable Value of the Senses—Limits of Sensitive Knowledge—Hypothesis and Faith—Theory and Faith—Essential Difference of Scientific (Natural) and Religious (Supernatural) Faith—Superstition of Savage and of Civilized Races—Confessions of Faith—Unsectarian Schools—The Faith of Our Fathers—Spiritism—Revelation

EVERY effort of genuine science makes for a knowledge of the truth. Our only real and valuable knowledge is a knowledge of nature itself, and consists of presentations which correspond to external things. We are incompetent, it is true, to penetrate into the innermost nature of this real world—the " thing in itself "—but impartial critical observation and comparison inform us that, in the normal action of the brain and the organs of sense, the impressions received by them from the outer world are the same in all rational men, and that in the normal function of the organs of thought certain presentations are formed which are everywhere the same. These presentations we call *true*, and we are convinced that their content corresponds to the knowable aspect of things. We *know* that these facts are not imaginary, but real.

KNOWLEDGE AND BELIEF

All knowledge of the truth depends on two different, but intimately connected, groups of human physiological functions: firstly, on the *sense-impressions* of the object by means of sense-action, and, secondly, on the combination of these impressions by an association into *presentations* in the subject. The instruments of sensation are the sense-organs (*sensilla* or *aestheta*); the instruments which form and link together the presentations are the organs of thought (*phroneta*). The latter are part of the central, and the former part of the peripheral, nervous system—that important and elaborate system of organs in the higher animals which alone effects their entire psychic activity.

Man's sense-activity, which is the starting-point of all knowledge, has been slowly and gradually developed from that of his nearest mammal relatives, the primates. The sense-organs are of substantially the same construction throughout this highest animal group, and their function takes place always according to the same physical and chemical laws. They have had the same historical development in all cases. In the mammals, as in the case of all other animals, the *sensilla* were originally parts of the skin; the sensitive cells of the epidermis are the sources of all the different sense-organs, which have acquired their specific energy by adaptation to different stimuli (light, heat, sound, chemical action, etc.). The rod-cells in the retina of the eye, the auditory cells in the cochlea of the ear, the olfactory cells in the nose, and the taste-cells on the tongue, are all originally derived from the simple, indifferent cells of the epidermis, which cover the entire surface of the body. This significant fact can be directly proved by observation of the embryonic development of man or any of the higher animals. And from this ontogenetic fact we confidently infer, in virtue of the great biogenetic law, the important phylogenetic proposition, that in the long historical evolution of our ancestors, likewise, the higher sense-organs with their specific energies were originally derived from the epidermis of lower animals, from a simple layer of cells which had no trace of such differentiated sensilla.

A particular importance attaches to the circumstance that different nerves are qualified to perceive different properties of the environment, and these only. The optic nerve accomplishes only the perception of light, the auditory nerve the perception of sound, the olfactory nerve the perception of smell, and so on. No matter what stimuli impinge on and irritate a given sense-organ, its reaction is always of the same character. From this specific energy of the sense-nerves, which was first fully appreciated by Johannes Müller, very erroneous inferences have been drawn, especially in favor of a dualistic and *à priori* theory of knowledge. It has been affirmed that the brain, or the soul, only perceives a certain condition of the stimulated nerve, and that, consequently, no conclusion can be drawn from the process as to the existence and nature of the stimulating environment. Sceptical philosophy concluded that the very existence of an outer world is doubtful, and extreme idealism went on positively to deny it, contending that things only exist in our impressions of them.

In opposition to these erroneous views, we must recall the fact that the "specific energy" was not originally an innate, special quality of the various nerves, but it has arisen by adaptation to the particular activity of the epidermic cells in which they terminate In harmony with the great law of "division of labor"

KNOWLEDGE AND BELIEF

the originally indifferent "sense-cells of the skin" undertook different tasks, one group of them taking over the stimulus of the light rays, another the impress of the sound waves, a third the chemical impulse of odorous substances, and so on. In the course of a very long period these external stimuli effected a gradual change in the physiological, and later in the morphological, properties of these parts of the epidermis, and there was a correlative modification of the sensitive nerves which conduct the impressions they receive to the brain. Selection improved, step by step, such particular modifications as proved to be useful, and thus eventually, in the course of many million years, created those wonderful instruments, the eye and the ear, which we prize so highly; their structure is so remarkably purposive that they might well lead to the erroneous assumption of a "creation on a preconceived design." The peculiar character of each sense-organ and its specific nerve has thus been gradually evolved by use and exercise—that is, by *adaptation*—and has then been transmitted by *heredity* from generation to generation. Albrecht Rau has thoroughly established this view in his excellent work on *Sensation and Thought*, a physiological inquiry into the nature of the human understanding (1896). It points out the correct significance of Müller's law of specific sense-energies, adding searching investigations into their relation to the brain, and in the last chapter there is an able "philosophy of sensitivity" based on the ideas of Ludwig Feuerbach. I thoroughly agree with his convincing work.

Critical comparison of sense-action in man and the other vertebrates has brought to light a number of extremely important facts, the knowledge of which we

THE RIDDLE OF THE UNIVERSE

owe to the penetrating research of the nineteenth century, especially of the second half of the century. This is particularly true of the two most elaborate "æsthetic" organs, the eye and the ear. They present a different and more complicated structure in the vertebrates than in the other animals, and have also a characteristic development in the embryo. This typical ontogenesis and structure of the sensilla of all the vertebrates is only explained by *heredity* from a common ancestor. Within the vertebrate group, however, we find a great variety of structure in points of detail, and this is due to *adaptation* to their manner of life on the part of the various species, to the increasing or diminishing use of various parts.

In respect of the structure of his sense-organs man is by no means the most perfect and most highly-developed vertebrate. The eye of the eagle is much keener, and can distinguish small objects at a distance much more clearly than the human eye. The hearing of many mammals, especially of the carnivora, ungulata, and rodentia of the desert, is much more sensitive than that of man, and perceives slight noises at a much greater distance; that may be seen at a glance by their large and very sensitive cochlea. Singing birds have attained a higher grade of development, even in respect of musical endowment, than the majority of men. The sense of smell is much more developed in most of the mammals, especially in the carnivora and the ungulata, than in man, if the dog could compare his own fine scent with that of man, he would look down on us with compassion. Even with regard to the lower senses—taste, sex-sense, touch, and temperature—man has by no means reached the highest stage in every respect.

KNOWLEDGE AND BELIEF

We can naturally only pass judgment on the sensations which we ourselves experience. However, anatomy informs us of the presence in the bodies of many animals of other senses than those we are familiar with. Thus fishes and other lower aquatic vertebrates have peculiar sensilla in the skin which are in connection with special sense-nerves. On the right and left sides of the fish's body there is a long canal, branching into a number of smaller canals at the head. In this "mucous canal" there are nerves with numerous branches, the terminations of which are connected with peculiar nerve-aggregates. This extensive epidermic sense-organ probably serves for the perception of changes in the pressure, or in other properties, of the water. Some groups are distinguished by the possession of other peculiar sensilla, the meaning of which is still unknown to us.

But it is already clear from the above facts that our human sense-activity is limited, not only in quantity, but in quality also. We can thus only perceive with our senses, especially with the eye and the sense of touch. a part of the qualities of the objects in our environment. And even this partial perception is incomplete, in the sense that our organs are imperfect, and our sensory nerves, acting as interpreters, communicate to the brain only a translation of the impressions received.

However, this acknowledged imperfection of our senses should not prevent us from recognizing their instruments, and especially the eye, to be organs of the highest type; together with the thought-organs in the brain, they are nature's most valuable gift to man. Very truly does Albrecht Rau say: "All science is sensitive knowledge in the ultimate analysis; it does not deny, but interpret, the data of the senses. The senses are our first and best friends. Long before the mind is developed the senses tell man what he must do and avoid. He who makes a general disavowal of the senses in order to meet their dangers acts as thoughtlessly and as foolishly as the man who plucks out his eyes because they once fell on shameful things, or the man who cuts off his hand lest at any time it should reach out to the goods of his neighbor." Hence Feuerbach is quite right in calling all philosophies, religions, and systems which oppose the principle of sense-action not only erroneous, but really pernicious. Without the senses there is no knowledge—"*Nihil est in intellectu, quod non fuerit in sensu*," as Locke said. Twenty years ago I pointed out, in my chapter " On the Origin and Development of the Sense-Organs,"* the great service of Darwinism in giving us a profounder knowledge and a juster appreciation of the senses.

The thirst for knowledge of the educated mind is not contented with the defective acquaintance with the outer world which is obtained through our imperfect sense-organs. He endeavors to build up the sense-impressions which they have brought him into valuable knowledge. He transforms them into specific sense-perceptions in the sense-centres of the cortex of the brain, and combines them into presentations, by association, in the thought-centres. Finally, by a further concatenation of the groups of presentations he attains to connected knowledge. But this knowledge remains defective and unsatisfactory until the imagination supplements the inadequate power of combination of the intelligence, and, by the association of stored-up

* *Collected Popular Lectures*; Bonn, 1878.

KNOWLEDGE AND BELIEF

images, unites the isolated elements into a connected whole. Thus are produced new general presentative images, and these suffice to interpret the facts perceived and satisfy "reason's feeling of causality."

The presentations which fill up the gaps in our knowledge, or take its place, may be called, in a broad sense, "faith." That is what happens continually in daily life. When we are not sure about a thing we say, I *believe* it. In this sense we are compelled to make use of faith even in science itself; we conjecture or assume that a certain relation exists between two phenomena, though we do not know it for certain. If it is a question of a *cause*, we form a *hypothesis;* though in science only such hypotheses are admitted as lie within the sphere of human cognizance, and do not contradict known facts. Such hypotheses are, for instance—in physics the theory of the vibratory movement of ether, in chemistry the hypothesis of atoms and their affinity, in biology the theory of the molecular structure of living protoplasm, and so forth.

The explanation of a great number of connected phenomena by the assumption of a common cause is called a *theory*. Both in theory and hypothesis "faith" (in the scientific sense) is indispensable; for here again it is the imagination that fills up the gaps left by the intelligence in our knowledge of the connection of things. A theory, therefore, must always be regarded only as an approximation to the truth; it must be understood that it may be replaced in time by another and better-grounded theory. But, in spite of this admitted uncertainty, theory is indispensable for all true science; it elucidates facts by postulating a cause for them. The man who renounces theory altogether, and seeks to construct a pure science with certain facts alone (as often happens with wrong-headed representatives of our "exact sciences"), must give up the hope of any knowledge of causes, and, consequently, of the satisfaction of reason's demand for causality.

The theory of gravitation in astronomy (Newton), the nebular theory in cosmogony (Kant and Laplace), the principle of energy in physics (Meyer and Helmholtz), the atomic theory in chemistry (Dalton), the vibratory theory in optics (Huyghens), the cellular theory in histology (Schleiden and Schwann), and the theory of descent in biology (Lamarck and Darwin), are all important theories of the first rank, they explain a whole world of natural phenomena by the assumption of a common cause for all the several facts of their respective provinces, and by showing that all the phenomena thereof are inter-connected and controlled by laws which issue from this common cause. Yet the cause itself may remain obscure in character, or be merely a "provisional hypothesis." The "force of gravity" in the theory of gravitation and in cosmogony, "energy" itself in its relation to matter, the "ether" of optics and electricity, the "atom" of the chemist, the living "protoplasm" of histology, the "heredity" of the evolutionist—these and similar conceptions of other great theories may be regarded by a sceptical philosophy as "mere hypotheses" and the outcome of scientific "faith," yet they are indispensable for us, until they are replaced by better hypotheses.

The dogmas which are used for the explanation of phenomena in the various religions, and which go by the name of "faith" (in the narrower sense), are of a very different character from the forms of scientific faith we have enumerated. The two types, however—the "natural" faith of science and the "supernatural"

KNOWLEDGE AND BELIEF

faith of religion — are not infrequently confounded, so that we must point out their fundamental difference. Religious faith means always belief in a miracle, and as such is in hopeless contradiction with the natural faith of reason. In opposition to reason it postulates supernatural agencies, and, therefore, may be justly called superstition. The essential difference of this superstition from rational faith lies in the fact that it assumes supernatural forces and phenomena, which are unknown and inadmissible to science, and which are the outcome of illusion and fancy; moreover, superstition contradicts the well-known laws of nature, and is therefore *irrational*.

Owing to the great progress of ethnology during the century, we have learned a vast quantity of different kinds and practices of superstition, as they still survive in uncivilized races. When they are compared with each other and with the mythological notion of earlier ages, a manifold analogy is discovered, frequently a common origin, and eventually one simple source for them all. This is found in the "demand of causality in reason," in the search for an explanation of obscure phenomena by the discovery of a cause. That applies particularly to such phenomena as threaten us with danger and excite fear, like thunder and lightning, earthquakes, eclipses, etc. The demand for a causal explanation of such phenomena is found in uncivilized races of the lowest grade, transmitted from their primate ancestors by heredity. It is even found in many other vertebrates. When a dog barks at the full moon, or at a ringing bell, of which it sees the hammer moving, or at a flag that flutters in the breeze, it expresses not only fear, but also the mysterious impulse to learn the cause of the obscure phenomenon.

THE RIDDLE OF THE UNIVERSE

The crude beginnings of religion among primitive races spring partly from this hereditary superstition of their primate ancestors, and partly from the worship of ancestors, from various emotional impulses, and from habits which have become traditional.

The religious notions of modern civilized peoples, which they esteem so highly, profess to be on a much higher level than the "crude superstition" of the savage; we are told of the great advance which civilization has made in sweeping it aside. That is a great mistake. Impartial comparison and analysis show that they only differ in their special "form of faith" and the outer shell of their creed. In the clear light of reason the refined faith of the most liberal ecclesiastical religion—inasmuch as it contradicts the known and inviolable laws of nature—is no less irrational a superstition than the crude spirit-faith of primitive fetichism on which it looks down with proud disdain.

And if, from this impartial stand-point, we take a critical glance at the kinds of faith that prevail to-day in civilized countries, we find them everywhere saturated with traditional superstition. The Christian belief in Creation, the Trinity, the Immaculate Conception, the Redemption, the Resurrection and Ascension of Christ, and so forth, is just as purely imaginative as the belief in the various dogmas of the Mohammedan, Mosaic, Buddhistic, and Brahmanic religions, and is just as incapable of reconciliation with a rational knowledge of nature. Each of these religions is for the sincere believer an indisputable truth, and each regards the other as heresy and damnable error. The more confidently a particular sect considers itself "the only ark of salvation," and the more ardently this conviction is cherished, the more zealously does it contend

KNOWLEDGE AND BELIEF

against all other sects and give rise to the fearful religious wars that form the saddest pages in the book of history. And all the time the unprejudiced "critique of pure reason" teaches us that all these different forms of faith are equally false and irrational, mere creatures of poetic fancy and uncritical tradition. Rational science must reject them all alike as the outcome of superstition.

The incalculable injury which irrational superstition has done to credulous humanity is conspicuously revealed in the ceaseless conflict of confessions of faith. Of all the wars which nations have waged against each other with fire and sword the religious wars have been the bloodiest; of all the forms of discord that have shattered the happiness of families and of individuals those that arise from religious differences are still the most painful. Think of the millions who have lost their lives in Christian persecutions, in the religious conflicts of Islam and of the Reformation, by the Inquisition, and under the charge of witchcraft. Or think of the still greater number of luckless men who, through religious differences, have been plunged into family troubles, have lost the esteem of their fellow-citizens and their position in the community, or have even been compelled to fly from their country. The official confession of faith becomes most pernicious of all when it is associated with the political aims of a modern state, and is enforced as "religious instruction" in our schools. The child's mind is thus early diverted from the pursuit of the truth and impregnated with superstition. Every friend of humanity should do all in his power to promote unsectarian schools as one of the most valuable institutions of the modern state.

The great value which is, none the less, still very

THE RIDDLE OF THE UNIVERSE

widely attached to sectarian instruction is not only due to the compulsion of a reactionary state and its dependence on a dominant clericalism, but also to the weight of old traditions and "emotional cravings" of various kinds. One of the strongest of these is the devout reverence which is extended everywhere to sectarian tradition, to the "faith of our fathers." In thousands of stories and poems fidelity to it is extolled as a spiritual treasure and a sacred duty. Yet a little impartial study of the history of faith suffices to show the absurdity of the notion. The dominant evangelical faith of the second half of the nineteenth century is essentially different from that of the first half, and this again from that of the eighteenth century. The faith of the eighteenth century diverges considerably from the "faith of our fathers" of the seventeenth, and still more from that of the sixteenth, century. The Reformation, releasing enslaved reason from the tyranny of the popes, is naturally regarded by them as darkest heresy; but even the faith of the papacy itself had been completely transformed in the course of a century. And how different is the faith of the Christian from that of his heathen ancestors. Every man with some degree of independent thought frames a more or less personal religion for himself, which is always different from that of his fathers; it depends largely on the general condition of thought in his day. The further we go back in the history of civilization, the more clearly do we find this esteemed "faith of our fathers" to be an indefensible superstition which is undergoing continual transformation.

One of the most remarkable forms of superstition, which still takes a very active part in modern life, is *spiritism*. It is a surprising and a lamentable fact

KNOWLEDGE AND BELIEF

that millions of educated people are still dominated by this dreary superstition; even distinguished scientists are entangled in it. A number of spiritualist journals spread the faith far and wide, and our "superior circles" do not scruple to hold *séances* in which "spirits" appear, rapping, writing, giving messages from "the beyond," and so on. It is a frequent boast of spiritists that even eminent men of science defend their superstition. In Germany, A. Zöllner and Fechner are quoted as instances; in England, Wallace and Crookes. The regrettable circumstance that physicists and biologists of such distinction have been led astray by spiritism is accounted for, partly by their excess of imagination and defect of critical faculty, and partly by the powerful influence of dogmas which a religious education imprinted on the brain in early youth. Moreover, it was precisely through the famous *séances* at Leipzig, in which the physicists, Zöllner, Fechner, and Wilhelm Weber, were imposed on by the clever American conjuror, Slade, that the fraud of the latter was afterwards fully exposed; he was discovered to be a common impostor. In other cases, too, where the alleged marvels of spiritism have been thoroughly investigated, they have been traced to a more or less clever deception; the mediums (generally of the weaker sex) have been found to be either smart swindlers or nervous persons of abnormal irritability. Their supposed gift of "telepathy" (or "action at a distance of thought without material medium") has no more existence than the "voices" or the "groans" of spirits, etc. The vivid pictures which Carl du Prel, of Munich, and other spiritists give of their phenomena must be regarded as the outcome of a lively imagination, together with a lack of critical power and of knowledge of physiology.

THE RIDDLE OF THE UNIVERSE

The majority of religions have, in spite of their great differences, one common feature, which is, at the same time, one of their strongest supports in many quarters. They declare that they can elucidate the problem of existence, the solution of which is beyond the natural power of reason, by the supernatural way of revelation; from that they derive the authority of the dogmas which in the guise of "divine laws" control morality and the practical conduct of life. "Divine" inspirations of that kind form the basis of many myths and legends, the human origin of which is perfectly clear. It is true that the God who reveals himself does not always appear in human shape, but in thunder and lightning, storm and earthquake, fiery bush or menacing cloud. But the revelation which he is supposed to bring to the credulous children of men is always anthropomorphic; it invariably takes the form of a communication of ideas or commands which are formulated and expressed precisely as is done in the normal action of the human brain and larynx. In the Indian and Egyptian religions, in the mythologies of Greece and Rome, in the Old and the New Testaments, the gods think, talk, and act just as men do; the revelations, in which they are supposed to unveil for us the secrets of existence and the solution of the great world-enigma, are creations of the human imagination. The "truth" which the credulous discover in them is a human invention; the "childlike faith" in these irrational revelations is mere superstition.

The true revelation—that is, the true source of rational knowledge—is to be sought in nature alone. The rich heritage of truth which forms the most valuable part of human culture is derived exclusively from the experiences acquired in a searching study of nature,

KNOWLEDGE AND BELIEF

and from the rational conclusions which it has reached by the just association of these empirical presentations. Every intelligent man with normal brain and senses finds this true revelation in nature on impartial study, and thus frees himself from the superstition with which the "revelations" of religion had burdened him.

CHAPTER XVII

SCIENCE AND CHRISTIANITY

Increasing Opposition between Modern Science and Christian Theology—The Old and the New Faith—Defence of Rational Science against the Attacks of Christian Superstition, especially against Catholicism—Four Periods in the Evolution of Christianity: I. Primitive Christianity (the First Three Centuries)—The Four Canonical Gospels—The Epistles of Paul —II. The Papacy (Ultramontane Christianity)—Retrogression of Civilization in the Middle Ages—Ultramontane Falsification of History—The Papacy and Science—The Papacy and Christianity—III. The Reformation—Luther and Calvin —The Year of Emancipation—IV. The Pseudo-Christianity of the Nineteenth Century—The Papal Declaration of War against Reason and Science : (a) Infallibility, (b) The Encyclica, (c) The Immaculate Conception

ONE of the most distinctive features of the expiring century is the increasing vehemence of the opposition between science and Christianity. That is both natural and inevitable. In the same proportion in which the victorious progress of modern science has surpassed all the scientific achievements of earlier ages has the untenability been proved of those mystic views which would subdue reason under the yoke of an alleged revelation; and the Christian religion belongs to that group. The more solidly modern astronomy, physics, and chemistry have established the sole dominion of inflexible natural laws in the universe at

SCIENCE AND CHRISTIANITY

large, and modern botany, zoology, and anthropology have proved the validity of those laws in the entire kingdom of organic nature, so much the more strenuously has the Christian religion, in association with dualistic metaphysics, striven to deny the application of these natural laws in the province of the so-called "spiritual life"—that is, in one section of the physiology of the brain.

No one has more clearly, boldly, and unanswerably enunciated this open and irreconcilable opposition between the modern scientific and the outworn Christian view than David Friedrich Strauss, the greatest theologian of the nineteenth century. His last work, *The Old Faith and the New*, is a magnificent expression of the honest conviction of all educated people of the present day who understand this unavoidable conflict between the discredited, dominant doctrines of Christianity and the illuminating, rational revelation of modern science—all those who have the courage to defend the right of reason against the pretensions of superstition, and who are sensible of the philosophic demand for a unified system of thought. Strauss, as an honorable and courageous free-thinker, has expounded far better than I could the principal points of difference between "the old and the new faith." The absolute irreconcilability of the opponents and the inevitability of their struggle ("for life or death") have been ably presented on the philosophic side by E. Hartmann, in his interesting work on *The Self-Destruction of Christianity*.

When the works of Strauss and Feuerbach and *The History of the Conflict between Religion and Science* of J. W. Draper have been read, it may seem superfluous for us to devote a special chapter to the subject. Yet we think it useful, and even necessary for our purpose, to cast a critical glance at the historical course of this great struggle; especially seeing that the attacks of the "Church militant" on science in general, and on the theory of evolution in particular, have become extremely bitter and menacing of late years. Unfortunately, the mental relaxation which has lately set in, and the rising flood of reaction in the political, social, and ecclesiastical world, are only too well calculated to give point to those dangers. If any one doubts it, he has only to look over the conduct of Christian synods and of the German Reichstag during the last few years. Quite in harmony are the recent efforts of many secular governments to get on as good a footing as possible with the "spiritual regiment," their deadly enemy—that is, to submit to its yoke The two forces find a common aim in the suppression of free thought and free scientific research, for the purpose of thus more easily securing a complete despotism.

Let us first emphatically protest that it is a question for us of the necessary defence of science and reason against the vigorous attacks of the Christian Church and its vast army, not of an unprovoked attack of science on religion. And, in the first place, our defence must be prepared against Romanism or Ultramontanism. This "one ark of salvation," this Catholic Church "destined for all," is not only much larger and more powerful than the other Christian sects, but it has the exceptional advantage of a vast, centralized organization and an unrivalled political ability. Men of science are often heard to say that the Catholic superstition is no more astute than the other forms of supernatural faith, and that all these insiduous institutions are equally inimical to reason and science. As a matter of general theoretical principle the statement may pass,

SCIENCE AND CHRISTIANITY

but it is certainly wrong when we look to its practical side. The deliberate and indiscriminate attacks of the ultramontane Church on science, supported by the apathy and ignorance of the masses, are, on account of its powerful organization, much more severe and dangerous than those of other religions.

In order to appreciate correctly the extreme importance of Christianity in regard to the entire history of civilization, and particularly its fundamental opposition to reason and science, we must briefly run over the principal stages of its historical evolution. It may be divided into four periods: (1) primitive Christianity (the first three centuries), (2) papal Christianity (twelve centuries, from the fourth to the fifteenth), (3) the Reformation (three centuries, from the sixteenth to the eighteenth), and (4) modern pseudo-Christianity.

I.—PRIMITIVE CHRISTIANITY

Primitive Christianity embraces the first three centuries. Christ himself, the noble prophet and enthusiast, so full of the love of humanity, was far below the level of classical culture; he knew nothing beyond the Jewish traditions; he has not left a single line of writing. He had, indeed, no suspicion of the advanced stage to which Greek philosophy and science had progressed five hundred years before.

All that we know of him and of his original teaching is taken from the chief documents of the New Testament—the four gospels and the Pauline epistles. As to the four canonical gospels, we now know that they were selected from a host of contradictory and forged manuscripts of the first three centuries by the three hundred and eighteen bishops who assembled at the

Council of Nicæa in 327. The entire list of gospels numbered forty; the canonical list contains four. As the contending and mutually abusive bishops could not agree about the choice, they determined to leave the selection to a miracle. They put all the books (according to the *Synodicon* of Pappus) together underneath the altar, and prayed that the apocryphal books, of human origin, might remain there, and the genuine, inspired books might be miraculously placed on the table of the Lord. And that, says tradition, really occurred! The three synoptic gospels (Matthew, Mark, and Luke—all written *after* them, not *by* them, at the beginning of the second century) and the very different fourth gospel (ostensibly "after" John, written about the middle of the second century) leaped on the table, and were thenceforth recognized as the inspired (with their thousand mutual contradictions) foundations of Christian doctrine. If any modern "unbeliever" finds this story of the " leap of the sacred books " incredible, we must remind him that it is just as credible as the table-turning and spirit-rapping that are believed to take place to-day by millions of educated people; and that hundreds of millions of Christians believe just as implicitly in their personal immortality; their "resurrection from the dead," and the Trinity of God—dogmas that contradict pure reason no more and no less than that miraculous bound of the gospel manuscripts.

The most important sources after the gospels are the fourteen separate (and general y forged) epistles of Paul. The genuine Pauline epistles (*three* in number, according to recent criticism—to the Romans, Galatians, and Corinthians) were written before the canonical gospels, and contain less incredible miraculous matter than they. They are also more concerned than the

SCIENCE AND CHRISTIANITY

gospels to adjust themselves with a rational view of the world. Hence the advanced theology of modern times constructs its "ideal Christianity" rather on the base of the Pauline epistles than on the gospels, so that it has been called "Paulinism."

The remarkable personality of Paul, who possessed much more culture and practical sense than Christ, is extremely interesting, from the anthropological point of view, from the fact that the racial origin of the two great religious founders is very much the same. Recent historical investigation teaches that Paul's father was of Greek nationality, and his mother of Jewish.* The half-breeds of these two races, which are so very distant in origin (although they are branches of the same species, the *homo mediterraneus*), are often distinguished by a happy blending of talents and temperament, as we find in many recent and actual instances. The plastic Oriental imagination and the critical Western reason often admirably combine and complete each other. That is visible in the Pauline teaching, which soon obtained a greater influence than the earliest Christian notions. Hence it is not incorrect to consider Paulinism a new phenomenon, of which the father was the philosophy of the Greeks, and the mother the religion of the Jews. Neoplatonism is an analogous combination.

As to the real teaching and aims of Christ (and as to many important aspects of his life) the views of conflicting theologians diverge more and more, as historical criticism (Strauss, Feuerbach, Baur, Renan, etc.) puts the accessible facts in their true light, and draws impartial conclusions from them. Two things, cer-

* As to the Greek paternity of Christ, *vide* p. 328.

tainly, remain beyond dispute—the lofty principle of universal charity and the fundamental maxim of ethics, the "golden rule," that issues therefrom; both, however, existed in theory and in practice centuries before the time of Christ (cf. chap. xix.). For the rest, the Christians of the early centuries were generally pure Communists, sometimes "Social Democrats," who, according to the prevailing theory in Germany to-day, ought to have been exterminated with fire and sword.

II.—PAPAL CHRISTIANITY

Latin Christianity, variously called Papistry, Romanism, Vaticanism, Ultramontanism, or the Roman Catholic Church, is one of the most remarkable phenomena in the history of civilized man; in spite of the storms that have swept over it, it still exerts a most powerful influence. Of the four hundred and ten million Christians who are scattered over the earth the majority—that is, two hundred and twenty-five millions—are Roman Catholics; there are seventy-five million Greek Catholics and one hundred and ten million Protestants. During a period of one thousand two hundred years, from the fourth to the sixteenth century, the papacy has almost absolutely controlled and tainted the spiritual life of Europe; on the other hand, it has won but little territory from the ancient religions of Asia and Africa. In Asia Buddhism still counts five hundred and three million followers, the Brahmanic religion one hundred and thirty-eight millions, and Islam one hundred and twenty millions.

It is the despotism of the papacy that lent its darkest character to the Middle Ages; it meant death to all freedom of mental life, decay to all science, corruption

SCIENCE AND CHRISTIANITY

to all morality. From the noble height to which the life of the human mind had attained in classical antiquity, in the centuries before Christ and the first century after Christ, it soon sank, under the rule of the papacy, to a level which, in respect of the knowledge of the truth, can only be termed barbarism. It is often protested that other aspects of mental life—poetry and architecture, scholastic learning and patristic philosophy—were richly developed in the Middle Ages. But this activity was in the service of the Church, it did not tend to the cultivation, but to the suppression, of free mental research. The exclusive preparing for an unknown eternity beyond the tomb, the contempt of nature, the withdrawal from the study of it, which are essential elements of Christianity, were urged as a sacred duty by the Roman hierarchy. It was not until the beginning of the sixteenth century that a change for the better came in with the Reformation.

It is impossible for us here to describe the pitiful retrogression of culture and morality during the twelve centuries of the spiritual despotism of Rome. It is very pithily expressed in a saying of the greatest and the ablest of the Hohenzollerns; Frederick the Great condensed his judgment in the phrase that the study of history led one to think that from Constantine to the date of the Reformation the whole world was insane. L. Büchner has given us an admirable, brief description of this "period of insanity" in his work on *Religious and Scientific Systems*. The reader who desires a closer acquaintance with the subject would do well to consult the historical works of Ranke, Draper, Kolb, Svoboda, etc. The truthful description of the awful condition of the Christian Middle Ages, which is given by these and other unprejudiced historians, is confirmed by all the reliable sources of investigation, and by the historical monuments which have come down from the saddest period of human history. Educated Catholics, who are sincere truth-seekers, cannot be too frequently recommended to study these historical sources for themselves. This is the more necessary as ultramontane literature has still a considerable influence. The old trick of deceiving the faithful by a complete reversal of facts and an invention of miraculous circumstances is still worked by it with great success. We will only mention Lourdes and the "Holy Coat" of Trêves. The ultramontane professor of history at Frankfurt, Johannes Janssen, affords a striking example of the length they will go in distorting historical truth; his much-read works (especially his *History of the German People since the Middle Ages*) are marred by falsification to an incredible extent. The untruthfulness of these Jesuitical productions is on a level with the credulity and the uncritical judgment of the simple German nation that takes them for gospel.

One of the most interesting of the historical facts which clearly prove the evil of the ultramontane despotism is its vigorous and consistent struggle with science. This was determined on, in principle, from the very beginning of Christianity, inasmuch as it set faith above reason and preached the blind subjection of the one to the other; that was natural, seeing that our whole life on earth was held to be only a preparation for the legendary life beyond, and thus scientific research was robbed of any real value. The deliberate and successful attack on science began in the early part of the fourth century, particularly after the Council of Nicæa (327), presided over by Constantine—called the "Great" because he raised Christianity to the po-

SCIENCE AND CHRISTIANITY

sition of a state religion, and founded Constantinople, though a worthless character, a false-hearted hypocrite, and a murderer. The success of the papacy in its conflict with independent scientific thought and inquiry is best seen in the distressing condition of science and its literature during the Middle Ages. Not only were the rich literary treasures that classical antiquity had bequeathed to the world destroyed for the most part, or withdrawn from circulation, but the rack and the stake insured the silence of every heretic—that is, every independent thinker. If he did not keep his thoughts to himself, he had to look forward to being burned alive, as was the fate of the great monistic philosopher, Giordano Bruno, the reformer, John Huss, and more than a hundred thousand other "witnesses to the truth." The history of science in the Middle Ages teaches us on every page that independent thought and empirical research were completely buried for twelve sad centuries under the oppression of the omnipotent papacy.

All that we esteem in true Christianity, in the sense of its founder and of his noblest followers, and that we must endeavor to save from the inevitable wreck of this great world religion for our new monistic religion, lies on its ethical and social planes. The principles of true humanism, the golden rule, the spirit of tolerance, the love of man, in the best and highest sense of the word—all these true graces of Christianity were not, indeed, first discovered and given to the world by that religion, but were successfully developed in the critical period when classical antiquity was hastening to its doom. The papacy, however, has attempted to convert all those virtues into the direct contrary, and still to hang out the sign of the old firm. Instead of Christian char-

THE RIDDLE OF THE UNIVERSE

ity, it introduced a fanatical hatred of the followers of all other religions; with fire and sword it has pursued, not only the heathen, but every Christian sect that dared resist the imposition of ultramontane dogma. Tribunals for heretics were erected all over Europe, yielding unnumbered victims, whose torments seemed only to fill their persecutors, with all their Christian charity, with a peculiar satisfaction. The power of Rome was directed mercilessly for centuries against everything that stood in its way. Under the notorious Torquemada (1481-98), in Spain alone eight thousand heretics were burned alive and ninety thousand punished with the confiscation of their goods and the most grievous ecclesiastical fines; in the Netherlands, under the rule of Charles V., at least fifty thousand men fell victims to the clerical bloodthirst. And while the heavens resounded with the cry of the martyrs, the wealth of half the world was pouring into Rome, to which the whole of Christianity paid tribute, and the self-styled representatives of God on earth and their accomplices (not infrequently Atheists themselves) wallowed in pleasure and vice of every description. "And all these privileges," said the frivolous, syphilitic Pope, Leo X., "have been secured to us by the fable of Jesus Christ."

Yet, with all the discipline of the Church and the fear of God, the condition of European society was pitiable. Feudalism, serfdom, the grace of God, and the favor of the monks ruled the land, the poor helots were only too glad to be permitted to raise their miserable huts under the shadow of the castle or the cloister, their secular and spiritual oppressors and exploiters. Even to-day we suffer from the aftermath of these awful ages and conditions, in which there was no ques-

SCIENCE AND CHRISTIANITY

tion of care for science or higher mental culture save in rare circumstances and in secret. Ignorance, poverty, and superstition combined with the immoral operation of the law of celibacy, which had been introduced in the eleventh century, to consolidate the ever-growing power of the papacy. It has been calculated that there were more than ten million victims of fanatical religious hatred during this "Golden Age" of papal domination; and how many more million human victims must be put to the account of celibacy, oral confession, and moral constraint, the most pernicious and accursed institutions of the papal despotism! Unbelieving philosophers, who have collected disproofs of the existence of God, have overlooked one of the strongest arguments in that sense—the fact that the Roman "Vicar of Christ" could for twelve centuries perpetrate with impunity the most shameful and horrible deeds "in the name of God."

III.—THE REFORMATION

The history of civilization, which we are so fond of calling "the history of the world," enters upon its third period with the Reformation of the Christian Church, just as its second period begins with the founding of Christianity. With the Reformation begins the new birth of fettered reason, the reawakening of science, which the iron hand of the Christian papacy had relentlessly crushed for twelve hundred years. At the same time the spread of general education had already commenced, owing to the invention of printing about the middle of the fifteenth century; and towards its close several great events occurred, especially the discovery of America in 1492, which prepared the way for the "renaissance" of science in company with that of art. Indeed, certain very important advances were made in the knowledge of nature during the first half of the sixteenth century, which shook the prevailing system to its very foundations. Such were the circumnavigation of the globe by Magellan in 1522, which afforded empirical proof of its rotundity, and the founding of the new system of the world by Copernicus in 1543.

Yet the 31st of October in the year 1517, the day on which Martin Luther nailed his ninety-five theses to the wooden door of Wittenburg Cathedral, must be regarded as the commencement of a new epoch; for on that day was forced the iron door of the prison in which the Papal Church had detained fettered reason for twelve hundred years. The merits of the great reformer have been partly exaggerated, partly underestimated. It has been justly pointed out that Luther, like all the other reformers, remained in manifold subjection to the deepest superstition. Thus he was throughout life a supporter of the rigid dogma of the verbal inspiration of the Bible; he zealously maintained the doctrines of the resurrection, original sin, predestination, justification by faith, etc. He rejected as folly the great discovery of Copernicus, because in the Bible "Joshua bade the sun, not the earth, stand still." He utterly failed to appreciate the great political revolutions of his time, especially the profound and just agitation of the peasantry. Worse still was the fanatical Calvin, of Geneva, who had the talented Spanish physician, Serveto, burned alive in 1553, because he rejected the absurd dogma of the Trinity. The fanatical "true believers" of the reformed Church followed only too frequently in the blood-stained footsteps of their papal enemies; as they do even in our own day.

SCIENCE AND CHRISTIANITY

Deeds of unparalleled cruelty followed in the train of the Reformation—the massacre of St. Bartholomew and the persecution of the Huguenots in France, bloody heretic-hunts in Italy, civil war in England, and the Thirty Years War in Germany. Yet, in spite of those grave blemishes, to the sixteenth and seventeenth centuries belongs the honor of once more opening a free path to the thoughtful mind, and delivering reason from the oppressive yoke of the papacy. Thus only was made possible that great development of different tendencies in critical philosophy and of new paths in science which won for the subsequent eighteenth century the honorable title of "the century of enlightenment."

IV.—THE PSEUDO-CHRISTIANITY OF THE NINETEENTH CENTURY

As the fourth and last stage in the history of Christianity we oppose our nineteenth century to all its predecessors. It is true that the enlightenment of preceding centuries had promoted critical thought in every direction, and the rise of science itself had furnished powerful empirical weapons; yet it seems to us that our progress along both lines has been quite phenomenal during the nineteenth century. It has inaugurated an entirely new period in the history of the human mind, characterized by the development of the monistic philosophy of nature. At its very commencement the foundations were laid of a new anthropology (by the comparative anatomy of Cuvier) and of a new biology (by the *Philosophie Zoologique* of Lamarck). The two great French scientists were quickly succeeded by two contemporary German scholars—Baer, the founder of the science of evolution, and Johannes Müller, the founder of comparative morphology and physiology. A pupil of Müller, Theodor Schwann, created the far-reaching cellular theory in 1838, in conjunction with M. Schleiden. Lyell had already traced the evolution of the earth to natural causes, and thus proved the application to our planet of the mechanical cosmogony which Kant had sketched with so much insight in 1755. Finally, Robert Mayer and Helmholtz established the principle of energy in 1842—the second, complementary half of the great law of substance, the first half of which (the persistence of matter) had been previously discovered by Lavoisier. Forty years ago Charles Darwin crowned all these profound revelations of the intimate nature of the universe by his new theory of evolution, the greatest natural-philosophical achievement of our century.

What is the relation of modern Christianity to this vast and unparalleled progress of science? In the first place, the deep gulf between its two great branches, conservative Romanism and progressive Protestantism, has naturally widened. The ultramontane clergy (and we must associate with them the orthodox "evangelical alliance") had naturally to offer a strenuous opposition to this rapid advance of the emancipated mind; they continued unmoved in their rigid literal belief, demanding the unconditional surrender of reason to dogma. Liberal Protestantism, on the other hand, took refuge in a kind of monistic pantheism, and sought a means of reconciling two contradictory principles. It endeavored to combine the unavoidable recognition of the established laws of nature, and the philosophic conclusions that followed from them, with a purified form of religion, in which scarcely anything remained of the distinctive teaching of faith. There

SCIENCE AND CHRISTIANITY

were many attempts at compromise to be found between the two extremes; but the conviction rapidly spread that dogmatic Christianity had lost every foundation, and that only its valuable ethical contents should be saved for the new monistic religion of the twentieth century. As, however, the existing external forms of the dominant Christian religion remained unaltered, and as, in spite of a progressive political development, they are more intimately than ever connected with the practical needs of the State, there has arisen that widespread religious profession in educated spheres which we can only call " pseudo-Christianity "—at the bottom it is a " religious lie " of the worst character. The great dangers which attend this conflict between sincere conviction and the hypocritical profession of modern pseudo-Christians are admirably described in Max Nordau's interesting work on *The Conventional Lies of Civilization*.

In the midst of this obvious falseness of prevalent pseudo-Christianity there is one favorable circumstance for the progress of a rational study of nature: its most powerful and bitterest enemy, the Roman Church, threw off its mask of ostensible concern for higher mental development about the middle of the nineteenth century, and declared a *guerre à l'outrance* against independent science. This happened in three important challenges to reason, for the explicitness and resoluteness of which modern science and culture cannot but be grateful to the " Vicar of Christ." (1) In December, 1854, the pope promulgated the dogma of the immaculate conception of Mary. (2) Ten years afterwards—in December, 1864—the pope published, in his famous *encyclica*, an absolute condemnation of the whole of modern civilization and culture; in the *sylla-*

bus that accompanied it he enumerated and anathematized all the rational theses and philosophical principles which are regarded by modern science as lucid truths. (3) Finally, six years afterwards—on July 13, 1870—the militant head of the Church crowned his folly by claiming *infallibility* for himself and all his predecessors in the papal chair. This triumph of the Roman *curia* was communicated to the astonished world five days afterwards, on the very day on which France declared war with Prussia. Two months later the temporal power of the pope was taken from him in consequence of the war.

These three stupendous acts of the papacy were such obvious assaults on the reason of the nineteenth century that they gave rise, from the very beginning, to a most heated discussion even within orthodox Catholic circles. When the Vatican Council proceeded to define the dogma of infallibility on July 13, 1870, only three-fourths of the bishops declared in its favor, 451 out of 601 assenting; many other bishops, who wished to keep clear of the perilous definition, were absent from the council. But the shrewd pontiff had calculated better than the timid " discreet Catholics ": even this extraordinary dogma was blindly accepted by the credulous and uneducated masses of the faithful.

The whole history of the papacy, as it is substantiated by a thousand reliable sources and accessible documents, appears to the impartial student as an unscrupulous tissue of lying and deceit, a reckless pursuit of absolute mental despotism and secular power, a frivolous contradiction of all the high moral precepts which true Christianity enunciates—charity and toleration, truth and chastity, poverty and self-denial. When we judge the long series of popes and of the Ro-

SCIENCE AND CHRISTIANITY

man princes of the Church, from whom the pope is chosen, by the standard of pure Christian morality, it is clear that the great majority of them were pitiful impostors, many of them utterly worthless and vicious. These well-known historical facts, however, do not prevent millions of educated Catholics from admitting the infallibility which the pope has claimed for himself; they do not prevent Protestant princes from going to Rome, and doing reverence to the pontiff (their most dangerous enemy); they do not prevent the fate of the German people from being intrusted to-day to the hands of the servants and followers of this "pious impostor" in the Reichstag—thanks to the incredible political indolence and credulity of the nation.

The most interesting of the three great events by which the papacy has endeavored to maintain and strengthen its despotism in the nineteenth century is the publication of the encyclica and the syllabus in December, 1864. In these remarkable documents all independent action was forbidden to reason and science, and they were commanded to submit implicitly to faith —that is, to the decrees of the infallible pope. The great excitement which followed this sublime piece of effrontery in educated and independent circles was in proportion with the stupendous contents of the encyclica. Draper has given us an excellent discussion of its educational and political significance in his *History of the Conflict between Science and Religion*.

The dogma of the immaculate conception seems, perhaps, to be less audacious and significant than the encyclica and the dogma of the infallibility of the pope. Yet not only the Roman hierarchy, but even some of the orthodox Protestants (the Evangelical Alliance, for instance), attach great importance to this thesis.

THE RIDDLE OF THE UNIVERSE

What is known as the " immaculate oath "—that is, the confirmation of faith by an oath taken on the immaculate conception of Mary—is still regarded by millions of Christians as a sacred obligation. Many believers take the dogma in a twofold application; they think that the mother of Mary was impregnated by the Holy Ghost as well as Mary herself. Comparative and critical theology has recently shown that this myth has no greater claim to originality than most of the other stories in the Christian mythology; it has been borrowed from older religions, especially Buddhism. Similar myths were widely circulated in India, Persia, Asia Minor, and Greece several centuries before the birth of Christ. Whenever a king's unwedded daughter, or some other maid of high degree, gave birth to a child, the father was always pronounced to be a god, or a demi-god; in the Christian case it was the Holy Ghost.

The special endowments of mind or body which often distinguished these " children of love " above ordinary offspring were thus partly explained by " heredity." Distinguished " sons of God " of this kind were held in high esteem both in antiquity and during the Middle Ages, while the moral code of modern civilization reproaches them with their want of honorable parentage. This applies even more forcibly to " daughters of God," though the poor maidens are just as little to blame for their want of a father. For the rest, every one who is familiar with the beautiful mythology of classical antiquity knows that these sons and daughters of the Greek and Roman gods often approach nearest to the highest ideal of humanity. Recollect the large legitimate family, and the still more numerous illegitimate offspring, of Zeus.

SCIENCE AND CHRISTIANITY

To return to the particular question of the impregnation of the Virgin Mary by the Holy Ghost, we are referred to the gospels for testimony to the fact. The only two evangelists who speak of it, Matthew and Luke, relate in harmony that the Jewish maiden Mary was betrothed to the carpenter Joseph, but became pregnant without his co-operation, and, indeed, "by the Holy Ghost." As we have already related, the four canonical gospels which are regarded as the only genuine ones by the Christian Church, and adopted as the foundation of faith, were deliberately chosen from a much larger number of gospels, the details of which contradict each other sometimes just as freely as the assertions of the four. The fathers of the Church enumerate from forty to fifty of these spurious or apocryphal gospels; some of them are written both in Greek and Latin—for instance, the gospel of James, of Thomas, of Nicodemus, and so forth. The details which these apocryphal gospels give of the life of Christ, especially with regard to his birth and childhood, have just as much (or, on the whole, just as little) claim to historical validity as the four canonical gospels.

Now we find in one of these documents an historical statement, confirmed, moreover, in the *Sepher Toldoth Jeschua*, which probably furnishes the simple and natural solution of the "world-riddle" of the supernatural conception and birth of Christ. The author curtly gives us in one sentence the remarkable statement which contains this solution: "Josephus Pandera, the Roman officer of a Calabrian legion which was in Judæa, seduced Miriam of Bethlehem, and was the father of Jesus." Other details given about Miriam (the Hebrew name for Mary) are far from being to the credit of the "Queen of Heaven."

Naturally, these historical details are carefully avoided by the official theologian, but they assort badly with the traditional myth, and lift the veil from its mystery in a very simple and natural fashion. That makes it the more incumbent on impartial research and pure reason to make a critical examination of these statements. It must be admitted that they have much more title to credence than all the other statements about the birth of Christ. When, on familiar principles of science, we put aside the notion of supernatural conception through an "overshadowing of the Most High" as a pure myth, there only remains the widely accepted version of modern rational theology—that Joseph, the Jewish carpenter, was the true father of Christ. But this assumption is explicitly contradicted by many texts of the gospels; Christ himself was convinced that he was a "Son of God," and he never recognized his foster-father, Joseph, as his real parent. Joseph, indeed, wanted to leave his betrothed when he found her pregnant without his interference. He gave up this idea when an angel appeared to him in a dream and pacified him. As it is expressly stated in the first chapter of Matthew (vv. 24, 25), there was no sexual intercourse between Joseph and Mary until after Jesus was born.

The statement of the apocryphal gospels, that the Roman officer, Pandera, was the true father of Christ, seems all the more credible when we make a careful anthropological study of the personality of Christ. He is generally regarded as purely Jewish. Yet the characteristics which distinguish his high and noble personality, and which give a distinct impress to his religion, are certainly not Semitical; they are rather features of the higher Arian race, and especially of its noblest branch, the Hellenes. Now, the name of Christ's real

SCIENCE AND CHRISTIANITY

father, "Pandera," points unequivocally to a Greek origin; in one manuscript, in fact, it is written "Pandora." Pandora was, according to the Greek mythology, the first woman, born of the earth by Vulcan and adorned with every charm by the gods, who was espoused by Epimetheus, and sent by Zeus to men with the dread "Pandora-box," containing every evil, in punishment for the stealing of divine fire from heaven by Prometheus.

And it is interesting to see the different reception that the love-story of Miriam has met with at the hands of the four great Christian nations of civilized Europe. The stern morality of the Teutonic races entirely repudiates it; the righteous German and the prudish Briton prefer to believe blindly in the impossible thesis of a conception "by the Holy Ghost." It is well known that this strenuous and carefully paraded prudery of the higher classes (especially in England) is by no means reflected in the true condition of sexual morality in high quarters. The revelations which the *Pall Mall Gazette*, for instance, made on the subject twelve years ago vividly recalled the condition of Babylon.

The Romantic races, which ridicule this prudery and take sexual relations less seriously, find *Mary's Romance* attractive enough; the special cult which "Our Lady" enjoys in France and Italy is often associated with this love-story with curious naïveté. Thus, for example, Paul de Regla (Dr. Desjardin), author of *Jesus of Nazareth considered from a Scientific, Historical, and Social Standpoint* (1894), finds precisely in the illegitimate birth of Christ a special "title to the halo that irradiates his noble form."

It seemed to me necessary to enter fully into this important question of the origin of Christ in the sense of impartial historical science, because the Church militant itself lays great emphasis on it, and because it regards the miraculous structure which has been founded on it as one of its strongest weapons against modern thought. The highest ethical value of pure primitive Christianity and the ennobling influence of this "religion of love" on the history of civilization are quite independent of those mythical dogmas. The so-called "revelations" on which these myths are based are incompatible with the firmest results of modern science.

CHAPTER XVIII

OUR MONISTIC RELIGION

Monism as a Connecting Link between Religion and Science—
The *Cultur-Kampf*—The Relations of Church and State—
Principles of the Monistic Religion—Its Three-fold Ideal: the
Good, the True, and the Beautiful—Contradiction between
Scientific and Christian Truth—Harmony of the Monistic
and the Christian Idea of Virtue—Opposition between Monistic
and Christian Views of Art—Modern Expansion and Enrichment of Our Idea of the World—Landscape-Painting and the
Modern Enjoyment of Nature—The Beauties of Nature—This
World and Beyond—Monistic Churches

MANY distinguished scientists and philosophers of the day, who share our monistic views, consider that religion is generally played out. Their meaning is that the clear insight into the evolution of the world which the great scientific progress of the nineteenth century has afforded us will satisfy, not only the causal feeling of our reason, but even our highest emotional cravings. This view is correct in the sense that the two ideas, religion and science, would indeed blend into one if we had a perfectly clear and consecutive system of monism. However, there are but a few resolute thinkers who attain to this most pure and lofty conception of Spinoza and Goethe. Most of the educated people of our time (as distinct from the uncultured masses) remain in the conviction that religion is a separate branch of our mental life, independent of science, and not less valuable and indispensable.

If we adopt this view, we can find a means of reconciling the two great and apparently quite distinct branches in the idea I put forward in "Monism, as a Connecting-Link between Religion and Science," in 1892. In the preface to this *Confession of Faith of a Man of Science* I expressed myself in the following words with regard to its double object: "In the first place, I must give expression to the rational system which is logically forced upon us by the recent progress of science; it dwells in the intimate thoughts of nearly every impartial and thoughtful scientist, though few have the courage or the disposition to avow it. In the second place, I would make of it a connecting-link between religion and science, and thus do away with the antithesis which has been needlessly maintained between these two branches of the highest activity of the human mind. The ethical craving of our emotion is satisfied by monism no less than the logical demand for causality on the part of reason."

The remarkable interest which the discourse enkindled is a proof that in this monistic profession of faith I expressed the feeling not only of many scientists, but of a large number of cultured men and women of very different circles. Not only was I rewarded by hundreds of sympathetic letters, but by a wide circulation of the printed address, of which six editions were required within six months. I had the more reason to be content with this unexpected success, as this "confession of faith" was originally merely an occasional speech which I delivered unprepared on October 9, 1892, at Altenburg, during the jubilee of the Scientific Society of East Germany. Naturally there was

OUR MONISTIC RELIGION

the usual demonstration on the other side; I was fiercely attacked, not only by the ultramontane press, the sworn defenders of superstition, but also by the "liberal" controversialists of evangelical Christianity, who profess to defend both scientific truth and purified faith. In the seven years that have ensued since that time the great struggle between modern science and orthodox Christianity has become more threatening; it has grown more dangerous for science in proportion as Christianity has found support in an increasing mental and political reaction. In some countries the Church has made such progress that the freedom of thought and conscience, which is guaranteed by the laws, is in practice gravely menaced (for instance, in Bavaria). The great historic struggle which Draper has so admirably depicted in his *Conflict between Religion and Science* is to-day more acute and significant than ever. For the last twenty-seven years it has been rightly called the "*cultur-kampf.*"

The famous encyclica and syllabus which the militant pope, Pius IX., sent out into the entire world in 1864 were a declaration of war on the whole of modern science; they demanded the blind submission of reason to the dogmas of the infallible pope. The enormity of this crude assault on the highest treasures of civilization even roused many indolent minds from the slumber of belief. Together with the subsequent promulgation of the papal infallibility (1870), the encyclica provoked a deep wave of irritation and an energetic repulse which held out high hopes. In the new German empire, which had attained its indispensable national unity by the heavy sacrifices of the wars of 1866 and 1871, the insolent attacks of the pope were felt to be particularly offensive. On the one hand,

THE RIDDLE OF THE UNIVERSE

Germany is the cradle of the Reformation and the modern emancipation of reason; on the other hand, it unfortunately has in its 18,000,000 Catholics a vast host of militant believers, who are unsurpassed by any other civilized people in blind obedience to their chief shepherd.

The dangers of such a situation were clearly recognized by the great statesman who had solved the political "world-riddle" of the dismemberment of Germany, and had led us by a marvellous statecraft to the long-desired goal of national unity and power. Prince Bismarck began the famous struggle with the Vatican, which is known as the *cultur-kampf*, in 1872, and it was conducted with equal ability and energy by the distinguished Minister of Worship, Falk, author of the May laws of 1873. Unfortunately, Bismarck had to desist six years afterwards. Although the great statesman was a remarkable judge of men and a realistic politician of immense tact, he had underestimated the force of three powerful obstacles—first, the unsurpassed cunning and unscrupulous treachery of the Roman *curia*; secondly, the correlative ingratitude and credulity of the uneducated Catholic masses, on which the papacy built; and, thirdly, the power of apathy, the continuance of the irrational, simply because it is in possession. Hence, in 1878, when the abler Leo XIII. had ascended the pontifical throne, the fatal "To Canossa" was heard once more. From that time the newly established power of Rome grew in strength; partly through the unscrupulous intrigues and serpentine bends of its slippery Jesuitical politics, partly through the false Church-politics of the German government and the marvellous political incompetence of the German people. We have, therefore, at the close

OUR MONISTIC RELIGION

of the nineteenth century to endure the pitiful spectacle of the Catholic "Centre" being the most important section of the Reichstag, and the fate of our humiliated country depending on a papal party, which does not constitute numerically a third part of the nation.

When the *cultur-kampf* began in 1872, it was justly acclaimed by all independent thinkers as a political renewal of the Reformation, a vigorous attempt to free modern civilization from the yoke of papal despotism. The whole of the Liberal press hailed Bismarck as a "political Luther"—as the great hero, not only of the national unity, but also of the rational emancipation of Germany. Ten years afterwards, when the papacy had proved victorious, the same "Liberal press" changed its colors, and denounced the *cultur-kampf* as a great mistake; and it does the same thing to-day. The facts show how short is the memory of our journalists, how defective their knowledge of history, and how poor their philosophic education. The so-called "Peace between Church and State" is never more than a suspension of hostilities. The modern papacy, true to the despotic principles it has followed for the last sixteen hundred years, is determined to wield sole dominion over the credulous souls of men; it must demand the absolute submission of the cultured State, which, as such, defends the rights of reason and science. True and enduring peace there cannot be until one of the combatants lies powerless on the ground. Either the Church wins, and then farewell to all "free science and free teaching"—then are our universities no better than jails, and our colleges become cloistral schools; or else the modern rational State proves victorious—then, in the twentieth century, human culture, freedom, and prosperity will continue their progressive development until they far surpass even the height of the nineteenth century.

In order to compass these high aims, it is of the first importance that modern science not only shatter the false structures of superstition and sweep their ruins from the path, but that it also erect a new abode for human emotion on the ground it has cleared—a " palace of reason," in which, under the influence of our new monistic views, we do reverence to the real trinity of the nineteenth century—the trinity of " the true, the good, and the beautiful." In order to give a tangible shape to the cult of this divine ideal, we must first of all compare our position with the dominant forms of Christianity, and realize the changes that are involved in the substitution of the one for the other. For, in spite of its errors and defects, the Christian religion (in its primitive and purer form) has so high an ethical value, and has entered so deeply into the most important social and political movements of civilized history for the last fifteen hundred years, that we must appeal as much as possible to its existing institutions in the establishment of our monistic religion. We do not seek a mighty *revolution*, but a rational *reformation*, of our religious life. And just as, two thousand years ago, the classic poetry of the ancient Greeks incarnated their ideals of virtue in divine shapes, so may we, too, lend the character of noble goddesses to our three rational ideals. We must inquire into the features of the three goddesses of the monist—truth, beauty, and virtue; and we must study their relation to the three corresponding ideals of Christianity which they are to replace.

I. The preceding inquiries (especially those of the first and third sections) have convinced us that truth

OUR MONISTIC RELIGION

unadulterated is only to be found in the temple of the study of nature, and that the only available paths to it are critical observation and reflection—the empirical investigation of facts and the rational study of their efficient causes. In this way we arrive, by means of pure reason, at true science, the highest treasure of civilized man. We must, in accordance with the arguments of our sixteenth chapter, reject what is called " revelation," the poetry of faith, that affirms the discovery of truth in a supernatural fashion, without the assistance of reason. And since the entire structure of the Judæo-Christian religion, like that of the Mohammedan and the Buddhistic, rests on these so-called revelations, and these mystic fruits of the imagination directly contradict the clear results of empirical research, it is obvious that we shall only attain to a knowledge of the truth by the rational activity of genuine science, not by the poetic imagining of a mystic faith. In this respect it is quite certain that the Christian system must give way to the monistic. The goddess of truth dwells in the temple of nature, in the green woods, on the blue sea, and on the snowy summits of the hills—not in the gloom of the cloister, nor in the narrow prisons of our jail-like schools, nor in the clouds of incense of the Christian churches. The paths which lead to the noble divinity of truth and knowledge are the loving study of nature and its laws, the observation of the infinitely great star-world with the aid of the telescope, and the infinitely tiny cell-world with the aid of the microscope—not senseless ceremonies and unthinking prayers, not alms and Peter's Pence. The rich gifts which the goddess of truth bestows on us are the noble fruits of the tree of knowledge and the inestimable treasure of a clear, unified view of the world—

not belief in supernatural miracles and the illusion of an eternal life.

II. It is otherwise with the divine ideal of eternal goodness. In our search for the truth we have entirely to exclude the " revelation " of the churches, and devote ourselves solely to the study of nature; but, on the other hand, the idea of the good, which we call virtue, in our monistic religion coincides for the most part with the Christian idea of virtue. We are speaking, naturally, of the primitive and pure Christianity of the first three centuries, as far as we learn its moral teaching from the gospels and the epistles of Paul; it does not apply to the Vatican caricature of that pure doctrine which has dominated European civilization, to its infinite prejudice, for twelve hundred years. The best part of Christian morality, to which we firmly adhere, is represented by the humanist precepts of charity and toleration, compassion and assistance. However, these noble commands, which are set down as " Christian " morality (in its best sense), are by no means original discoveries of Christianity; they are derived from earlier religions. The Golden Rule, which sums up these precepts in one sentence, is centuries older than Christianity. In the conduct of life this law of natural morality has been followed just as frequently by non-Christians and atheists as it has been neglected by pious believers. Moreover, Christian ethics was marred by the great defect of a narrow insistence on altruism and a denunciation of egoism. Our monistic ethics lays equal emphasis on the two, and finds perfect virtue in the just balance of love of self and love of one's neighbor (cf. chap. xix.).

III. But monism enters into its strongest opposition to Christianity on the question of beauty. Primi-

OUR MONISTIC RELIGION

tive Christianity preached the worthlessness of earthly life, regarding it merely as a preparation for an eternal life beyond. Hence it immediately followed that all we find in the life of man here below, all that is beautiful in art and science, in public and in private life, is of no real value. The true Christian must avert his eyes from them; he must think only of a worthy preparation for the life beyond. Contempt of nature, aversion from all its inexhaustible charms, rejection of every kind of fine art, are Christian duties; and they are carried out to perfection when a man separates himself from his fellows, chastises his body, and spends all his time in prayer in the cloister or the hermit's cell.

History teaches us that this ascetical morality that would scorn the whole of nature had, as a natural consequence, the very opposite effect to that it intended. Monasteries, the homes of chastity and discipline, soon became dens of the wildest orgies; the sexual commerce of monks and nuns has inspired shoals of novels, as it is so faithfully depicted in the literature of the Renaissance. The cult of the "beautiful," which was then practised, was in flagrant contradiction with the vaunted "abandonment of the world"; and the same must be said of the pomp and luxury which soon developed in the immoral private lives of the higher ecclesiastics and in the artistic decoration of Christian churches and monasteries.

It may be objected that our view is refuted by the splendor of Christian art, which, especially in the best days of the Middle Ages, created works of undying beauty. The graceful Gothic cathedrals and Byzantine basilicas, the hundreds of magnificent chapels, the thousands of marble statues of saints and martyrs, the millions of fine pictures of saints, of profoundly conceived representations of Christ and the madonna —all are proofs of the development of a noble art in the Middle Ages, which is unique of its kind. All these splendid monuments of mediæval art are untouched in their high æsthetic value, whatever we say of their mixture of truth and fancy. Yes; but what has all that to do with the pure teaching of Christianity—with that religion of sacrifice that turned scornfully away from all earthly parade and glamour, from all material beauty and art; that made light of the life of the family and the love of woman; that urged an exclusive concern as to the immaterial goods of eternal life? The idea of a Christian art is a contradiction in terms—a *contradictio in adjecto*. The wealthy princes of the Church who fostered it were candidly aiming at very different ideals, and they completely attained them. In directing the whole interest and activity of the human mind in the Middle Ages to the Christian Church and its distinctive art they were diverting it *from nature* and from the knowledge of the treasures that were hidden in it, and would have conducted to independent science. Moreover, the daily sight of the huge images of the saints and of the scenes of " sacred history " continually reminded the faithful of the vast collection of myths that the Church had made. The legends themselves were taught and believed to be true narratives, and the stories of miracles to be records of actual events. It cannot be doubted that in this respect Christian art has exercised an immense influence on general culture, and especially in the strengthening of Christian belief—an influence which still endures throughout the entire civilized world.

The diametrical opposite of this dominant Christian

OUR MONISTIC RELIGION

art is the new artistic tendency which has been developed during the present century in connection with science. The remarkable expansion of our knowledge of nature, and the discovery of countless beautiful forms of life, which it includes, have awakened quite a new æsthetic sense in our generation, and thus given a new tone to painting and sculpture. Numerous scientific voyages and expeditions for the exploration of unknown lands and seas, partly in earlier centuries, but more especially in the nineteenth, have brought to light an undreamed abundance of new organic forms. The number of new species of animals and plants soon became enormous, and among them (especially among the lower groups that had been neglected before) there were thousands of forms of great beauty and interest, affording an entirely new inspiration for painting, sculpture, architecture, and technical art. In this respect a new world was revealed by the great advance of microscopic research in the second half of the century, and especially by the discovery of the marvellous inhabitants of the deep sea, which were first brought to light by the famous expedition of the *Challenger* (1872-76). Thousands of graceful radiolaria and thalamophora, of pretty medusæ and corals, of extraordinary molluscs, and crabs, suddenly introduced us to a wealth of hidden organisms beyond all anticipation, the peculiar beauty and diversity of which far transcend all the creations of the human imagination. In the fifty large volumes of the account of the *Challenger* expedition a vast number of these beautiful forms are delineated on three thousand plates; and there are millions of other lovely organisms described in other great works that are included in the fast-growing literature of zoology and botany of the last ten years. I began on a small scale to select a number of these beautiful forms for more popular description in my *Art Forms in Nature* (1899).

However, there is now no need for long voyages and costly works to appreciate the beauties of this world. A man needs only to keep his eyes open and his mind disciplined. Surrounding nature offers us everywhere a marvellous wealth of lovely and interesting objects of all kinds. In every bit of moss and blade of grass, in every beetle and butterfly, we find, when we examine it carefully, beauties which are usually overlooked. Above all, when we examine them with a powerful glass or, better still, with a good microscope, we find everywhere in nature a new world of inexhaustible charms.

But the nineteenth century has not only opened our eyes to the æsthetic enjoyment of the microscopic world; it has shown us the beauty of the greater objects in nature. Even at its commencement it was the fashion to regard the mountains as magnificent but forbidding, and the sea as sublime but dreaded. At its close the majority of educated people—especially they who dwell in the great cities—are delighted to enjoy the glories of the Alps and the crystal splendor of the glacier world for a fortnight every year, or to drink in the majesty of the ocean and the lovely scenery of its coasts. All these sources of the keenest enjoyment of nature have only recently been revealed to us in all their splendor, and the remarkable progress we have made in facility and rapidity of conveyance has given even the less wealthy an opportunity of approaching them. All this progress in the æsthetic enjoyment of nature—and, proportionately, in the scientific understanding of nature—implies an equal advance in higher mental development and, consequently, in the direction of our monistic religion.

OUR MONISTIC RELIGION

The opposite character of our *naturalistic* century to that of the *anthropistic* centuries that preceded is especially noticeable in the different appreciation and spread of illustrations of the most diverse natural objects. In our own days a lively interest in artistic work of that kind has been developed, which did not exist in earlier ages; it has been supported by the remarkable progress of commerce and technical art which have facilitated a wide popularization of such illustrations. Countless illustrated periodicals convey along with their general information a sense of the inexhaustible beauty of nature in all its departments. In particular, landscape-painting has acquired an importance that surpassed all imagination. In the first half of the century one of our greatest and most erudite scientists, Alexander Humboldt, had pointed out that the development of modern landscape-painting is not only of great importance as an incentive to the study of nature and as a means of geographical description, but that it is to be commended in other respects as a noble educative medium. Since that time the taste for it has considerably increased. It should be the aim at every school to teach the children to enjoy scenery at an early age, and to give them the valuable art of imprinting on the memory by a drawing or water-color sketch.

The infinite wealth of nature in what is beautiful and sublime offers every man with open eyes and an æsthetic sense an incalculable sum of choicest gifts. Still, however valuable and agreeable is the immediate enjoyment of each single gift, its worth is doubled by a knowledge of its meaning and its connection with the rest of nature. When Humboldt gave us the "outline of a physical description of the world" in his magnificent *Cosmos* forty years ago, and when he combined

THE RIDDLE OF THE UNIVERSE

scientific and æsthetic consideration so happily in his standard *Prospects of Nature*, he justly indicated how closely the higher enjoyment of nature is connected with the " scientific establishment of cosmic laws," and that the conjunction of the two serves to raise human nature to a higher stage of perfection The astonishment with which we gaze upon the starry heavens and the microscopic life in a drop of water, the awe with which we trace the marvellous working of energy in the motion of matter, the reverence with which we grasp the universal dominance of the law of substance throughout the universe—all these are part of our emotional life, falling under the heading of "natural religion."

This progress of modern times in knowledge of the true and enjoyment of the beautiful expresses, on the one hand, a valuable element of our monistic religion, but is, on the other hand, in fatal opposition to Christianity. For the human mind is thus made to live on this side of the grave; Christianity would have it ever gaze beyond. Monism teaches that we are perishable children of the earth, who for one or two, or, at the most, three generations, have the good fortune to enjoy the treasures of our planet, to drink of the inexhaustible fountain of its beauty, and to trace out the marvellous play of its forces. Christianity would teach us that the earth is "a vale of tears," in which we have but a brief period to chasten and torment ourselves in order to merit the life of eternal bliss beyond. Where this " beyond " is, and of what joys the glory of this eternal life is compacted, no revelation has ever told us. As long as " heaven " was thought to be the blue vault that hovers over the disk of our planet, and is illumined by the twinkling light of a few thousand stars,

OUR MONISTIC RELIGION

the human imagination could picture to itself the ambrosial banquets of the Olympic gods above or the laden tables of the happy dwellers in Valhalla. But now all these deities and the immortal souls that sat at their tables are " houseless and homeless," as David Strauss has so ably described; for we know from astrophysical science that the immeasurable depths of space are filled with a prosaic ether, and that millions of heavenly bodies, ruled by eternal laws of iron, rush hither and thither in the great ocean, in their eternal rhythm of life and death.

The places of devotion, in which men seek the satisfaction of their religious emotions and worship the objects of their reverence, are regarded as sacred "churches." The pagodas of Buddhistic Asia, the Greek temples of classical antiquity, the synagogues of Palestine, the mosques of Egypt, the Catholic cathedrals of the south, and the Protestant cathedrals of the north, of Europe—all these " houses of God " serve to raise man above the misery and the prose of daily life, to lift him into the sacred, poetic atmosphere of a higher, ideal world. They attain this end in a thousand different ways, according to their various forms of worship and their age. The modern man who " has science and art "—and, therefore, " religion "—needs no special church, no narrow, enclosed portion of space. For through the length and breadth of free nature, wherever he turns his gaze, to the whole universe or to any single part of it, he finds, indeed, the grim " struggle for life," but by its side are ever " the good, the true, and the beautiful "; his church is commensurate with the whole of glorious nature. Still, there will always be men of special temperament who will desire to have decorated temples or churches as places of devotion

345

to which they may withdraw. Just as the Catholics had to relinquish a number of churches to the Reformation in the sixteenth century, so a still larger number will pass over to " free societies " of monists in the coming years.

CHAPTER XIX

OUR MONISTIC ETHICS

Monistic and Dualistic Ethics—Contradiction of Pure and Practical Reason in Kant—His Categorical Imperative—The Neo-Kantians—Herbert Spencer—Egoism and Altruism—Equivalence of the Two Instincts—The Fundamental Law of Ethics. the Golden Rule—Its Antiquity—Christian Ethics—Contempt of Self, the Body, Nature, Civilization, the Family, Woman—Roman Catholic Ethics—Immoral Results of Celibacy—Necessity for the Abolition of the Law of Celibacy, Oral Confession, and Indulgences—State and Church—Religion a Private Concern—Church and School—State and School—Need of School Reform

THE practical conduct of life makes a number of definite ethical claims on a man which can only be duly and naturally satisfied when they are in complete harmony with his view of the world. In accordance with this fundamental principle of our monistic philosophy, our whole system of ethics must be rationally connected with the unified conception of the cosmos which we have formed by our advanced knowledge of the laws of nature. Just as the infinite universe is one great whole in the light of our monistic teaching, so the spiritual and moral life of man is a part of this cosmos, and our naturalistic ordering of it must also be monistic. There are not two different, separate worlds—the one physical and material, and the other moral and immaterial.

THE RIDDLE OF THE UNIVERSE

The great majority of philosophers and theologians still hold the contrary opinion. They affirm, with Kant, that the moral world is quite independent of the physical, and is subject to very different laws; hence a man's conscience, as the basis of his moral life, must also be quite independent of our scientific knowledge of the world, and must be based rather on his religious faith. On that theory the study of the moral world belongs to *practical* reason, while that of nature, or of the physical world, is referred to *pure* or theoretical reason. This unequivocal and conscious dualism of Kant's philosophy was its greatest defect; it has caused, and still causes, incalculable mischief. First of all the " critical Kant " had built up the splendid and marvellous palace of pure reason, and convincingly proved that the three great central dogmas of metaphysics—a personal God, free will, and the immortal soul—had no place whatever in it, and that no rational proof could be found of their reality. Afterwards, however, the "dogmatic Kant" superimposed on this true crystal palace of *pure* reason the glittering, ideal castle in the air of *practical* reason, in which three imposing church-naves were designed for the accommodation of those three great mystic divinities. When they had been put out at the front door by rational knowledge they returned by the back door under the guidance of irrational faith.

The cupola of his great cathedral of faith was crowned by Kant with his curious idol, the famous " categorical imperative." According to it, the demand of the universal moral law is unconditional, independent of any regard to actuality or potentiality. It runs: " Act at all times in such wise that the maxim (or the subjective law of thy will) may hold good as a principle of a uni-

OUR MONISTIC ETHICS

versal law." On that theory all normal men would have the same sense of duty. Modern anthropology has ruthlessly dissipated that pretty dream; it has shown that conceptions of duty differ even more among uncivilized than among civilized nations All the actions and customs which we regard as sins or loathsome crimes (theft, fraud, murder, adultery, etc) are considered by other nations in certain circumstances to be virtues, or even sacred duties.

Although the obvious contradiction of the two forms of reason in Kant's teaching, the fundamental antagonism of pure and practical reason, was recognized and attacked at the very beginning of the century, it is still pretty widely accepted. The modern school of neo-Kantians urges a " return to Kant " so pressingly precisely on account of this agreeable dualism; the Church militant zealously supports it because it fits in admirably with its own mystic faith. But it met with an effective reverse at the hands of modern science in the second half of the nineteenth century, which entirely demolished the theses of the system of practical reason. Monistic cosmology proved, on the basis of the law of substance, that there is no personal God; comparative and genetic psychology showed that there cannot be an immortal soul; and monistic physiology proved the futility of the assumption of " free will." Finally, the science of evolution made it clear that the same eternal iron laws that rule in the inorganic world are valid too in the organic and moral world.

But modern science gives not only a negative support to practical philosophy and ethics in demolishing the Kantian dualism, but it renders the positive service of substituting for it the new structure of ethical monism. It shows that the feeling of duty does not rest on an illusory " categorical imperative," but on the solid ground of *social instinct*, as we find in the case of all social animals. It regards as the highest aim of all morality the re-establishment of a sound harmony between egoism and altruism, between self-love and the love of one's neighbor. It is to the great English philosopher, Herbert Spencer, that we owe the founding of this monistic ethics on a basis of evolution.

Man belongs to the social vertebrates, and has, therefore, like all social animals, two sets of duties — first to himself, and secondly to the society to which he belongs. The former are the behests of self-love or egoism, the latter of love for one's fellows or altruism. The two sets of precepts are equally just, equally natural, and equally indispensable. If a man desire to have the advantage of living in an organized community, he has to consult not only his own fortune, but also that of the society, and of the " neighbors " who form the society. He must realize that its prosperity is his own prosperity, and that it cannot suffer without his own injury. This fundamental law of society is so simple and so inevitable that one cannot understand how it can be contradicted in theory or in practice; yet that is done to-day, and has been done for thousands of years.

The equal appreciation of these two natural impulses, or the moral equivalence of self-love and love of others, is the chief and the fundamental principle of our morality. Hence the highest aim of all ethics is very simple—it is the re-establishment of " the natural equality of egoism and altruism, of the love of one's self and the love of one's neighbor." The Golden Rule says: " Do unto others as you would that they should do unto

OUR MONISTIC ETHICS

you." From this highest precept of Christianity it follows of itself that we have just as sacred duties towards ourselves as we have towards our fellows. I have explained my conception of this principle in my *Monism,* and laid down three important theses. (1) Both these concurrent impulses are natural laws, of equal importance and necessity for the preservation of the family and the society; egoism secures the self-preservation of the individual, altruism that of the species which is made up of the chain of perishable individuals. (2) The social duties which are imposed by the social structure of the associated individuals, and by means of which it secures its preservation, are merely higher evolutionary stages of the social instincts, which we find in all higher social animals (as "habits which have become hereditary"). (3) In the case of civilized man all ethics, theoretical or practical, being "a science of rules," is connected with his view of the world at large, and consequently with his religion.

From the recognition of the fundamental principle of our morality we may immediately deduce its highest precept, that noble command, which is often called the Golden Rule of morals, or, briefly, the Golden Rule. Christ repeatedly expressed it in the simple phrase: "Thou shalt love thy neighbor as thyself." Mark adds that "there is no greater commandment than this," and Matthew says: "In these two commandments is the whole law and the prophets." In this greatest and highest commandment our monistic ethics is completely at one with Christianity. We must, however, recall the historical fact that the formulation of this supreme command is not an original merit of Christ, as the majority of Christian theologians affirm and their uncritical supporters blindly accept. The Golden Rule is five hundred years older than Christ; it was laid down as the highest moral principle by many Greek and Oriental sages. Pittacus, of Mylene, one of the seven wise men of Greece, said six hundred and twenty years before Christ: " Do not that to thy neighbor that thou wouldst not suffer from him." Confucius, the great Chinese philosopher and religious founder (who rejected the idea of a personal God and of the immortality of the soul), said five hundred years B.C.: "Do to every man as thou wouldst have him do to thee; and do not to another what thou wouldst not have him do to thee. This precept only dost thou need; it is the foundation of all other commandments." Aristotle taught about the middle of the fourth century B.C.: "We must act towards others as we wish others to act towards us." In the same sense, and partly in the same words, the Golden Rule was given by Thales, Isocrates, Aristippus, Sextus, the Pythagorean, and other philosophers of classic antiquity—several centuries before Christ. From this collection it is clear that the Golden Rule had a *polyphyletic* origin—that is, it was formulated by a number of philosophers at different times and in different places, quite independently of each other. Otherwise it must be assumed that Jesus derived it from some other Oriental source, from ancient Semitic, Indian, Chinese, or especially Buddhistic traditions, as has been proved in the case of most of the other Christian doctrines.

As the great ethical principle is thus twenty-five hundred years old, and as Christianity itself has put it at the head of its moral teaching as the highest and all-embracing commandment, it follows that our monistic ethics is in complete harmony on this important point, not only with the ethics of the ancient heathens, but also

OUR MONISTIC ETHICS

with that of Christianity. Unfortunately this harmony is disturbed by the fact that the gospels and the Pauline epistles contain many other points of moral teaching, which contradict our first and supreme commandment. Christian theologians have fruitlessly striven to explain away these striking and painful contradictions by their ingenious interpretations. We need not enter into that question now, but we must briefly consider those unfortunate aspects of Christian ethics which are incompatible with the better thought of the modern age, and which are distinctly injurious in their practical consequences. Of that character is the contempt which Christianity has shown for self, for the body, for nature, for civilization, for the family, and for woman.

I. The supreme mistake of Christian ethics, and one which runs directly counter to the Golden Rule, is its exaggeration of love of one's neighbor at the expense of self-love. Christianity attacks and despises egoism on principle. Yet that natural impulse is absolutely indispensable in view of self-preservation; indeed, one may say that even altruism, its apparent opposite, is only an enlightened egoism. Nothing great or elevated has ever taken place without egoism, and without the passion that urges us to great sacrifices. It is only the excesses of the impulse that are injurious. One of the Christian precepts that were impressed upon us in our early youth as of great importance, and that are glorified in millions of sermons, is: "Love your enemies, bless them that curse you, do good to them that hate you, and pray for them which despitefully use you and persecute you." It is a very ideal precept, but as useless in practice as it is unnatural. So it is with the counsel, "If any man will take away thy coat, let him have thy cloak also." Translated into the terms of modern life, that means: "When some unscrupulous scoundrel has defrauded thee of half thy goods, let him have the other half also." Or, again, in the language of modern politics: "When the pious English take from you simple Germans one after another of your new and valuable colonies in Africa, let them have all the rest of your colonies also —or, best of all, give them Germany itself." And, while we touch on the marvellous world-politics of modern England, we may note in passing its direct contradiction of every precept of Christian charity, which is more frequently on the lips of that great nation than of any other nation in the world. However, the glaring contradiction between the theoretical, *ideal*, altruistic morality of the human individual and the *real*, purely selfish morality of the human community, and especially of the civilized Christian state, is a familiar fact. It would be interesting to determine mathematically in what proportion among organized men the altruistic ethical ideal of the individual changes into its contrary, the purely egoistic "real politics" of the state and the nation.

II. Since the Christian faith takes a wholly dualistic view of the human organism and attributes to the immortal soul only a temporary sojourn in the mortal frame, it very naturally sets a much greater value on the soul than on the body. Hence results that neglect of the care of the body, of training, and of cleanliness which contrasts the life of the Christian Middle Ages so unfavorably with that of pagan classical antiquity. Christian ethics contains none of those firm commands as to daily ablutions which are theoretically laid down and practically fulfilled in the Mohammedan, Hindoo,

OUR MONISTIC ETHICS

and other religions In many monasteries the ideal of the pious Christian is the man who does not wash and clothe himself properly, who never changes his malodorous gown, and who, instead of regular work, fills up his useless life with mechanical prayers, senseless fasts, and so forth. As a special outgrowth of this contempt of the body we have the disgusting discipline of the flagellants and other ascetics.

III. One source of countless theoretical errors and practical blemishes, of deplorable crudity and privation, is found in the false anthropism of Christianity—that is, in the unique position which it gives to man, as the image of God, in opposition to all the rest of nature. In this way it has contributed, not only to an extremely injurious isolation from our glorious mother "nature," but also to a regrettable contempt of all other organisms. Christianity has no place for that well-known love of animals, that sympathy with the nearly related and friendly mammals (dogs, horses, cattle, etc.), which is urged in the ethical teaching of many of the older religions, especially Buddhism. Whoever has spent much time in the south of Europe must have often witnessed those frightful sufferings of animals which fill us friends of animals with the deepest sympathy and indignation. And when one expostulates with these brutal "Christians" on their cruelty, the only answer is, with a laugh: "But the beasts are not Christians." Unfortunately Descartes gave some support to the error in teaching that man only has a sensitive soul, not the animal.

How much more elevated is our monistic ethics than the Christian in this regard! Darwinism teaches us that we have descended immediately from the primates, and, in a secondary degree, from a long series of earlier mammals, and that, therefore, they are "our brothers"; physiology informs us that they have the same nerves and sense-organs as we, and the same feelings of pleasure and pain. No sympathetic monistic scientist would ever be guilty of that brutal treatment of animals which comes so lightly to the Christian in his anthropistic illusion—to the "child of the God of love." Moreover, this Christian contempt of nature on principle deprives man of an abundance of the highest earthly joys, especially of the keen, ennobling enjoyment of nature.

IV. Since, according to Christ's teaching, our planet is "a vale of tears," and our earthly life is valueless and a mere preparation for a better life to come, it has succeeded in inducing men to sacrifice all happiness on this side of eternity and make light of all earthly goods. Among these "earthly goods," in the case of the modern civilized man, we must include the countless great and small conveniences of technical science, hygiene, commerce, etc., which have made modern life cheerful and comfortable; we must include all the gratifications of painting, sculpture, music, and poetry, which flourished exceedingly even during the Middle Ages (in spite of its principles), and which we esteem as "ideal pleasures"; we must include all that invaluable progress of science, especially the study of nature, of which the nineteenth century is justly proud. All these "earthly goods," that have so high a value in the eyes of the monist, are worthless—nay, injurious—for the most part, according to Christian teaching; the stern code of Christian morals should look just as unfavorably on the pursuit of these pleasures as our humanistic ethics fosters and encourages it. Once more, therefore, Christianity is found to be an enemy to civili-

OUR MONISTIC ETHICS

zation, and the struggle which modern thought and science are compelled to conduct with it is, in this additional sense, a "*cultur-kampf.*"

V. Another of the most deplorable aspects of Christian morality is its belittlement of the life of the family, of that natural living together with our next of kin which is just as necessary in the case of man as in the case of all the higher social animals. The family is justly regarded as the "foundation of society," and the healthy life of the family is a necessary condition of the prosperity of the State. Christ, however, was of a very different opinion: with his gaze ever directed to "the beyond," he thought as lightly of woman and the family as of all other goods of "this life." Of his infrequent contact with his parents and sisters the gospels have very little to say; but they are far from representing his relations with his mother to have been so tender and intimate as they are poetically depicted in so many thousands of pictures. He was not married himself. Sexual love, the first foundation of the family union, seems to have been regarded by Jesus as a necessary evil. His most enthusiastic apostle, Paul, went still farther in the same direction, declaring it to be better not to marry than to marry: "It is good for a man not to touch a woman." If humanity were to follow this excellent counsel, it would soon be rid of all earthly misery and suffering; it would be killed off by such a "radical cure" within half a century.

VI. As Christ never knew the love of woman, he had no personal acquaintance with that refining of man's true nature that comes only from the intimate life of man with woman. The intimate sexual union, on which the preservation of the human race depends, is just as important on that account as the spiritual

THE RIDDLE OF THE UNIVERSE

penetration of the two sexes, or the mutual complement which they bring to each other in the practical wants of daily life as well as in the highest ideal functions of the soul. For man and woman are two different organisms, equal in worth, each having its characteristic virtues and defects. As civilization advanced, this ideal value of sexual love was more appreciated, and woman held in higher honor, especially among the Teutonic races; she is the inspiring source of the highest achievements of art and poetry. But Christ was as far from this view as nearly the whole of antiquity; he shared the idea that prevailed everywhere in the East—that woman is subordinate to man, and intercourse with her is " unclean." Long-suffering nature has taken a fearful revenge for this blunder; its sad consequences are written in letters of blood in the history of the papal Middle Ages.

The marvellous hierarchy of the Roman Church, that never disdained any means of strengthening its spiritual despotism, found an exceptionally powerful instrument in the manipulation of this " unclean " idea, and in the promotion of the ascetic notion that abstinence from intercourse with women is a virtue of itself. In the first few centuries after Christ a number of priests voluntarily abstained from marriage, and the supposed value of this celibacy soon rose to such a degree that it was made obligatory. In the Middle Ages the seduction of women of good repute and of their daughters by Catholic priests (the confessional was an active agency in the business) was a public scandal: many communities, in order to prevent such things, pressed for a license of concubinage to be given to the clergy. And it was done in many, and sometimes very romatic, ways. Thus, for instance, the canon law that

OUR MONISTIC ETHICS

the priest's cook should not be less than forty years old was very cleverly "explained" in the sense that the priest might have two cooks, one in the presbytery, another without; if one was twenty-four and the other eighteen, that made forty-two together — two years above the prescribed age. At the Christian councils, at which heretics were burned alive, the cardinals and bishops sat down with whole troops of prostitutes. The private and public debauchery of the Catholic clergy was so scandalous and dangerous to the commonwealth that there was a general rebellion against it before the time of Luther, and a loud demand for a "reformation of the church in head and members." It is well known that these immoral relations still continue in Roman Catholic lands, although more in secret. Formerly proposals were made from time to time for the definitive abrogation of celibacy, as was done, for instance, in the chambers of Baden, Bavaria, Hesse, Saxony, and other lands; but they have, unfortunately, hitherto proved unavailing. In the German Reichstag, in which the ultramontane Centre is now proposing the most ridiculous measures for the suppression of sexual immorality, there is now no party that will urge the abolition of celibacy in the interest of public morality. The so-called "Freethought" Party and the utopian social democracy coquette with the favor of the Centre.

The modern state that would lift not only the material, but the moral, life of its people to a higher level is entitled, and indeed bound, to sweep away such unworthy and harmful conditions. The obligatory celibacy of the Catholic clergy is as pernicious and immoral as the practice of auricular confession or the sale of indulgences. All three have nothing what-

THE RIDDLE OF THE UNIVERSE

ever to do with primitive Christianity. All three are directly opposed to true Christian morality. All three are disreputable inventions of the papacy, designed for the sole purpose of strengthening its despotic rule over the credulous masses and making as much material profit as possible out of them

The Nemesis of history will sooner or later exact a terrible account of the Roman papacy, and the millions who have been robbed of their happiness by this degenerate religion will help to give it its death-blow in the coming twentieth century—at least, in every truly civilized state. It has been recently calculated that the number of men who lost their lives in the papal persecutions of heretics, the Inquisition, the Christian religious wars, etc., is much more than ten millions. But what is this in comparison with the tenfold greater number of the unfortunate *moral* victims of the institutions and the priestly domination of the degenerate Christian Church—with the unnumbered millions whose higher mental life was extinguished, whose conscience was tortured, whose family life was destroyed, by the Church? We may with truth apply the words of Goethe in his *Bride of Corinth* :

> "Victims fall, nor lambs nor bulls,
> But human victims numberless."

In the great *cultur-kampf*, which must go on as long as these sad conditions exist, the first aim must be the absolute separation of Church and State. There shall be "a free Church in a free State"—that is, every Church shall be free in the practice of its special worship and ceremonies, and in the construction of its fantastic poetry and superstitious dogmas — with the sole condition that they contain no danger to social order or

OUR MONISTIC ETHICS

morality. Then there will be equal rights for all. Free societies and monistic religious bodies shall be equally tolerated, and just as free in their movements as Liberal Protestant and orthodox ultramontane congregations. But for all these "faithful" of the most diverse sects religion will have to be a private concern. The state shall supervise them, and prevent excesses; but it must neither oppress nor support them. Above all, the ratepayers shall not be compelled to contribute to the support and spread of a "faith" which they honestly believe to be a harmful superstition. In the United States such a complete separation of Church and State has been long accomplished, greatly to the satisfaction of all parties. They have also the equally important separation of the Church from the school; that is, undoubtedly, a powerful element in the great advance which science and culture have recently made in America.

It goes without saying that this exclusion of the Church from the school only refers to its sectarian principles, the particular form of belief which each Church has evolved in the course of its life. This sectarian education is purely a private concern, and should be left to parents and tutors, or to such priests or teachers as may have the personal confidence of the parents. Instead of the rejected sectarian instruction, two important branches of education will be introduced —monistic or humanist ethics and comparative religion. During the last thirty years an extensive literature has appeared dealing with the new system of ethics which has been raised on the basis of modern science —especially evolutionary science. Comparative religion will be a natural companion to the actual elementary instruction in "biblical history" and in the

THE RIDDLE OF THE UNIVERSE

mythology of Greece and Rome. Both of these will remain in the curriculum. The reason for that is obvious enough; the whole of our painting and sculpture, the chief branches of monistic æsthetics, are intimately blended with the Christian, Greek, and Roman mythologies. There will only be this important difference—that the Christian myths and legends will not be taught as truths, but as poetic fancies, like the Greek and Roman myths; the high value of the ethical and æsthetical material they contain will not be lessened, but increased, by this means. As regards the Bible, the "book of books" will only be given to the children in carefully selected extracts (a sort of "school Bible"); in this way we shall avoid the besmirching of the child's imagination with the unclean stories and passages which are so numerous in the Old Testament.

Once the modern State has freed itself and its schools from the fetters of the Church, it will be able to devote more attention to the improvement of education. The incalculable value of a good system of education has forced itself more and more upon us as the many aspects of modern civilized life have been enlarged and enriched in the course of the century. But the development of the educational methods has by no means kept pace with life in general The necessity for a comprehensive reform of our schools is making itself felt more and more. On this question, too, a number of valuable works have appeared in the course of the last forty years. We shall restrict ourselves to making a few general observations which we think of special importance.

1. In all education up to the present time *man* has played the chief part, and especially the grammatical

study of his language; the study of *nature* was entirely neglected.

2. In the school of the future nature will be the chief object of the study; a man shall learn a correct view of the world he lives in; he will not be made to stand outside of and opposed to nature, but be represented as its highest and noblest product.

3. The study of the classical tongues (Latin and Greek), which has hitherto absorbed most of the pupils' time and energy, is indeed valuable; but it will be much restricted, and confined to the mere elements (obligatory for Latin, optional for Greek).

4. In consequence, modern languages must be all the more cultivated in all the higher schools (English and French to be obligatory, Italian optional).

5. Historical instruction must pay more attention to the inner mental and spiritual life of a nation, and to the development of its civilization, and less to its external history (the vicissitudes of dynasties, wars, and so forth).

6. The elements of evolutionary science must be learned in conjunction with cosmology, geology must go with geography, and anthropology with biology.

7. The first principles of biology must be familiar to every educated man; the modern training in observation furnishes an attractive introduction to the biological sciences (anthropology, zoology, and botany). A start must be made with descriptive system (in conjunction with ætiology or bionomy); the elements of anatomy and physiology to be added later on.

8. The first principles of physics and chemistry must also be taught, and their exact establishment with the aid of mathematics.

9. Every pupil must be taught to draw well, and

from nature; and, wherever it is possible, the use of water-colors. The execution of drawings and of water-color sketches from nature (of flowers, animals, landscapes, clouds, etc.) not only excites interest in nature and helps memory to enjoy objects, but it gives the pupil his first lesson in *seeing* correctly and understanding what he has seen.

10. Much more care and time must be devoted than has been done hitherto to corporal exercise, to gymnastics and swimming; but it is especially important to have walks in common every week, and journeys on foot during the holidays. The lesson in observation which they obtain in this way is invaluable.

The chief aim of higher education up to the present time, in most countries, has been a preparation for the subsequent profession, and the acquisition of a certain amount of information and direction for civic duties. The school of the twentieth century will have for its main object the formation of independent thought, the clear understanding of the knowledge acquired, and an insight into the natural connection of phenomena. If the modern state gives every citizen a vote, it should also give him the means of developing his reason by a proper education, in order to make a rational use of his vote for the commonweal.

CHAPTER XX

SOLUTION OF THE WORLD-PROBLEMS

A Glance at the Progress of the Nineteenth Century in Solving Cosmic Problems—I. Progress of Astronomy and Cosmology—Physical and Chemical Unity of the Universe—Cosmic Metamorphoses—Evolution of the Planetary System—Analogy of the Phylogenetic Processes on the Earth and on Other Planets—Organic Inhabitants of Other Heavenly Bodies—Periodic Variation in the Making of Worlds—II. Progress of Geology and Palæontology—Neptunism and Vulcanism—Theory of Continuity—III. Progress of Physics and Chemistry—IV. Progress of Biology—Cellular Theory and Theory of Descent—V. Anthropology—Origin of Man—General Conclusion

AT the close of our philosophic study of the riddles of the universe we turn with confidence to the answer to the momentous question, How nearly have we approached to a solution of them? What is the value of the immense progress which the passing nineteenth century has made in the knowledge of nature? And what prospect does it open out to us for the future, for the further development of our system in the twentieth century, at the threshold of which we pause? Every unprejudiced thinker who impartially considers the solid progress of our empirical science, and the unity and clearness of our philosophic interpretation of it, will share our view: the nineteenth century has made greater progress in knowledge of the world and

THE RIDDLE OF THE UNIVERSE

in grasp of its nature than all its predecessors; it has solved many great problems that seemed insoluble a hundred years ago; it has opened out to us new provinces of learning, the very existence of which was unsuspected at the beginning of the century Above all, it has put clearly before our eyes the lofty aim of monistic cosmology, and has pointed out the path which alone will lead us towards it—the way of the exact empirical investigation of facts, and of the critical genetic study of their causes. The great abstract law of mechanical causality, of which our cosmological law— the law of substance—is but another and a concrete expression, now rules the entire universe, as it does the mind of man; it is the steady, immovable pole-star, whose clear light falls on our path through the dark labyrinth of the countless separate phenomena. To see the truth of this more clearly, let us cast a brief glance at the astonishing progress which the chief branches of science have made in this remarkable period.

I.—PROGRESS OF ASTRONOMY

The study of the heavens is the oldest, the study of man the youngest, of the sciences. With regard to himself and the character of his being man only obtained a clear knowledge in the second half of the present century; with regard to the starry heavens, the motions of the planets, and so on, he had acquired astonishing information forty-five hundred years ago. The ancient Chinese, Hindoos, Egyptians, and Chaldæans in the distant East knew more of the science of the spheres than the majority of educated Christians did in the West four thousand years after them. An eclipse of the sun was astronomically observed in China in the

SOLUTION OF THE WORLD-PROBLEMS

year 2697 B.C., and the plane of the ecliptic was determined by means of a gnome eleven hundred years B.C., while Christ himself had no knowledge whatever of astronomy—indeed, he looked out upon heaven and earth, nature and man, from the very narrowest geocentric and anthropocentric point of view. The greatest advance of astronomy is generally, and rightly, said to be the founding of the heliocentric system of Copernicus, whose famous work, *De Revolutionibus Orbium Celestium*, of itself caused a profound revolution in the minds of thoughtful men. In overthrowing the Ptolemaic system, he destroyed the foundation of the Christian theory, which regarded the earth as the centre of the universe and man as the godlike ruler of the earth. It was natural, therefore, that the Christian clergy, with the pope at its head, should enter upon a fierce struggle with the invaluable discovery of Copernicus. Yet it soon cleared a path for itself, when Kepler and Galileo grounded on it their true "mechanics of the heavens," and Newton gave it a solid foundation by his theory of gravitation (1686).

A further great advance, comprehending the entire universe, was the application of the idea of evolution to astronomy. It was done by the youthful Kant in 1755; in his famous general natural history and theory of the heavens he undertook the discussion, not only of the "constitution," but also of the "mechanical origin" of the whole world-structure on Newtonian principles. The splendid *Système du Monde* of Laplace, who had independently come to the same conclusions as Kant on the world-problem, gave so firm a basis to this new *Mécanique Celeste* in 1796 that it looked as if nothing entirely new of equal importance was left to be discovered in the nineteenth century. Yet here again it had the honor of opening out entirely new paths and infinitely enlarging our outlook on the universe. The invention of photography and photometry, and especially of spectral analysis (in 1860 by Bunsen and Kirchoff), introduced physics and chemistry into astronomy and led to cosmological conclusions of the utmost importance. It was now made perfectly clear that matter is the same throughout the universe, and that its physical and chemical properties in the most distant stars do not differ from those of the earth under our feet.

The monistic conviction, which we thus arrived at, of the physical and chemical unity of the entire cosmos is certainly one of the most valuable general truths which we owe to astrophysics, the new branch of astronomy which is honorably associated with the name of Friedrich Zöllner. Not less important is the clear knowledge we have obtained that the same laws of mechanical development that we have on the earth rule throughout the infinite universe. A vast, all-embracing metamorphosis goes on continuously in all parts of the universe, just as it is found in the geological history of the earth; it can be traced in the evolution of its living inhabitants as surely as in the history of peoples or in the life of each human individual. In one part of space we perceive, with the aid of our best telescopes, vast nebulæ of glowing, infinitely attenuated gas; we see in them the embryos of heavenly bodies, billions of miles away, in the first stage of their development. In some of these "stellar embryos" the chemical elements do not seem to be differentiated yet, but still buried in the homogeneous primitive matter (*prothyl*) at an enormous temperature (calculated to run into millions of degrees); it is possible that the origi-

SOLUTION OF THE WORLD-PROBLEMS

nal basic "substance" (*vide* p. 229) is not yet divided into ponderable and imponderable matter. In other parts of space we find stars that have cooled down into glowing fluid, and yet others that are cold and rigid; we can tell their stage of evolution approximately by their color. We find stars that are surrounded with rings and moons like Saturn; and we recognize in the luminous ring of the nebula the embryo of a new moon, which has detached itself from the mother-planet, just as the planet was released from the sun.

Many of the stars, the light of which has taken thousands of years to reach us, are certainly suns like our own mother-sun, and are girt about with planets and moons, just as in our own solar system. We are justified in supposing that thousands of these planets are in a similar stage of development to that of our earth—that is, they have arrived at a period when the temperature at the surface lies between the freezing and boiling point of water, and so permits the existence of water in its liquid condition. That makes it possible that carbon has entered into the same complex combinations on those planets as it has done on our earth, and that from its nitrogenous compounds protoplasm has been evolved—that wonderful substance which alone, as far as our knowledge goes, is the possessor of organic life. The monera (for instance, chromacea and bacteria), which consist only of this primitive protoplasm, and which arise by spontaneous generation from these inorganic nitrocarbonates, may thus have entered upon the same course of evolution on many other planets as on our own; first of all, living cells of the simplest character would be formed from their homogeneous protoplasmic body by the separation of an inner nucleus from the outer cell body (cytostoma). Further, the analogy that we find in the life of all cells—whether plasmodomous plant-cells or plasmophagous animal-cells—justifies the inference that the further course of organic evolution on these other planets has been analogous to that of our own earth—always, of course, given the same limits of temperature which permit water in a liquid form. In the glowing liquid bodies of the stars, where water can only exist in the form of steam, and on the cold extinct suns, where it can only be in the shape of ice, such organic life as we know is impossible.

The similarity of phylogeny, or the analogy of organic evolution, which we may thus assume in many stars which are at the same stage of biogenetic development, naturally opens out a wide field of brilliant speculation to the constructive imagination. A favorite subject for such speculation has long been the question whether there are men, or living beings like ourselves, perhaps much more highly developed, in other planets? Among the many works which have sought to answer the question, those of Camille Flammarion, the Parisian astronomer, have recently been extremely popular; they are equally distinguished by exuberant imagination and brilliant style, and by a deplorable lack of critical judgment and biological knowledge. We may condense in the following thesis the present condition of our knowledge on the subject:

I. It is very probable that a similar biogenetic process to that of our own earth is taking place on some of the other planets of our solar system (Mars and Venus), and on many planets of other solar systems; first simple monera are formed by spontaneous generation, and from these arise unicellular protists (first plasmodomous primitive plants, and then plasmophagous primitive animals).

SOLUTION OF THE WORLD-PROBLEMS

II. It is very probable that from these unicellular protists arise, in the further course of evolution, first social cell-communities (cœnobia), and subsequently tissue-forming plants and animals (metaphyta and metazoa).

III. It is also very probable that thallophyta (algæ and fungi) were the first to appear in the plant-kingdom, then diaphyta (mosses and ferns), finally anthophyta (gymnosperm and angiosperm flowering plants).

IV. It is equally probable that the biogenetic process took a similar course in the animal kingdom—that from the blastæads (catallacta) first gastræads were formed, and from these lower animal forms (cœlenteria) higher organisms (cœlomaria) were afterwards evolved.

V. On the other hand, it is very questionable whether the different stems of these higher animals (and those of the higher plants as well) run through the same course of development on other planets as on our earth.

VI. In particular, it is wholly uncertain whether there are vertebrates on other planets, and whether, in the course of their phyletic development, taking millions of years, mammals are formed as on earth, reaching their highest point in the formation of man; in such an event, millions of changes would have to be just the same in both cases.

VII. It is much more probable, on the contrary, that other planets have produced other types of the higher plants and animals, which are unknown on our earth; perhaps from some higher animal stem, which is superior to the vertebrate in formation, higher beings have arisen who far transcend us earthly men in intelligence.

VIII. The possibility of our ever entering into direct communication with such inhabitants of other planets seems to be excluded by the immense distance of our earth from the other heavenly bodies, and the absence of the requisite atmosphere in the intervening space, which contains only ether.

But while many of the stars are probably in a similar stage of biogenetic development to that of our earth (for the last one hundred million years at least), others have advanced far beyond this stage, and, in their planetary old age, are hastening towards their end—the same end that inevitably awaits our own globe. The radiation of heat into space gradually lowers the temperature until all the water is turned into ice; that is the end of all organic life. The substance of the rotating mass contracts more and more; the rapidity of its motion gradually falls off. The orbits of the planets and of their moons grow narrower. At length the moons fall upon the planets, and the planets are drawn into the sun that gave them birth. The collision again produces an enormous quantity of heat. The pulverized mass of the colliding bodies is distributed freely through infinite space, and the eternal drama of sun-birth begins afresh

The sublime picture which modern astrophysics thus unveils before the mind's eye shows us an eternal birth and death of countless heavenly bodies, a periodic change from one to the other of the different cosmogenetic conditions, which we observe side by side in the universe. While the embryo of a new world is being formed from a nebula in one corner of the vast stage of the universe, another has already condensed into a rotating sphere of liquid fire in some far distant spot; a third has already cast off rings at its equator,

SOLUTION OF THE WORLD-PROBLEMS

which round themselves into planets; a fourth has become a vast sun whose planets have formed a secondary retinue of moons, and so on. And between them are floating about in space myriads of smaller bodies, meteorites, or shooting-stars, which cross and recross the paths of the planets apparently like lawless vagabonds, and of which a great number fall onto the planets every day. Thus there is a continuous but slow change in the velocities and the orbits of the revolving spheres. The frozen moons fall onto the planets, the planets onto their suns. Two distant suns, perhaps already stark and cold, rush together with inconceivable force and melt away into nebulous clouds. And such prodigious heat is generated by the collision that the nebula is once more raised to incandescence, and the old drama begins again. Yet in this " perpetual motion " the infinite substance of the universe, the sum total of its matter and energy, remains eternally unchanged, and we have an eternal repetition in infinite time of the periodic dance of the worlds, the metamorphosis of the cosmos that ever returns to its starting-point. Over all rules the law of substance.

II.—PROGRESS OF GEOLOGY

The earth and its origin were much later than the heavens in becoming the object of scientific investigation. The numerous ancient and modern cosmogonies do, indeed, profess to give us as good an insight into the origin of the earth as into that of the heavens; but the mythological raiment, in which all alike are clothed, betrays their origin in poetic fancy. Among the countless legends of creation which we find in the history of religions and of thought there is one that soon took

THE RIDDLE OF THE UNIVERSE

precedence of all the rest—the Mosaic story of creation as told in the first book of the Hexateuch. It did not exist in its present form until long after the death of Moses (probably not until eight hundred years afterwards); but its sources are much older, and are to be found for the most part in Assyrian, Babylonian, and Hindoo legends. This Hebrew legend of creation obtained its great influence through its adoption into the Christian faith and its consecration as the " Word of God." Greek philosophers had already, five hundred years before Christ, explained the natural origin of the earth in the same way as that of other cosmic bodies. Xenophanes of Colophon had even recognized the true character of the fossils which were afterwards to prove of such moment; the great painter, Leonardo da Vinci, of the fifteenth century, also explained the fossils as the petrified remains of animals which had lived in earlier periods of the earth's history. But the authority of the Bible, especially the myth of the deluge, prevented any further progress in this direction, and insured the triumph of the Mosaic legend until about the middle of the last century. It survives even at the present day among orthodox theologians. However, in the second half of the eighteenth century, scientific inquiry into the structure of the crust of the earth set to work independently of the Mosaic story, and it soon led to certain conclusions as to the origin of the earth. The founder of geology, Werner of Freiberg, thought that all the rocks were formed in water, while Voigt and Hutton (1788) rightly contended that only the stratified, fossil-bearing rocks had had an aquatic origin, and that the Vulcanic or Plutonic mountain ranges had been formed by the cooling down of molten matter.

The heated conflict of these " Neptunian " and " Plu-

SOLUTION OF THE WORLD-PROBLEMS

tonic" schools was still going on during the first three decades of the present century; it was only settled when Karl Hoff (1822) established the principle of "actualism," and Sir Charles Lyell applied it with signal success to the entire natural evolution of the earth. The *Principles of Geology* of Lyell (1830) secured the full recognition of the supremely important theory of continuity in the formation of the earth's crust, as opposed to the catastrophic theory of Cuvier.* Palæontology, which had been founded by Cuvier's work on fossil bones (1812), was of the greatest service to geology; by the middle of the present century it had advanced so far that the chief periods in the history of the earth and its inhabitants could be established. The comparatively thin crust of the earth was now recognized with certainty to be the hard surface formed by the cooling of an incandescent fluid planet, which still continues its slow, unbroken course of refrigeration and condensation. The crumpling of the stiffened crust, "the reaction of the molten fiery contents on the cool surface," and especially the unceasing geological action of water, are the natural causes which are daily at work in the secular formation of the crust of the earth and its mountains.

To the brilliant progress of modern geology we owe three extremely important results of general import. In the first place, it has excluded from the story of the earth all questions of miracle, all questions of supernatural agencies, in the building of the mountains and the shaping of the continents. In the second place, our idea of the length of the vast period of time which had been absorbed in their formation has been consid-

*Cf. *The Natural History of Creation*, chaps. iii., vi., xv., and xvi.

erably enlarged. We now know that the huge mountains of the palæozoic, mesozoic, and cenozoic formations have taken, not thousands, but millions of years in their growth. In the third place, we now know that all the countless fossils that are found in those formations are not " sports of nature," as was believed one hundred and fifty years ago, but the petrified remains of organisms that lived in earlier periods of the earth's history, and arose by gradual transformation from a long series of ancestors.

III.—PROGRESS OF PHYSICS AND CHEMISTRY

The many important discoveries which these fundamental sciences have made during the nineteenth century are so well known, and their practical application in every branch of modern life is so obvious, that we need not discuss them in detail here. In particular, the application of steam and electricity has given to our nineteenth century its characteristic " machinist-stamp." But the colossal progress of inorganic and organic chemistry is not less important. All branches of modern civilization—medicine and technology, industry and agriculture, mining and forestry, land and water transport—have been so much improved in the course of the century, especially in the second half, that our ancestors of the eighteenth century would find themselves in a new world, could they return. But more valuable and important still is the great theoretical expansion of our knowledge of nature, which we owe to the establishment of the law of substance. Once Lavoisier (1789) had established the law of the persistence of matter, and Dalton (1808) had founded his new atomic theory with its assistance, a way was open to

SOLUTION OF THE WORLD-PROBLEMS

modern chemistry along which it has advanced with a rapidity and success beyond all anticipation. The same must be said of physics in respect of the law of the conservation of energy. Its discovery by Robert Mayer (1842) and Hermann Helmholtz (1847) inaugurated for this science also a new epoch of the most fruitful development; for it put physics in a position to grasp the universal unity of the forces of nature and the eternal play of natural processes, in which one force may be converted into another at any moment.

IV.—PROGRESS OF BIOLOGY

The great discoveries which astronomy and geology have made during the nineteenth century, and which are of extreme importance to our whole system, are, nevertheless, far surpassed by those of biology. Indeed, we may say that the greater part of the many branches which this comprehensive science of organic life has recently produced have seen the light in the course of the present century. As we saw in the first section, during the century all branches of anatomy and physiology, botany and zoology, ontogeny and phylogeny, have been so marvellously enriched by countless discoveries that the present condition of biological science is immeasurably superior to its condition a hundred years ago. That applies first of all *quantitatively* to the colossal growth of our positive information in all those provinces and their several parts. But it applies with even greater force *qualitatively* to the deepening of our comprehension of biological phenomena, and our knowledge of their efficient causes. In this Charles Darwin (1859) takes the palm of victory; by his theory of selection he has solved the great problem of "organic creation," of the natural origin of the countless forms of life by gradual transformation. It is true that Lamarck had recognized fifty years earlier that the mode of this transformation lay in the reciprocal action of heredity and adaptation. However, Lamarck was hampered by his lack of the principle of selection, and of that deeper insight into the true nature of organization which was only rendered possible after the founding of the theory of evolution and the cellular theory. When we collated the results of these and other disciplines, and found the key to their harmonious interpretation in the ancestral development of living beings, we succeeded in establishing the monistic biology, the principles of which I have endeavored to lay down securely in my *General Morphology*.

V.—PROGRESS OF ANTHROPOLOGY

In a certain sense, the true science of man, rational anthropology, takes precedence of every other science. The saying of the ancient sage, "Man, know thyself," and that other famous maxim, "Man is the measure of all things," have been accepted and applied from all time. And yet this science—taking it in its widest sense—has languished longer than all other sciences in the fetters of tradition and superstition. We saw in the first section how slowly and how late the science of the human organism was developed. One of its chief branches—embryology—was not firmly established until 1828 (by Baer), and another, of equal importance—the cellular theory—until 1838 (by Schwann). And it was even later still when the answer was given to the "question of all questions," the great riddle of the origin of man. Although Lamarck had pointed out

SOLUTION OF THE WORLD-PROBLEMS

the only path to a correct solution of it in 1809, and had affirmed the descent of man from the ape, it fell to Darwin to establish the affirmation securely fifty years afterwards, and to Huxley to collect the most important proofs of it in 1863, in his *Place of Man in Nature*. I have myself made the first attempt, in my *Anthropogeny* (1874), to present in their historical connection the entire series of ancestors through which our race has been slowly evolved from the animal kingdom in the course of many millions of years.

CONCLUSION

THE number of world-riddles has been continually diminishing in the course of the nineteenth century through the aforesaid progress of a true knowledge of nature. Only one comprehensive riddle of the universe now remains—the problem of substance. What is the real character of this mighty world-wonder that the realistic scientist calls Nature or the Universe, the idealist philosopher calls Substance or the Cosmos, the pious believer calls Creator or God? Can we affirm to-day that the marvellous progress of modern cosmology has solved this "problem of substance," or at least that it has brought us nearer to the solution?

The answer to this final question naturally varies considerably according to the stand-point of the philosophic inquirer and his empirical acquaintance with the real world. We grant at once that the innermost character of nature is just as little understood by us as it was by Anaximander and Empedocles twenty-four hundred years ago, by Spinoza and Newton two hundred years ago, and by Kant and Goethe one hundred years ago. We must even grant that this essence of substance becomes more mysterious and enigmatic the deeper we penetrate into the knowledge of its attributes, matter and energy, and the more thoroughly we study its countless phenomenal forms and their evolution. We do not know the "thing in itself" that lies behind these knowable phenomena. But why trouble about this

CONCLUSION

enigmatic "thing in itself" when we have no means of investigating it, when we do not even clearly know whether it exists or not? Let us, then, leave the fruitless brooding over this ideal phantom to the "pure metaphysician," and let us instead, as "real physicists," rejoice in the immense progress which has been actually made by our monistic philosophy of nature.

Towering above all the achievements and discoveries of the century we have the great, comprehensive "law of substance," the fundamental law of the constancy of matter and force. The fact that substance is everywhere subject to eternal movement and transformation gives it the character also of the universal law of evolution. As this supreme law has been firmly established, and all others are subordinate to it, we arrive at a conviction of the universal unity of nature and the eternal validity of its laws. From the gloomy *problem* of substance we have evolved the clear *law* of substance. The monism of the cosmos which we establish thereon proclaims the absolute dominion of "the great eternal iron laws" throughout the universe. It thus shatters, at the same time, the three central dogmas of the dualistic philosophy—the personality of God, the immortality of the soul, and the freedom of the will.

Many of us certainly view with sharp regret, or even with a profound sorrow, the death of the gods that were so much to our parents and ancestors. We must console ourselves in the words of the poet:

> "The times are changed, old systems fall,
> And new life o'er their ruins dawns."

The older view of idealistic dualism is breaking up with all its mystic and anthropistic dogmas; but upon

THE RIDDLE OF THE UNIVERSE

the vast field of ruins rises, majestic and brilliant, the new sun of our realistic monism, which reveals to us the wonderful temple of nature in all its beauty. In the sincere cult of "the true, the good, and the beautiful," which is the heart of our new monistic religion, we find ample compensation for the anthropistic ideals of "God, freedom, and immortality" which we have lost.

Throughout this discussion of the riddles of the universe I have clearly defined my consistent monistic position and its opposition to the still prevalent dualistic theory. In this I am supported by the agreement of nearly all modern scientists who have the courage to accept a rounded philosophical system. I must not, however, take leave of my readers without pointing out in a conciliatory way that this strenuous opposition may be toned down to a certain degree on clear and logical reflection — may, indeed, even be converted into a friendly harmony. In a thoroughly logical mind, applying the highest principles with equal force in the entire field of the cosmos—in both organic and inorganic nature—the antithetical positions of theism and pantheism, vitalism and mechanism, approach until they touch each other. Unfortunately, consecutive thought is a rare phenomenon in nature. The great majority of philosophers are content to grasp with the right hand the pure knowledge that is built on experience, but they will not part with the mystic faith based on revelation, to which they cling with the left. The best type of this contradictory dualism is the conflict of pure and practical reason in the critical philosophy of the most famous of modern thinkers, Immanuel Kant.

On the other hand, the number is always small of

CONCLUSION

the thinkers who will boldly reject dualism and embrace pure monism. That is equally true of consistent idealists and theists, and of logical realists and pantheists. However, the reconciliation of these apparent antitheses, and, consequently, the advance towards the solution of the fundamental riddle of the universe, is brought nearer to us every year in the ever-increasing growth of our knowledge of nature. We may, therefore, express a hope that the approaching twentieth century will complete the task of resolving the antitheses, and, by the construction of a system of pure monism, spread far and wide the long-desired unity of world-conception. Germany's greatest thinker and poet, whose one hundred and fiftieth anniversary will soon be upon us—Wolfgang Goethe—gave this "philosophy of unity" a perfect poetic expression, at the very beginning of the century, in his immortal poems, *Faust, Prometheus,* and *God and the World*:

> "By eternal laws
> Of iron ruled,
> Must all fulfil
> The cycle of
> Their destiny."

INDEX

Abiogenesis, 257, 369.
Abortive organs, 264.
Accidents, 216.
Acrania, 166.
Action at a distance, 217.
Actualism, 249.
Æsthesis, 225.
Affinity, 224.
Altruism, 350.
Amphibia, 167.
Amphimixis, 141.
Ampitheism, 278.
Ananke, 272.
Anatomy, 22, etc.
    comparative, 24.
Anaximander, 289, 379.
Anthropism, 11.
Anthropistic illusion, 14, etc.
    world-theory, 13.
Anthropocentric dogma, 11, etc.
Anthropogeny, 83.
Anthropolatric dogma, 12.
Anthropomorpha, 36.
Anthropomorphic dogma, 12.
Apes, 36, 37, 167.
    anthropoid, 37.
Archæus, 43.
Archigony, 257.
Aristotle, 23, 268.
Association, centres of, 183.
    of ideas, 121.
    of presentations, 121, 122.
Astronomy, progress of, 366.
Astrophysics, 368.
Atavism, 142.
Athanatism, 189.

Athanatistic illusions, 205.
Atheism, 290.
Atheistic science, 260.
Atom, the, 222.
Atomism, 223.
Atomistic consciousness, 187.
Attributes of ether, 227.
    of substance, 216.
Augustine of Hippo, 130.
Auricular confession, 319, 359.
Autogony, 257.

Baer (Carl Ernst), 57.
Bastian (Adolf), 103.
Beginning of the world, 240, 247.
Bible, the, 282, 362.
Biogenesis, 257.
Biogenetic law, 81, 143.
Bismarck, 334.
Blastoderm, 150, 155.
Blastosphere, 153.
Blastula, 153.
Bruno (Giordano), 290, 317.
Büchner (Ludwig), 93.
Buddhism, 326, 355.

Calvin, 130.
Canonical gospels, 312.
Carbon as creator, 256.
    theory, 257.
Catarrhinæ, 35.
Catastrophic theory, 74.
Categorical imperative, 350.
Causes, efficient, 258.
    final, 258.

INDEX

Celibacy, 358.
Cell-love, 137.
    community, soul of the, 155.
    soul, 151.
    state, 157.
Cellular pathology, 50.
    physiology, 48.
    psychology, 153, 177.
    theory, 26.
Cenobitic soul, 155.
Cenogenesis, 82.
    of the psyche, 144.
Chance, 274.
Chemicotropism, 64, 136.
Chordula, 64.
Chorion, 68.
Christ, father of, 327.
Christian art, 339.
    civilization, 356.
    contempt of the body, 354.
        animals, 355.
        nature, 355.
        self, 353.
        the family, 357.
        woman, 358.
    ethics, 352.
Christianity, 347.
Church and school, 362.
    state, 361.
Cnidaria, 161.
Conception, 64.
Concubinage of the clergy, 358.
Confession of faith, 302.
Consciousness, 170.
    animal, 176.
    atomistic, 178.
    biological, 176.
    cellular, 177.
    development of, 185.
    dualistic, 182.
    human, 173.
    monistic, 182.
    neurological, 174.
    ontogeny of, 186.
    pathology of, 182.
    physiological, 180.
    transcendental, 180.
Constancy of energy, 212, 231.
    matter, 212.
Constantine the Great, 316.

Constellations of substance, 218.
Conventional lies, 323.
Copernicus, 24, 320, 367.
Cosmic immortality, 191.
Cosmogonies, 234.
Cosmological dualism, 257.
    creationism, 235.
    law, 211.
    perspective, 14.
Cosmos, the, 229.
Creation, 73, 79, 234.
    cosmological, 235.
    dualistic, 236.
    heptameral, 237.
    individual, 237.
    myths of, 236.
    periodic, 237.
    trialistic, 237.
Cultur-kampf, 334.
Cuvier, 74.
Cyclostomata, 167.
Cynopitheci, 46.
Cytology, 26, etc.
Cytopsyche, 151.
Cytula, 64.

Darwin (Charles), 78, etc.
Decidua, 69.
Deduction, 16.
Demonism, 276.
Descartes, 99, 355.
Descent of the ape, 85, etc.
    of man, 87.
    theory of, 77.
Design, 264, 266.
    in nature, 260.
    in organisms, 266.
    in selection, 261.
Destruction of heavenly bodies, 243.
Determinists, 130.
Diaphragm, 31.
Division of labor in matter, 229.
Draper, 309, 333.
Dualism, 20, etc.
Du Bois-Reymond, 15, 180, 235.
Du Prel (Carl), 305.
Duty, feeling of, 350.
Dynamodes, 216.
Dysteleology, 260.

INDEX

Echinodermata, 62.
Ectoderm, 160.
    sense-cells in the, 293
Egoism, 350.
Elements, chemical, 222.
    system of the, 222.
Embryo, human, 64.
Embryology, 54.
Embryonic psychogeny, 144.
    sleep, 146.
Empedocles, 23, 224.
Encyclica (of Pius IX.), 323.
End of the world, 247.
Energy, kinetic, 231.
    potential, 231.
    principle of, 230.
    specific, 294.
Entelecheia, 268.
Entoderm, 160.
Entropy of the universe, 247.
Epigenesis, 56, 133.
Ergonomy of matter, 229.
Eternity of the world, 242.
Ether, 225
Etheric souls, 199.
Ethics, fundamental law of, 350.
Evolution, theory of, 54, 239, 243.
    chief element in, 267.
Experience, 16.
Extra-mundane God, 288.

Faith, confession of, 303.
    of our fathers, 304.
Family, the, and Christianity, 357.
Fate, 272.
Fechner, 97, etc.
Fecundation, 63.
Fetishism, 276.
Feuerbach (Ludwig), 295.
Flechsig, 183.
Fœtal membranes, 66.
Folk-psychology, 103.
Forces, conversion of, 231.
Frederick the Great, 194, 315.

Galen, 23, 40.
Gaseous souls, 199.
    vertebrates, 288.

Gastræa, 160.
    theory of the, 60.
Gastræads, 159.
Gastrula, 61.
Gegenbaur, 25, 30.
Generation, theory of, 55.
Genus, 73.
Geology, periods of, 270.
    progress of, 373.
Germinal disk, 57.
Gills, 65.
God, 275.
    the father, 277.
    the son, 277, 328.
Goethe, 20, etc.
Goethe's monism, 331.
Golden Rule, the, 351.
Gospels, 312.
Gravitation, theory of, 217.
Gut-layer, 159.

Haller, 42.
Harvey, 42.
Helmholtz (Hermann), 213, 230.
Heredity, psychic, 138.
Hertz (Heinrich), 225.
Hippocrates, 23.
Histology, 26.
Histopsyche, 156.
Hoff (Carl), 250.
Holbach (Paul), 193.
Holy Ghost, 277, 326.
Humboldt (Alexander), 343.
Hydra, 161.
Hylozoism, 289.
Hypothesis, 299.

Iatrochemicists, 45.
Iatromechanicists, 45.
Ideal of beauty, 338.
    of truth, 337.
    of virtue, 339.
Ignorabimus, 180.
Immaculate conception, 326.
Immaterial substance, 221.
Immortality of animals, 201.
    of the human soul, 188.
    of unicellular organisms, 190.
    personal, 192.

INDEX

Imperfection of nature, 264.
Imponderable matter, 225.
Impregnation, 64.
Indeterminists, 130.
Induction, 16.
Indulgences, 359.
Infallibility of the pope, 324.
Instinct, 105, 123.
Intellect, 125, etc.
Intramundane God, 288.
Introspective psychology, 95.
Islam, 284.

Janssen (Johannes), 316.
Jehovah, 283.
Journeys on foot, 364.

Kant, 258, etc.
Kant's metamorphosis, 92, etc.
Kinetic energy, 231.
    theory of substance, 216.
Kölliker, 26, 48.

Lamarck, 76, etc.
Lamettrie, 194.
Landscape-painting, 343.
Language, 126.
    study of, 363.
Last judgment, 209.
Lavoisier, 212.
Leap of the gospels, miraculous, 312.
Leydig, 27.
Life, definition of, 39.
Limits of our knowledge, 182.
Love, 357.
    of animals, 355.
    of neighbor, 350.
    of self, 350.
Lucretius Carus, 290.
Lunarism, 281.
Luther, 320.
Lyell, 77, 250.

Madonna, cult of the, 284, 327.
Malphigi, 54.
Mammals, 30, etc.
Mammary glands, 31.
Man, ancestors of, 82.
Marsupials, 32, 86.

Mass, 222.
Materialism, 20.
Mayer (Robert), 213, 377.
Mechanical causality, 366.
    explanation, 259.
    theory of heat, 247.
Mechanicism, 259.
Mediterranean religions, the, 282.
Memory, cellular, 120.
    conscious, 121.
    histionic, 121
    unconscious, 121.
Mephistopheles, 279.
Metabolism, 232.
Metamorphoses of the cosmos, 372.
    of philosophers, 92.
Metaphyta, 156.
Metasitism, 153.
Metazoa, 60, 157.
Middle Ages, 315, 358.
Mixotheism, 286.
Mohammedanism, 284.
Mohr (Friedrich), 213.
Monera, 257, 369.
Monism, 20, and *passim*.
    of energy, 254.
    of Spinoza, 331.
    of the cosmos, 255.
Monistic anthropogeny, 252.
    art, 341.
    biogeny, 251.
    churches, 345.
    cosmology, 368.
    ethics, 347.
    geogeny, 248.
Monotheism, 279.
Monotrema, 32.
Moon-worship, 281.
Moral order of the universe, 269
Morula, 155.
Mosaism, 283.
Müller (Johannes), 25, 45, 262.
Mythology of the soul, 135.

Natural religion, 344.
Navel-cord, 69.
Neo-kantians, 349.
Neovitalism, 264.
Neptunian geology, 375.

INDEX

Neuro-muscular cells, 114.
Neuroplasm, 91, 109.
Neuropsyche, 162.
Nomocracy, 9.

Ontogenetic psychology, 103.
Ontological creationism, 235.
    methods, 249.
Orbits of the heavenly bodies, 241.
Origin of movement, 15, 241.
    of feeling, 15, 241.
Ovary, 63.

Palingenesis, 82.
    of the psyche, 143.
Pandera (the father of Christ), 328.
Pantheism, 288.
Papacy, 314.
Papal ethics, 359.
Papiomorpha, 37.
Paul, 313, 357.
    epistles of, 312.
Paulinism, 313.
Pedicle of the allantois, 69.
Perpetual motion, 245.
Persistence of force, 212, 231.
    of matter, 212.
Phroneta, 293.
Phylogeny, 71, 81.
    of the apes, 51.
    systematic, 81.
Physiology, 39.
Phytopsyche, 157.
Pithecanthropus, 87.
Pithecoid theory, 82, etc.
Pithecometra-thesis, 69, 85.
Placenta, 32, 68.
Placentals, 32, 86.
Plasmodoma, 153.
Plasmogony, 257.
Plasmophaga, 154.
Plato, 99, 197.
Plato's theory of ideas, 269.
Platodaria, 160.
Platodes, 160.
Platyrrhinæ, 35.
Pneuma zoticon, 40.
Polytheism, 276.

Ponderable matter, 222.
Preformation theory, 54.
Primaria, 33.
Primates, 33, 86.
Primitive Christianity, 311.
    gut, 61, 161.
Prodynamis, 216.
Progaster, 161.
Proplacentals, 85.
Prosimiæ, 34.
Prostoma, 161.
Prothyl, 223.
Protoplasm, 90.
Protozoa, 60.
Provertebræ, 166.
Pseudo-Christianity, 321.
Psychade theory, 178.
Psyche, 88.
Psychogeny, 135.
    phyletic, 149.
    post-embryonic, 146.
Psychology, 88 et seqq.
    ontogenetic, 104.
    phylogenetic, 104.
Psychomonism, 226.
Psychophysics, 97.
Psychoplasm, 91, 110.
Pupa, sleep of the, 146.
Pyknosis, 218.
Pyknotic theory of substance, 218.

Reason, 17, 125.
Reflex action, 112.
    arches, 114.
Reformation, the, 319.
Religion a private concern, 361.
Remak, 58.
Revelation, 306.
Reversion, 142.
Romance of the Virgin Mary, 327.
Romanes, 106.
Rudimentary organs, 264.

Saints, 284.
Scale of emotion, 127.
    of memory, 120.
    of movement, 111.
    of presentation, 118.

INDEX

Scale of reason, 122.
    of reflex action, 113.
    of will, 127.
Scatulation theory, 55.
Schleiden, 26, 47.
School, and Church, 361.
    and State, 362.
    reform of the, 363.
Schwann, 26, 47.
Selachii, 166.
Selection, theory of, 79.
Self-consciousness, 171.
Sense-knowledge, 297.
    organs, 293
Senses, philosophy of the, 295.
Sentiment, 17, etc., 331.
Siebold, 27.
Simiæ, 34.
Social duties, 351.
    instincts, 350.
Solar systems, 241, 369.
Solarism, 280.
Soul, 88 *et seqq.*
    apparatus of the, 162.
    blending of the, 141.
    creation of the, 135.
    division of the, 135.
    etheric, 199.
    gaseous, 199.
    histionic, 157.
    history of the, 167.
    hydra, 161.
    life of the, 90.
    liquid, 200.
    mammal, 167.
    nerve, 162.
    origin of the, 135.
    of the plant, 157.
    personal, 162.
    solid, 201.
    substance of the, 198.
    transmigration of the, 135.
Sources of knowledge, 293.
Space and time, 244.
    infinity of, 242.
    reality of. 244.
Species, 73.
Spectral analysis, 241.
Spermarium, 63.
Spermatozoa, 58.

Spinal cord, 165.
Spinoza, 21, 215, 290.
Spirit world, 221.
Spirit-rapping, 305.
Spiritism, 304.
Spiritualism, 20.
Sponge, soul of the, 161.
Stem-cell, 63, 138, 151.
Stimulated movement, 113, 116
Stimuli, conduction of, 158.
Strauss (David), 309, 313.
Struggle for life, 270.
Substance, 215.
    law of, 211, etc.
    structure of, 229.
Superstition, 301.
Suss (Edward), 250.
Syllabus, 323.
Synodikon (of Pappus), 312.

Table-turning, 305.
Teleological explanation, 259.
Teleology, 258.
Tetrapoda, 29.
Thanatism, 189.
    primary, 192.
    secondary, 192.
Theism, 276.
Theocracy, 9.
Theory, 299.
Thought, organs of, 126, 183, 293.
Time and space, 244.
    reality of, 246.
Tissue, theory of, 26.
Tissue-forming animals, 157.
    plants, 156.
Transformism, 76.
Trimurti, 278.
Trinity, dogma of the, 277.
    monistic, 336.
Triplotheism, 277.
Tropesis, 225.
Tropismata, 128.
Tunicata, 165.
Turbellaria, 161.

Ultramontanism, 310.
Understanding, 125.
Unity of natural forces, 231.
    of substance, 214.

INDEX

Universum perpetuum mobile, 245.
Uterus, 34.

Vaticanism, 314.
Vertebrates, 27, *passim*.
Verworn (Max), 48, 116.
Vesalius, 24.
Vibration, theory of, 216.
Virchow, 26, 50.
Virchow's metamorphosis, 93.
Vital force, 42, 262.
Vitalism, 43, 262.

Vivisection, 41.
Vogt (Carl), 93.
Vogt (J.E.), 218.

Water-color drawing, 364.
Weismann, 190.
Will, liberty of the, 129.
    scale of the, 128.
Wolff (C.F.), 56.
Woman and Christianity, 358.
World-consciousness, 171.
World-riddles, number of, 15.
Wundt (Wilhelm), 100, 171.

THE END

BIBLIOLIFE

Old Books Deserve a New Life
www.bibliolife.com

Did you know that you can get most of our titles in our trademark **EasyScript**™ print format? **EasyScript**™ provides readers with a larger than average typeface, for a reading experience that's easier on the eyes.

Did you know that we have an ever-growing collection of books in many languages?

Order online:
www.bibliolife.com/store

Or to exclusively browse our **EasyScript**™ collection:
www.bibliogrande.com

At BiblioLife, we aim to make knowledge more accessible by making thousands of titles available to you – quickly and affordably.

Contact us:
BiblioLife
PO Box 21206
Charleston, SC 29413